enGendered

*en*Gendered

God's Gift of
Gender Difference
in Relationship

SAM A. ANDREADES

WEAVER BOOK
C O M P A N Y

WOOSTER, OHIO

enGendered: God's Gift of Gender Difference in Relationship
© 2015 by Sam A. Andreades

First edition published by
Weaver Book Company
1190 Summerset Dr.
Wooster, OH 44691
Visit us at weaverbookcompany.com

DISCLAIMER: Personal names used in this book have been changed to protect privacy.

Unless otherwise indicated, all Scripture quotations are from the ESV® Bible (The Holy Bible, English Standard Version®), copyright © 2001 by Crossway, a publishing ministry of Good News Publishers. Used by permission. All rights reserved.

Scripture quotations marked (NIV) are taken from the Holy Bible, New International Version®, NIV®. Copyright © 1973, 1978, 1984, 2011 by Biblica, Inc.™ Used by permission of Zondervan. All rights reserved worldwide. www.zondervan.com. The "NIV" and "New International Version" are trademarks registered in the United States Patent and Trademark Office by Biblica, Inc.™

Scripture quotations marked (RSV) are taken from the Revised Standard Version of the Bible, copyright © 1946, 1952, and 1971 National Council of the Churches of Christ in the United States of America. Used by permission. All rights reserved.

Italics in Scripture quotations indicate emphasis added by the author. Verse numbers appear in some Scripture quotations when the author refers to or comments on specific verses. Verses prefaced by "literally" or the like are the author's translation from the original language.

Cover: Frank Gutbrod
Interior design and typesetting: Frank Gutbrod
Editing: Paul J. Brinkerhoff

ISBN: 978-1-941337-11-0
ISBN (e-book): 978-1-941337-31-8

Library of Congress Cataloging-in-Publication Data

Andreades, Sam A., 1962-

enGendered : God's gift of gender difference in relationship / Sam A. Andreades. -- First Edition.
pages cm

Includes bibliographical references and index.
ISBN 978-1-941337-11-0 (pbk.) -- ISBN 978-1-941337-31-8 (e-book)

1. Man-woman relationships--Religious aspects--Christianity. 2. Sex role--Religious aspects--Christianity. 3. Intimacy (Psychology) --Religious aspects--Christianity. 4. Homosexuality--Religious aspects--Christianity. I. Title.
BT705.8.A53 2015
230.081--dc23

2014042986

Printed in the United States of America
15 16 17 18 19 / 5 4 3 2 1

Contents

● ● ● **Part 3**
The Inner Wood: The Dynamics of Getting Close

Scenic Overlooks
from the Bible

Preface

This preface is for those readers who like to get down to the brass tacks and know what they are getting themselves into before they start reading. It gives the layout of the book and an explanation of its parts and chapters. Readers who are not in the same hurry may skip this preview and simply discover the trail the author has blazed for you in the pages following.

This book attempts to explain the importance of gender in relationships. It is born of a pastor's attempts to help people navigate the current relationship scene in light of biblical truth. In our times the shifting cultural landscape on gender, the normalization of same-sex relationships, and feminist critiques of difference in men and women's roles has yielded increasing numbers of people finding biblical injunctions in the area of gender puzzling, which produces an increasing need among Christians for guidance on close relationships. Praying and preaching, counseling and convincing, failing and succeeding in aiding and arguing have supplied the answers found herein. The pastoral work underlying these answers continued through a doctoral dissertation studying successful Christian marriages of husband and wife where the husband had a history of same-sex attraction.

The book proceeds upon the premise that the issues of homosexuality and whether women and men should behave differently are cut of the same cloth: the role of gender in relationships. The introduction argues the need for a theology of gender, positively expressed, to guide us in these issues, while explaining the author's journey to it.

The book then builds a theology of gender in six propositions through addressing gender questions about close relationships one chapter at a time. Each chapter begins with questions we typically hear on people's lips today, representing problems the chapter then addresses. Some of the book's chapters are introduced by dramatic tellings of Bible narratives illustrating gender in action. These "Scenic Overlooks," opening part 1 and then punctuating six chapters in part 2, give vistas of the trail of gendered relationship we are navigating.

Part 1 (chapters 1–6), after the first of these biblical imaginings, unfolds the first four propositions:

Chapter 1 prepares the terrain of our truth-seeking by highlighting how hard such thinking is in light of the current cultural direction of minimizing gender or casting it as mere social construct. For the trail of relational love, this book recommends the Scriptures as our guide. Chapter 2 then explains the first proposition by showing where relationships come from. God has intimacy within His Trinitarian Self and so likewise intends for us to know emotional intimacy with one another and with Him.

The classic though now nonstandard practice of capitalizing pronouns and nouns referring to God, as in the previous sentence, finds particular prominence in chapter 2, and is employed thereafter. Though perhaps unfamiliar, this convention is used to honor the Giver of the gift of gender, setting Him apart in the writing as a singular Deity deserves. The convention extends to plural pronouns referring to God's three Persons in community (as in, "Let Us make man in Our own Image" or "God is a community of love inside Themself"), phrasing that is itself unfamiliar, but possessing warrant in God's plural Self within a unity.

Chapter 3 offers hope by finding the meaning of gender in our being created in God's image. It thereby yields the second proposition: Gender is part of the image of God in us. Chapter 4 emphasizes the Bible's insistence on the parity of the genders, a third proposition: Women and men are equal partners in bearing God's image. Chapter 5 explains the fourth proposition, namely, that gender matters in relationship. Chapter 6 elaborates on these four propositions by distinguishing sexual differences (male/female) from gender differences (masculine/feminine).

Part 2 (chapters 7–13) explores the fifth proposition, that God's gift of gender creates asymmetries in our posture and behavior. The gift calls us to specialties for one another. Traversing this ground carries us to resilient definitions of true womanliness and real manhood.

Specifically, chapter 7 introduces the three grand asymmetries found in the apostle Paul's reading of the Genesis creation of gender. Chapter 8 explains the asymmetry arising from how men and women were made differently for one another. Chapters 9 and 10 discuss the asymmetry in the sequence of origin and its implications for how men and women help one another. Chapter 11 takes up the third asymmetry, that is, how God's stated purposes in creating men and women helps us take part together in His mission of redemption in the world. Chapter 12 follows through the implication of specialties in producing healthy dependence between us, and chapter 13 takes up the interaction of gender with culture.

The final section, part 3 (chapters 14–18), expounds upon the final proposition, namely, that gender is a gift to foster emotional intimacy between us. Chapter 14 explains the genius behind God's design, and chapter 15 dissects its dynamics. Chapter 16 builds on the dichotomy of chapter 6, once more visiting how to understand and respect the physical differences that form the platform for gender differences. Chapter 17 elaborates on the continuum of relationships, first to help decide when gender does and doesn't matter, and second, to highlight the intimacy God intends for single people. Finally, Chapter 18 pursues the hints in Scripture of an invitation to ever-greater intimacy.

To help review, appendix 1 lays out the six propositions of this theology of gender in statement form, with their subpoints and supporting Scriptures. Appendix 2 supplies a chiasmus or chiasm (a common device in Hebrew narratives) showing the relationship between the narrative elements in the book of Judges, used at several points in this book.

This work is a poor offering, but it is the author's great hope that through it the reader seeking to love well might acquire some inkling of the profound wisdom in what God has created and in what He commands.

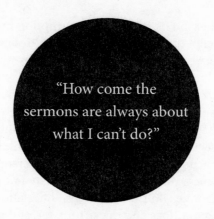

"How come the sermons are always about what I can't do?"

Introduction:
Prohibitions Are Not Enough

Okay. I got it but it doesn't help me." I had just finished the Sunday sermon, a careful explication of one of the New Testament passages limiting church eldership to men. Rachel, the perceptive young woman, recently married and faithfully active in our little New York City congregation, was front and center to deliver her heartfelt response to my brilliant teaching. But it was not praise. I did not mind this. I had been a preacher long enough to stop caring much whether people thought I was good and to start caring very much whether what I was saying was actually helping anyone change. Sermon reactions, even negative ones, help me understand my preaching through my listeners' ears. But I was still not expecting this.

The topic of gender distinctions is never popular. I thought I had been as sensitive as possible to women in delivering this message. I previewed it with my wife, Mary K., to be sure that the points were attentive to women's concerns. I tried to be faithful to the text and revealing of its wisdom. But my congregant was not impressed. "It doesn't help me," she repeated to my silence. "I have heard plenty of times what I cannot do. Okay. Even if I accept that, it doesn't move me an inch toward knowing what I *should* be doing." It was really a gentle criticism. Sometimes, after sermons, the criticism I receive says more about the hearer than the message, complaints arising from deep hurt over past abuse, or an unwillingness to trust God. But this one was none of that. It was a key rebuke for me. With her two sentences, I saw my failure, and the church's failure in general, to give Rachel what she really needed.

What did Rachel need? Something to embrace. Something to pursue. A positive vision for how she, specifically as a woman, furthered God's purposes, how she, as a woman, meant something to the kingdom of heaven. I could not give her that by just telling her what she shouldn't be doing. I was not giving her a reason to rejoice in the commands the Bible gives her. I was not giving her a theology of gender.

Reading the Bible for a while teaches one something. Each negative command in the Bible points to a corresponding affirmation of some good thing. The command "You shall not commit adultery"[1] is really a way of exalting marriage. The demand to not steal is really a valuing of personal property and a call to stewardship. The more one reads, the more one finds a call to pursue the positive alongside a warning to eschew the negative. This pattern should lead us to ask, if the apostle Paul tells Timothy to not permit a woman to teach a man in church (1 Tim. 2:12), and if the apostle really means to generalize the instruction to "in every place" (v. 8),[2] what is he trying to affirm? The failure of my Sunday sermon spurred a long quest to answer that question for my congregation. This quest transformed what is a sore subject, for many reasons, into a reason to rejoice, as I discovered God's love for us within the precepts.

Not long before that Sunday, I found myself in my office with another member of my church—we'll call him Mark—having a hard conversation about his recently disclosed same-sex relationship with a friend. Talking about this personal issue is a painful thing for a church member to do. The position of our church was that same-sex unions are not God's way for us,[3] and he knew it. The only reason that Mark opened up to me was because of an unrelated event earlier that year that had launched us to a new level of friendship. That gave him the courage to at least talk to me about this secret. Although he knew that his relationship with this guy, who occasionally attended our church, had to eventually come out, it was still a big step for him into the pastor's office. I was relieved to find enough trust there for him to initiate the conversation.

But it did not end well. In fact, the conversation was agonizing. Mark is a gentle soul. Our church had been instrumental in his coming to faith. He was heavily involved in the life of the congregation and had shown great kindness to me. His church was not something he felt he could give up. But neither was this relationship. It did not help that his intelligent partner had convinced him that God sanctioned and blessed their union. I did the best I could, relating respectfully about what he was choosing and explaining from the Scriptures why we disagreed. But merely explaining that the Bible calls it wrong was not enough to help him. As author Wesley Hill puts it, "Demands can seem harsh and deadly if the rhyme or reason for the rules isn't easy to discern."[4] I can still remember the look in Mark's eyes as he pleaded, "Meet me halfway, Sam!" I had no way to respond. Because I did not really understand why the Bible said what it said. I did not have a theology of gender.

Events like these—and there were many others—focused my attention as pastor of The Village Church in New York City. For ten years I searched out how God directs us in close relationships and why. That search meant befriending people, helping them in their difficulties in following those directions. The pain surrounding issues of homosexuality, and the stunning silence of churches in my tradition addressing it, precipitated our Greenwich Village church's ministry called Higher Ground (originally G.A.M.E., Gender Affirming Ministry Endeavor), to walk beside those who saw conflict between their same-sex attraction and following Christ. Our church did this to help folks stand against defining themselves by their desires and to provide a place for them to reaffirm gender in relationship. In addition, my wife, Mary K., and I took great care with each man and woman beginning their lives together as a couple, giving them as much time as possible to see what marriage was about. We all learned a great deal. Furthermore, it seemed there were always relationship mouths chirping for help. A church full of holy, struggling saints is a great instructor. Women who do not feel their worth. Men who struggle to grow up. Couples crying in candlelit cafes. Overcoming odds and lasting loves. Meltdowns and breakups. I had a front-row ticket to the surging rhythms of urban combats and conciliations.

This book is the result. As feeble an offering as it is, it would be much poorer if not for these many counselors whose stories (with all names changed) shine through these pages. The greatest thing I learned was the quality of people following Christ. For one thing, I witnessed wise decisions that led people into redeemed relationships. For another, I recognized hidden champions—women and men with a history of same-sex attraction (SSA) who are following Christ. I have come to consider them the unsung heroes of what God is doing in our day. They showed me what it means to walk and mature while getting meager support from your surroundings. They showed me what it is to carry a heavier cross in their walk of discipleship. They showed me that where God commands, He empowers.

When it came time for me to do doctoral work, I found myself wanting to talk to more of these exceptional people. Let's say that there are two kinds of romantic relationships: "monogendered" (sometimes called, same-sex) relationships between a man and a man, or a woman and a woman, and "intergendered" ones, that is, across the genders, between a man and a woman. Some with a history of monogendered relationships self-consciously go for an intergendered marriage. While there could be many reasons for this arrangement, I wanted to study if happily married Christian couples who are doing this perceived some benefit to gender difference in marriage.

How many "mixed orientation couples,"[5] intergendered marriages where one partner experiences SSA, reside in America is unknown,[6] but author and ex-wife of a gay man, Amity Pierce Buxton, who founded the Straight Spouse Network servicing thousands of spouses like herself, estimates the number to be two million.[7] Not all of these are Christian or happy, of course, but there seem to be plenty that are. I know because they were not hard to find for my study.

Little research has been done on these intact, happily married, mixed-orientation couples, but there are indications of an unexplored dynamic that meets the extra challenge of same-sex attraction in one of the partners to deliver a happy marriage. Mark A. Yarhouse, the clinical psychologist who formed the Institute for the Study of Sexual Identity at Regent University, published four studies on mixed-orientation couples. In three of his studies performed over five years on sixteen stable couples, the love between the husband and wife is the most frequently cited reason for staying together.[8] Another study of 267 people involved in mixed-orientation relationships reveals several themes, including trust and love, to be a feature of the couples' longevity.[9] Participants with good marriages most often cited friendship and companionship as the best aspects of their marriage.[10] I wondered. These folks may uniquely understand if an opposite-gendered spouse brings something different to an intergendered marriage.

I did my own qualitative study[11] on a small number of husbands, diverse in place of residence, denominational background, age, and relationship background, who had a history of monogendered relationships and yet were now in thriving intergendered marriages lasting five years or more. These men indeed turned out to be a trove of sensitive reflection on the difference that gender makes in a relationship. They answered the question: Does she matter? Does the "she-ness" in the "she" matter? I refer to the answers of these men as the "Does She Matter?" or DSM interviews, and they pepper this book. (Please do not confuse my abbreviation for the *Diagnostic and Statistical Manual* the psychiatry community uses to categorize mental disorders—I did not find these men disordered at all). Those from that study who get directly quoted herein are Nick, Ted, Theo, Silva, Fred, Fibeo, Edwin, Toseph, and Steven. (Again, their names and their wives' names have been changed.)

In addition to walking with such enlightening people, my search also meant reviewing academic literature to comb what I could from experienced researchers or those who have thought about these things a lot. I read many Christian writers on gender issues. So references to different studies and authorities also make an appearance here. Of course, my own marriage is itself exposed in these pages. Twenty-four years of learning how to love her and receive her love has shaped me as a man in a way I can hardly begin to describe. But statistical studies, interviewing, the wisdom of the saints, and even personal experience was not enough. A quest needs a guide. Yet when it comes to gender, guides into this deep wood are lacking.

PART 1
The Way through the Thicket

Who We Are and Where
Relationships Come From

The Big Frolicking Circle on the Deep

I was racing faster than the speed of light, if you can imagine that.[1] Maybe you can't. But I was. It was moments after the unveiling, the explosion of His Big Idea, so long in planning between us. I had His blueprint, but blueprints are one thing. Actually building it, making it work in space and time, well, that is where I came in. I was in my element, begotten to go out. I sped forth fresh, as if in well-worn jeans and leather boots at a sunrise work site. I first set the expansion rate to fifty-five places, sighing deeply. In fact, I actually purred, visualizing His reaction to this law of the heavens—large enough to dispel cosmic lumps but small enough to keep things interesting. I didn't have to turn around. I knew His thrill.

I paused to ponder, should I, might I make the constant 0.0000000000667122. A flick of my wrist could diminish it to that last one twenty-two. What swirls would result! A glorious arrangement! I turned to look at Him, my One. He needed only to raise what you might call one of His eyebrows. It was enough. He did not approve. He cared about hotter stars for plenteous heavy elements. It was important to Him. So it was important to me. I laughed a final forty-eight to the wind and zoomed off in another direction. I will be His delight. That matters more to me than a few decimal points.

I knew what He wanted, drawing a circle on the face of the deep. I cartwheeled across what you would one day call the Lynx Supercluster, as I made it gorgeous and deadly. Most of my galaxies in it would be elliptical, like us. These bursts were not places fit to visit, but necessary for the stage of creation's crown.

He spoke to me then—that is, what you might call speaking. It is somewhat nonsensical to speak of speaking then, before the waters that would make speaking possible. Rather, He knew into me, conveyed across unseen bonds of love. It was our own private language, precise and poetic at the same time, every phrase laced with layers of meaning and music. The gist of it was that He wanted more white dwarf binary stars. I knew why. He liked Fluorine, which, I quickly surmised, would end up useful for teeth. This was the only way to get it. I beamed in agreement. Yes, so many pretty smiles to come.

There would be work by the Tender, Who would follow me. But, for the moment what needed to be there for the march to habitation was in place. The count of baryons, the particle ratios, the supernovae frequency, the distances within the Milky Way, the binding of beautiful Pleiades, all my work. I so wanted this to be a place of rest for our feet, and now, as I surveyed it, I think I had done it. I turned once again to Him. He smiled in pleasure and desire, with a look that said, beyond the sadness that will come, He would always keep me near. I, Holy Wisdom, didn't want to think about the sadness then. Then it was all fresh and beautiful and pure life. And they were coming, the biggest and strangest idea He ever had . . .

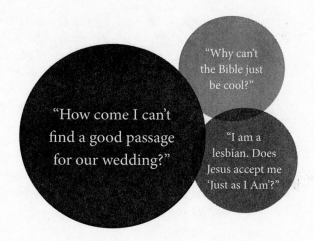

"Why can't the Bible just be cool?"

"How come I can't find a good passage for our wedding?"

"I am a lesbian. Does Jesus accept me 'Just as I Am'?"

CHAPTER 1

We Have Lost the Trail of Relational Love

I f you have ever gone through a pastoral search in your church, you know it is a long, drawn out business. Protestant congregations looking for a leader form committees to examine pastor candidates for visible strengths and hidden weaknesses. They must pay close attention to make sure the marriage of pastor to congregation will work. When I was the subject of one such search, after I preached at the Sunday service the first time, I was asked to field questions from the attendees. This was mostly fun, until a woman stood up and said, "We sing this song about how, when I come to Him, Jesus accepts me 'Just as I Am.' Well, I am a lesbian. If you are pastor here, will this church accept me just as I am?" The room of a few hundred people fell silent. The pause stretched to the length of that moment before the final pitch of the ninth inning when the score is down three and all the bases are loaded. What might the potential pastor say?

Relational love is like an inviting, verdant woods marked by trail-heads promising emerald glades. It draws us to explore. Rarely can you see what you are getting into before you wander into one, relationship or forest, and you surely cannot see very far ahead of you once you are involved. You can never be entirely certain where you are going. They are full of mystery, promising both delight and danger, depending on where you next place your boot. Since we cannot avoid the allure of love, we desperately need a guide and a path to steer us toward the beautiful hidden waterfalls and to keep us safe from lurking rattlesnakes.

I find it a helpful practice as a pastor to read through some recommended book on engagement or marriage with each couple I am counseling for marriage. This exercise, along with discussion about the couple's particular issues, provides perspective for them about what life together will really be like. So, over time I have built up an annotated bibliography of some two dozen marriage advice books. Most of these books have something helpful to say. Some counsel better on communication. Others adeptly advise on how marriage sanctifies us, showing us our need for redemption. One delves deeply into the mysteries of two people coming together sexually as one. Another offers valuable nuggets about conflict resolution. But there is one thing I have noticed about nearly all contemporary Christian books on marriage. They do not talk much about gender, or how it may power love. Gender might be touched on, or come up tangentially (as in, "Women tend to . . ." and "Men are likely to . . ."). It might even get a whole chapter (always tucked safely late in the book), but gender distinction does not arise in these books as anything fundamental to making a marriage work.

That's odd. Because when you open the New Testament to get counsel from passages explicitly about marriage, distinguishing gender is just about all the authors talk about! You can easily verify what I am saying by looking up "marry," "husbands," or "wives" in a concordance or online and then go and read the passages you find. This gender-marriage link in the Bible also creates an interesting Christian social phenomenon. Most Christian couples, when choosing a Scripture reading for their wedding, default to 1 Corinthians 13, also known as "The Love Chapter." You can see why. When they sit down to look through the New Testament for a nice passage that talks about marriage, that pesky issue of gender distinction keeps popping up. When Jesus brings up marriage, it is in response to a question of divorce, which is not an issue you tend to want to bring up at your wedding.

And the author of Hebrews, when touching on marriage, just seems concerned with sex. But in the main marriage passages, when Paul or Peter talk about it, they make uncomfortable statements that will offend the groom's Uncle Charlie, and others that will send Deirdre, the bride's sister, through the roof. So the couple sigh and decide it is best to simply quote 1 Corinthians 13, the chapter of love ("Love is patient, love is kind . . ."). This chapter commemorates their wedding even though it was not written about marriage at all but about church relationships.

Their decision is not a great tragedy. Certainly a passage like 1 Corinthians 13 bears on marriage. The principles from many different Scripture stories can help people love their spouses better. And the genderless Christian books can help us to do that too. But it is curious that, when marriage comes up as a point of instruction, the topic about which the New Testament shouts is one about which the Christian books barely whisper.

This difference between the Bible and Christian discourse compelled me to include Bible study in engagement and marriage counseling meetings. But it also meant that, in counseling couples, I do not get a lot of confirmation from other sources. Exploring gender distinction as power energizing a home or church is to hike an unfrequented trail. Trying to understand and apply, much less celebrate, what the Bible teaches about gender in relationships is like walking through the woods on a path that is overgrown and uncertain. You might have been sure at the trailhead that you were going down a marked route but, with so few visitors using it, overgrowth and underhangs have moved in to obscure it. The cultural relationship landscape has reclaimed the territory, leaving you, poor hiker, to wonder and fret as to whether you remain on a trail at all.

It is not as if gender is a nonissue in our time. In universities across the land, whole academic departments and college curriculums have sprung up, devoted to "Gender Studies," which used to be called "Women's Studies" in its maidenly years, before it found itself made matron of many other topics of human experience needing care: the use of language to deny others' legitimacy, the plight of those with unsanctioned sexual desires, the measure of how different men and women are or aren't. But in these departments and throughout their consequent journals, the meaning of gender is researched, tested, and fiercely debated, leading to little agreement on what makes a woman or what is the meaning of man.[1] This haze about what gender even is pervades the academy, both secular[2] and Christian,[3] and these clouds fog up our relationship practices. The mystery goes beyond argument about whether gender is inherent or socially constructed. It obscures how men and women should behave toward each other. Thus these departments, professors, and journals, grappling with some of the paradoxes of gender, tend to define it out of our lives.

Furthermore, laudable labors to secure gender equality and inclusion have gone in the unfortunate direction of minimizing gender distinction. Dartmouth philosophy professor Amy Allen astutely summarizes the conflict within American feminism from the 1970s forward that led to our current flattened gender landscape.[4] She explains how the academic second wave feminism (1970s–1980s) had two camps in tension. The first sought to empower women by showing them to be capable of supposed masculine traits (reason vs. emotion, culture-focus vs. nature-focus, tied-to-mind vs. tied-to-body, initiating and goal-oriented vs. passive). Alternatively, the second camp sought equality by valuing femininity and what women do, working to reconstruct society's values to value what women are. These two camps never reached a resolution about whose way was better. The second camp resisted the first camp's approach, arguing that helping women to be more like men continues the patriarchal sexism that subjugates women, tacitly agreeing that the masculine is better. The first camp responded with the critique that the second's "separate but equal" policy continues the subjugation, keeping women marginalized from the centers of male power. The 1990s' hybrid outcome, the third wave feminist theory, strenuously pushed to minimize any distinction between men and women and what they do in life. So here we are.

These results removed from our relationships the God-given gift.[5] It is as if these efforts cut down some of the trees that were marked with trail blazes and, instead, now highlight some uncertain deer trails. We are again left alone in the woods. The church has not found its footing in this dense thicket.

As a pastor, I choose what to preach about each Sunday. Sometimes this is exciting—I see how a passage about the Sabbath will address the lawyer spending too many hours at work or how Christ's birth narrative will comfort the brokenhearted girl freshly split up from her boyfriend. Other times sermon preparation weighs heavy on me, when, say, we are going through a Bible book and we come to a passage teaching an unpopular topic, "pew grippers" as my wife calls them. I have never felt at liberty to skip over such passages since, as Paul tells Timothy, "*all* Scripture is . . . profitable for teaching" (2 Tim. 3:16). Brushing aside difficult passages cheats the church. And experience urges me on because tackling those passages has often rewarded our church with needed though neglected wisdom.

But this decision costs. In our time specifically, preaching on gender distinction in relationship can be expensive. A church that makes it a topic of discussion is liable to uncover intense feelings and discord. People leave and the church loses members. Jerram Barrs, professor of Christian studies and contemporary culture at Covenant Theological Seminary, to publicize a book on women in the Bible, gave talks in recent years on the Bible's high view of women. He confessed being overwhelmed *on every speaking occasion* at the emotional response that that message evokes. This included, on one occasion, a several-minute cheering ovation from women, to the astonishment of the men present.[6]

The Bible's message that women are equally fashioned in God's image, by definition, has been available and without innovation for the last three or four thousand years. Yet it provokes an immediate and intense response whenever the topic is broached. It is as if the gender distinction practices of the church somehow obscure the message of equality. It is similarly telling that prominent pastor and author John Piper indicates disagreement in this area even in his former Minneapolis church, Bethlehem Baptist, an enclave of conservative thought and practice. He discreetly divulges, "Not all the women of our church see things exactly the same way."[7] One can see why, nowadays, many preachers feel like it is easier to just not bring gender up. Others may bring it up, defiantly rebutting the cultural minimizing, but not addressing legitimate concerns the culture has raised.

Yet if God has told people to make gender distinction a main point of relationships, as we see the New Testament doing, there must be rich benefits to doing so. Detecting those benefits could alleviate the smoldering discomfort with this topic that is present in churches. Women who feel increasingly conflicted about the evangelical teaching need to perceive a logic behind what their Bible says about how they should behave. Men who tend to go with the status quo need to examine whether what they are doing is really what the Bible teaches. And people struggling with same-sex attraction need a whole lot more than the condemnation that the church has often dispensed to them. We need a new trail guide, one that acknowledges the forest as it now is.

So, there I was, a pastoral candidate, standing in this silent, expectant church, just asked by this lovely young woman, whether she would be welcome, coming to Jesus just as she was, a lesbian. Somehow, I did not feel that this was a yes or no question. I could see nothing else to do but to start talking about relationships.

I said that I know that lesbian relationships provide a lot of good things. They must, because they are relationships and can involve love. God, in His common grace, gives blessings to us through all kinds of relationships. But I also confessed that I personally had to repent over how I conducted some of my own close relationships in the past because, even though they felt natural, they were not what God wanted for me. There was bad in there with the good. I found that there was a lot more I needed to understand about myself and Him. God accepted me as a sinner, but also corrected how I lived. If I really was following Him, I had to be open to that change. Otherwise, whatever I claimed, whether just as I am or not, I was not really *coming* to the Lord of the universe at all. I said that this kind of thing, allowing God to contradict what we thought was right, would be a common experience for everyone in the church I would pastor. In this way, I tried to convey to her that she would be welcome as she was, but not to stay as she was. That welcome meant joining us all in our repenting and learning about relationships God's way.

These are not easy issues. That church did hire me, but I realized back then that, what with the woods constantly changing, the guide we wanted was the unchanging Scriptures. The very book that stops us with its gender prohibitions also pushes us to gender celebration. So this book takes a systematic theological approach to the teaching on gender found in the Bible. I find that reading the Old and New Testaments as both unified and authoritative on this subject gives us a machete to hack a swath through the now dense foliage of the relationship jungle and, en route, to make sense of questions found on many lips today. I have now taken walks with a number of people through the shadowy relationship wood, identifying the Bible's main points and prevalent themes on the subject. With this guide, we struck out for the deep groves of the forest, to the mysterious troves of intimacy, discovering the ways of gender that God has given to make the journey.

There are choices of confidence in using any guide, so I want to note how I will read the Bible in this book. A systematic approach, gathering all passages on a topic, runs the risk of doing injustice to the voices of the individual biblical authors, so we will consult the text in a biblical-theological fashion, making great effort to understand the statements of the authors in their grammatical, historical, and literary context. Sometimes this takes a little more effort to do, rather than just quoting verses here and there. I beg the reader's patience and promise to relegate as much background information to endnotes as possible without sacrificing a clear understanding of these stories. I also reserve scholarly debate about passages for the endnotes, but disclose here that I accept both the authorship claimed by the individual New Testament texts themselves and the representation of the Old Testament authors of their narrative's time and place. I have confidence in the Gospel writers' accuracy in preserving the teaching of Jesus and in the historicity of the events covered by the biblical writers.

In fact, one finds that a systematic approach here, taking the Scriptures as a whole, does little harm to the individual biblical authors on account of their remarkable unity on this matter. Unlike the academics arguing in the universities, the biblical authors all seem to agree on the principles of gender. This unity is due, in part no doubt, to the strong Judaic-Christian value of rooting current expressions in the past Holy Writ. Later witnesses held earlier writings to be authoritative, so previous biblical authors shaped the latter's thoughts. But the consistency also comes of them having the same things to say. This fact alone, when appreciated, is staggering, considering the span of time over which the biblical books were composed, and the variety of cultural situations in which they were written. First Peter 3:4–6, from the first century CE, for example, calls for imitation of the matriarch Sarah in her gendered practice of 2000 BCE, declaring that her principles still benefit the people of God after two thousand years. First Corinthians 14:34, of the same New Testament era, recalls the Mosaic law of the mid- to late second millennium BCE in affirming the practice of gender distinction. These doctrines stood the test of time because the authors continued to find them true and practically valuable. The texts themselves, then, justify proceeding upon the principle that the Bible speaks with unified voices on gender. And, on this issue, that speaking begins in the very first chapter of Genesis and continues right on through.

"What does God have to do with my love life?"

CHAPTER 2

The God of Closeness Has Shown Himself

You don't want to have an affair with the mailman. At least, I hope that you don't. And you probably shouldn't be telling your economics professor your deepest secret about what happened in third grade. We do not want to be close with everybody. Suspicious strangers, recognizable acquaintances, waving neighbors, kind colleagues, fellow gym rats, faraway friends, bowling buddies, raucous roommates, odd extended family, chiding church members, loving life partners—we have varying nearness with each. Have you ever felt shock at an acquaintance revealing something about himself too personal for you to hear? That feeling was probably there because he shouldn't have. Different degrees of closeness are appropriate to each connection, the tightest ties being to our family and spouses (we hope).

So relationships run along a continuum and we especially want to care for the close ones. This book concerns the stuff of that closeness, how it is developed and preserved. Now, marriage is one of the closest human bonds possible. Not all of us marry, but marriage can be a means of discussing bonding principles because of its relational intensity. Marriage is union projected on a screen large enough to recognize the wrinkles of close ties.

People who study marriages tell us something surprising. What makes marriages flourish can be boiled down to one thing. Many studies on marital success from various disciplines converge on this one thing. It is not having children or lots of money. It is not good communication or setting up his and her bath towels. It is not even quality time together or date nights. No. It is emotional intimacy. According to marriage counseling researcher Everett L. Worthington Jr., marital success is not as much about how partners behave toward each other, whether they communicate effectively or manage conflict, or even about how they confess transgressions and forgive, as much as it is about the emotional bond that underlies these acts. After writing a widely used marriage counseling manual based on years of experience, and reviewing the text after seven years of further research and feedback from numerous counselors, Worthington's main self-criticism was that he should have written "more about emotion and emotional bonds."[1]

Likewise, University of Washington psychologist John M. Gottman, known for his close examination of married couples in the Seattle "Love Lab," claims to be able to predict divorce or marital success among couples with 91 percent accuracy.[2] After twenty-seven years of research, he concluded that successful marriages "are based on a deep friendship. . . . These couples tend to know each other intimately."[3] According to W. Bradford Wilcox, director of the National Marriage Project at the University of Virginia, a man's emotional involvement in a marriage matters far more to a wife's happiness than his level of commitment, his participation in household labor, the presence of children, or even perceptions of equality.[4] Wilcox and Steven L. Nock, the late University of Virginia professor of sociology and director of the Marriage Matters Project, phrase it academically: "The emotional functions . . . [are] particularly crucial for contemporary marital happiness and marital stability."[5] Worthington is simpler: "emotional intimacy is one of the best barometers of marital happiness."[6]

Conversely, the absence of intimacy shortens unions. Wilcox accounts for our higher divorce rates by people expecting "an intense emotional relationship," and not getting it.[7] Sociologist and Roman Catholic priest Andrew M. Greeley finds that, even though 40 percent of those in "bottoming out" marriages think of their spouse as kind and gentle, 60 percent of them do not consider their spouse to be their best friend. Failure to make best friends in spite of good qualities simply means a lack of intimacy. Thirty-nine percent of these floundering marriages consider their spouse "untrustworthy."[8] In fact, feeling unable to trust one's spouse and not being made to feel important by one's spouse are the two highest-ranking reasons given by Greeley for marriages ending.[9] Again, these are simply different windows into a house empty of intimacy. Couples' therapy suggests remedies to this emptiness. Emotionally focused therapy, based on the heavily researched view of relationships called attachment theory[10] and prevalent now for almost thirty years,[11] boasts the best results of any other measured form of couple intervention.[12] What accounts for this therapy's success? Its "ultimate goal . . . is to help couples create . . . secure emotional bonds."[13]

All of this research seems to be just catching up to what the Bible has said for thousands of years. When first defining marriage as it was meant to be, the Good Book paints a sublime picture of holistic intimacy: the two "shall become one flesh" (Gen. 2:24), a vision that has inspired—as well as held together—marriages for millennia.

Chapter 5 of the book of Ephesians, a letter celebrating the mysterious unity and ministry of Christ's people, takes up His salvation's impact on home relationships. Verses 22–33 of that chapter, the quintessential New Testament marriage passage, simply elaborates on the Genesis 2:24 "one flesh" verse (quoted in Eph. 5:31). The extended and lofty explanation of marriage responsibilities encourages husbands to think of their wives as their own bodies (v. 28). The text calls a husband to nourish and cherish his wife in the same way that he cares for his own skin and stomach (v. 29). One's body could be seen as a possession, but it is a possession unlike any other. For it is also one's self. Our identities are wrapped up in our bodies, nigh impossible to differentiate from them. Marriage, argues Ephesians, folds a spouse into one's own identity. A more profound image of intimacy is hard to imagine. Indeed, "he who loves his wife loves himself" (v. 28).

So both Bible and social science agree on the key: emotional intimacy. Come deeper though. The Bible understands intimacy as critical to close relationships because it constantly occurs in God's own Self. Christianity, unique among monotheistic religions, understands close relationship to be happening within God, in whom three discrete Persons of a Trinity nonetheless constitute one God (2 Cor. 13:14). The

Persons of God are sometimes articulated as Father, Son, and Spirit. Jesus Christ, in some of His last earthly words, commands baptism into the one God in the name of "the Father and the Son and the Holy Spirit" (Matt. 28:19). In this three-in-one, the First, Second, and Third Members of the Godhead are distinct but not separate, and this is why we have relationships.

Let us speak of them without their familiar labels to generalize the ties between them, because their society does encompass all human relationships, not just Father to Son. The First and the Second and the Third Persons of God's Trinity deeply love each other. Take the Second Person. We may not be used to thinking of Wisdom as a Person, but the Bible does (Luke 11:49). The apostle Paul calls the Second Person, whom we know as Jesus, the Wisdom of God (1 Cor. 1:30, 24). Jesus also pictures Himself as the person of Wisdom (Matt. 11:19; Luke 7:35). Although wisdom in the Old Testament book of Proverbs usually refers to the wise counsel of Solomon,[14] Proverbs 8 also personifies Wisdom interacting with the First Person of the Triune God. Wisdom, here portrayed as feminine, claims to have been begotten[15] by God (the First Person; v. 24, 25) and to have been with Him, at His side, through all His creating of the universe (vv. 25–29). As imagined in our book's opening to part 1, Wisdom participates in the creation as Master Workman and says, "I was daily his delight, rejoicing before him always" (v. 30). If this is indeed the Second Person speaking, consider what those words express. Besides seeing the Second as, in some manner, feminine to the First, the First delights daily in the Second and the Second rejoices merely to be in the presence of the First. They thoroughly enjoy just spending time with each other. It is as if the one brightens up when the other gets back from the store. The other glows in anticipation of when they will be together again. With these two simply delighting in each other, we glimpse the relational intimacy in God.

Intimate people like to sit next to each other. Psalm 110:1 reads, "The LORD says to my Lord: 'Sit at my right hand, until I make your enemies your footstool.'" Jesus, as the Second, chooses this Old Testament verse to highlight His Trinitarian relationship to the First. It is the only verse from the Psalms that we read Jesus quoting on two different occasions.[16] He puzzles His listeners with it:

> [35]And as Jesus taught in the temple, he said, "How can the scribes say that the Christ is the son of David? [36]David himself, in the Holy Spirit, declared,

> "'The Lord said to my Lord,
> "Sit at my right hand,
>   until I put your enemies under your feet."'
>
> [37]David himself calls him Lord. So how is he his son?"
>   (Mark 12:35–37)

Jesus asks them why David would call David's eventual son, his Lord. Nobody has an answer for Jesus because nobody suspects that very God the Second would come as David's son, the Christ. If we accept Jesus' exegesis, a powerful image of intimacy confronts us. The First beckons the Second to sit next to Him[17] while He does things for Him. "Sit down right here by Me while I arrange things for You to flourish in ruling. No, not over there—right here, close to Me."

In that scene of Mark 12, the Third Person, the Spirit of God, is there too, only you might miss Him if you do not look at the passage closely. He is in verse 36, moving to make this scene of intimacy known through David's prophetic expression. The Third Himself, in other places, exhibits intimacy by "resting on" the Second (Isa. 11:2; 42:1). In fact, in the famous messianic passage, the Second claims, "The Spirit of the Lord GOD is upon me, because the LORD has anointed me to bring good news . . ." (Isa. 61:1). You could easily read the Third here to enjoy lying upon the Second because He likes what the Second does, broadcasting the good news, binding the brokenhearted, and freeing the captives. The Second would feel the Third embracing Him, exulting, "I really love the things that You do."

The New Testament Gospels picture even more clearly the intimacy between the First and the Second. When the Second gets angry at slights to things that mean a lot to the First, yelling at the merchants and driving the money-changers out of the temple, the First's house (John 2:16); or when the great affection of the First for the Second is broadcast by the First, bellowing from the sky, "This is my beloved . . ." (Matt. 3:17; 17:5; Mark 1:11; 9:7; Luke 3:22; cf. 9:35; John 12:28), or cited by the Second, as when He tells a parable representing Himself as an only beloved (Mark 12:6; Matt. 12:18); or when the Second expresses how They enjoy doing the same things, declaring that He is working as the First is working, He gives life to people as the First does, and He assigns the kingdom just as the First does (John 5:17; 5:21; Luke 22:29; cf. John 14:31); or when They enjoy saying the same things, as when the Second speaks just as the First does (John

12:49–50; 14:10);[18] or when the First gives His own privileges to the Second (John 5:26–27); or even when a conflict of desires between the First and Second yields to constructive action, as the Second recoils from cross and death, but yields with, "Not as I will, but as you will" (Matt. 26:39; cf. vv. 42, 44; and perhaps a similar constructive divergence even between the Second and Third, where the Third must drive the Second into the wilderness, Mark 1:12); or when the Second announces Their unity with "I and the Father are one" (John 10:30); or how They share everything with, "All that the Father has is mine," and "all mine are yours" (John 16:15; 17:10). When we see these things, what are we seeing but Their intimacy?

When He is about to die, and His disciples are upset about His leaving them, Jesus allows Himself a moment of indulgence with them. He more than hints that, if His disciples really loved Him, they would be happy for Him, because departing from this world means that He gets to go be with the First. And the First is just so great (John 14:28)! It is a strange way to look at one's death. But if you anticipate the ecstasy of returning to someone you adore, even death is relativized. At least, it is for Jesus. That's how intimate They are.

Following the Gospels, the New Testament Letters ascribe this same close character to the Persons, where the Trinity is cited in connection with love and, specifically, fellowship (2 Cor. 13:14; Eph. 2:18). For example, They are pictured as possessing a penchant for the same pursuits: 2 Thessalonians 2:16–17 avows that the First and Second both comfort, and 1 Corinthians 12:4–6 avers that all three get into the same game of gifting people: varieties of gifts, yet the same Spirit; varieties of service, yet the same Lord; varieties of working of those gifts, yet the same God empowering them. Second Corinthians 3:17 rather starkly proclaims the Second and Third's unity: "Now the Lord is the Spirit." In case you missed it, the same proclamation is repeated in the next verse: "This comes from the Lord who is the Spirit" (v. 18). In other words, there is no way you are going to separate these two, They are so close. You want to make something of it? In the Bible's next letter, Galatians 4:6 somewhat confusingly portrays Them all involved in our shouting out in joy: "Abba! Father!" ("Abba" is like our word "Dad.") It is a bizarre statement: the First sends the Third of the Second into our hearts, says Paul, to help us cry out this phrase of intimacy. They all seem to tumble over each other in assuring familial closeness.

Matthew 11:27 gives another telling glimpse of the intimacy the first two of the three enjoy.[19] The Second, in the person of the Christ, in the course of praying to the First, exclaims, "No one knows the Son except the Father, and no one knows the Father except the Son . . . ," on the face of it, a puzzling pronouncement. Obviously, others "know" the Son, or "know" God. Many Scripture verses say that people know God the Father or know Jesus. So Jesus must rather, in this absolute-sounding statement, be describing an intimacy that only They share. The statement must mean something like, "Nobody knows Him like I know Him. And nobody knows Me like He does." It sounds like a song we might hear on the radio: "Our love is like no other . . ." The Second is the First's beloved (Eph. 1:6) and will sweat blood over the disruption of their bond (Luke 22:42–44). The apostle makes similar statements of exclusive knowing regarding the Third's familiarity with the First (1 Cor. 2:10–11) and the First's familiarity with the Third (Rom. 8:27). These Guys are tight!

So this splendid confederation is all very nice for God. But what does it have to do with us? It has to do with what we are. Being made in God's image has given us our ability and privilege to have human relationships. The communal side of God's command to "be holy, for I the LORD your God am holy" (Lev. 19:2) would be to "be in relationship, for We are in relationship." We display His Triune image when we get close to one another. So it is most instructive to understand our relationships this way.

Presbyterian churches are run by a group of elders called a session. One time our church's session, which included me, was trying to decide how to deal with a recalcitrant church member. It was tough. We each came at the conflict from a different viewpoint. The situation threatened to dissolve into a morass of disagreement. But, fortunately, we stuck with one another through many meetings to hammer out this decision. In an atmosphere of determined respect, meeting after meeting, we asserted our opinions back and forth, until we navigated a course of action we could all admire. The plan was compassionate to the person, honoring to God, and showed the church's heart to anyone watching. We made a much stronger decision than any of us could have made each on our own. But even more, we would all agree that this was one of our greatest moments, a highlight of our lives, to be solving this difficulty as a team, each one of us crucial and not one of us alone. We had grown in Trinitarian intimacy. Paul even compares human marriage to the union between the First and the Second (1 Cor. 11:3, 12). God has given relationships for us to discover more about Him.

But there is more than that. Jesus follows His thought about God's internal intimacy in Matthew 11:27 with a striking extension: "No one knows the Father except the Son *and anyone to whom the Son chooses to reveal him.*" God is not stopping with Their own delightful intimacy with each other, nor even with letting us see it in our close friendships with other people, as through a glass darkly. No. God intends to invite us into that same love, to have us in the family. Not just the windows but the doors to the divine bond are being flung open. The waiter, to our shock, is directing us to the restaurant table with the heavenly celebrities sloshing their glasses in raucous rapport, and chairs are being pulled up for us to sit. Jesus put it this way: "If anyone loves me, he will keep my word, and my Father will love him, and we will come to him and make our home with him" (John 14:23).[20] Their love proceeds from the Father through the Son to us. In other words, God wants us close. This tells us what relationships are all about.

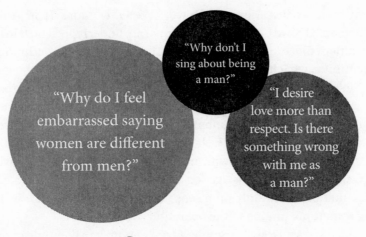

"Why don't I sing about being a man?"

"Why do I feel embarrassed saying women are different from men?"

"I desire love more than respect. Is there something wrong with me as a man?"

C H A P T E R 3

Gender Is Hard to Talk About for Good Reason

I don't feel that way at all. Is there something the matter with me?" asked Art. I was teaching our Marriage Checkup, a Bible study group for couples wanting to grow in their marriages. I was trying to help the wives see what their husbands needed, and referencing a popular Christian book, reporting the statistic that most men would rather feel respected than feel loved.[1] Desiring to prove the point, I asked for a show of hands from the husbands who would rather be respected than loved, confidently expecting all hands to rise. Art's hand stayed stubbornly down. The demonstration backfired. He not only wrecked my point, I had left him honestly concerned about what this revealed about him. Was he a real man?

Talking about gender is always awkward. The academy cannot agree on what it is: social construct or essential aspect or malleable covering. Popular books bounce back and forth about its importance. Polite conversation is always searching about for phraseology to speak about it. Consider the dance around what femininity is, and an inability to reach a definition, in a recent column of the newspaper of record by journalist Maureen Dowd, "We Offer More Than Ankles, Gentlemen."[2] Dowd bemoans how women are underrepresented in high government office. She at first suggests, quoting others' descriptions of the feminine, what it is about women that should recommend them for these jobs: "Women reach across the aisle, seek consensus, verbalize and empathize more, manage and listen better. Women are more pragmatic, risk-averse and, unburdened by testosterone, less bellicose." But then, in the next sentence, she must concede, "Unfortunately, these 'truisms' haven't held true with many of the top women I've covered in Washington." She must go on to make her argument for equal representation based only on a sense of fairness, *not* because women bring something unique to the operation.

Musing over Dowd's argument too long may make it miscarry. If women really are practically interchangeable with men, because there is hardly any difference, why would it be important to strive for equal representation in a presidential cabinet? The distinction becomes something equivalent to hair color. Would fairness demand an equal number of blondes and brunettes in government?

So then why does Dowd pull back from delineating feminine qualities? It is because she is also smart enough to know that such an argument would be vulnerable to contradiction. Because it is so hard to say what makes a woman a woman. (The same editorial page encountered similar difficulty, a year earlier, in an attempt to distinguish masculinity.[3]) Simply listen to the next conversation you hear touching on possible differences between women and men. If the conversation is at all public, its tone will be sheepish or tentative, as if the words themselves are nervously looking over their shoulders. This is true, inside or outside the church. Mississippi State University sociologist John P. Bartkowski, who studies Christians' gendered practices, finds the debate about gender in churches "remarkably similar to academic and popular disputes on the subject."[4]

Even the Bible, as definite and as unembarrassed as it is in describing gender's creation, sounds ungainly. Genesis cannot get through its first chapter without proclaiming a profound distinction of masculine and feminine, albeit awkwardly:

> Then God said, "Let us make man in our image, after our likeness. And let them have dominion . . ."

> So God created man in his own image,
>   in the image of God he created him;
>   male and female he created them. (Gen. 1:26–27)

Is it one thing God created or two? Is it him or them? Why are the singulars and plurals mixed up in the same sentence? If even the Bible cannot talk about it without some inelegance, maybe clumsiness is inherent in the matter itself. Let me suggest that this is indeed the case. Clumsiness is endemic because of what gender really is: a fundamental element of bearing the image of God. Gender is hard to understand because God is hard to understand.

This is important to think through. We ought to take the translation "male and female" to refer to a reality larger than simply physical sex differences. In chapter 2's more focused story on humanity's origins, the creation of Eve is distinct from that of Adam. Her genesis occurs after that of the animals, with their own sexual differences (Gen. 2:7; 2:18–22; 6:19). Thus, the second creation account of chapter 2 emphasizes what chapter 1 implies, that sexual differentiation existed in the world before the conferring of the divine image's "male and female." This latter distinction, arriving with people, was something new and different. So, even though the same Hebrew words for Adam and Eve's "male and female" (*zakar vunqebah*) are also used at times to describe animals' sexual difference, the text calls us to distinguish between man and beast. In this book, I will use "male and female" to mean the physical or biological or sexual differences we observe in ourselves, some of which we share with animals. But I will reserve the terms "gender," "man and woman," and "masculine and feminine" to mean that uniquely human bearing of the image of God. These latter terms more clearly designate God's specific work in humanity. This implied dichotomy may be why the male and female of the beasts and the broccoli are not deemed important enough to mention in chapter 1's creation story—the terms of division first appear in connection with humanity. But we can perceive the masculine-feminine to be a crucial point of bearing God's image since, in the creation recap of chapter 5, the author brings them up again, with all their awkwardness, to elaborate on people being in God's likeness: "When God created man, he made him in the likeness of God. Male and female he created them, and he blessed them and named them Man when they were created" (Gen. 5:1–2).

First and foremost, then, the Bible sees gender as a further gift added upon our biology, shaping our identities and deeply revealing of

God's Self. The New Testament repeats the profundity of Genesis. The apostle Paul writing to the Corinthians claims that both woman and man are, literally, "out of God" (*ek tou theou*). He says that, even though each comes out of the other—Eve initially coming out of Adam and men subsequently coming out of Eve and her daughters by birth—the source of both ("all things"), where they come out of, is God (1 Cor. 11:11–12). God, then, must contain both the masculine and feminine,[5] which is another way of saying that women and men both bear His image.

This is why it is hard to talk about what makes a man a man, or what a true woman is. These questions bear on the knowledge of God. So to describe manliness apart from something about God is bound to miss it. To reach for the essence of womanhood, like it's a perfume bottle on the second shelf, unrelated to Trinitarian godliness, is bound to fail and end up being insulting. You will be left with an evanescent whiff of something without substance. To say that men are from Mars and women are from Venus might capture a statistical distribution of some traits, but what do you say to the exceptionally sensitive man? Is he not a man? Or to a woman with high levels of testosterone? Is she less of a woman? Thankfully, the Bible gives us a better place to look for our manhood and womanliness.

And it is not in cultural practices. There are always masculine and feminine expressions in each culture, as we discuss in chapter 13, "Culture: The Clothes of Gender," but the Genesis and 1 Corinthians texts teach us right off that we must be careful not to use these expressions to define gender. Scripture would rebuke us for looking askance at women who like football or men who like show tunes. These are not contradictions of anything but the culture's consensus on what many men or women like to do. We mustn't confuse cultural preferences with gender.

On the other hand, if Genesis 1 and 1 Corinthians 11 are right, it also means that minimizing gender loses something very important. As explained in the previous chapter, many today seek to reduce gender distinction in an effort to promote women's equality, an understandable and laudable goal. But is the process of wiping out discrimination erasing part of who we are? Boys and girls, women and men, should be treated the same, we are told. Select grade schools in Stockholm, Sweden, for example, refuse to use the pronouns "he" and "she," instead referring to everyone as "hen."[6] A number of American college campuses are likewise linguistically experimenting with pronouns, avoiding "he" and "she" by substituting with "they," to the irritation of English teachers everywhere. Such gender neutrality, making people the same in all contexts, loses the biblical balance, along with a significant portion of what it means to be human.

At one point we lived in Park Slope, Brooklyn. In that neighborhood, people strive not to impose gender stereotypes, which is nice, but they can similarly go overboard. Once when my wife was working child care at our food co-op, a distinguished, professorial stay-at-home dad dropped off a five-year-old child that he and his wife had obviously dressed and groomed to be gender neutral. I know how these parents were thinking. They did not want to impose any preconceptions on what the child would become. In fact, the moms on duty could not tell exactly what the child was, girl or boy. But when another youngster went over to the mystery kid and proclaimed, "You're not a girl, you're a boy!" she (yes, alas, she was a girl) burst out crying. The problem was that children around ages four through six yearn to know what gender they are and to act accordingly. It is a time of life when it really matters to them. They truly like pink or blue.

"No I'm not!" she cried.

"Yes you are. You're wearing boys' sneakers," returned the accuser. Don't ask me how these five-year-olds knew the subtle difference in clothing but, as I said, the issue is very important to them. They notice. To this argument the poor little accused, confused girl had no answer, except to weep afresh.

The interesting thing was that the other workers on duty did not know what to say. Our neighborhood tended to discourage making distinctions. Should they say that it does not matter what she is? Should they affirm the little girl's right to be whatever she wanted? But neither of those were what the little girl was crying out for. Finally Mary K. blurted out, "Of course she's a girl. It's something inside!" This stopped the crying, rebuffed the skeptic, and happy play recommenced. Something lost was recovered.

If gender differences help to make us like God, our genders should inspire celebration. A man, properly oriented toward the Giver of his life, should arise in the morning, singing loudly in gratitude that he is a man, the image of God. A woman should exult in being a woman, as if it were the best thing in the world to be, the image of God. This is what it would mean to receive what we've been given as the weighty gift of God's Self. Sadly, gender is often today a thing of embarrassment or shame. Do you know many women who celebrate being women? Or men being men? Truth be told, people come closest to doing just that during sex, although they might not admit it. That is a clue to what gender really is, but the bed should not be the only possible place of celebration.

Mary K. has attended several groups for pastors' wives over the years. She began to notice that whenever the discussion came to one of the ten principal New Testament passages instructing on gender distinction,[7] these women, apparently the mature of the church, would spend all of the time talking about what the verses do not mean. It seemed to Mary K. that the passages were always held at arm's length. If you can only read Scriptures about gender and talk about what they don't mean, you're not experiencing the enlivening mission that God has given us. You're bypassing the beauty of the picture. You're missing out on the dance. If these verses are true, we cannot understand God's image in us without rejoicing in the gift He has given, and discovering why He has given it.

Many do not celebrate being who they are because the masculine and feminine are so cloudy. I can relate. I grew up with three older sisters. This was helpful in certain ways; I initially could relate better to women. But in a big way, my own sisters' struggles to define their femininity in an era of gender role upheaval left me often feeling guilty about being a boy. In our interactions, gender got minimized.

For others, celebration is out of the question because gender in them has been damaged. Far from seeing their gender as a gift, they hate being what they are. One woman who came to my church eventually disclosed that the youth group leader in another church had taken inappropriate liberties with her while she was growing up. Since then, she found it very hard to embrace being a woman. Isn't this perfectly understandable? Her womanliness was tied up with something bad. Another attender had been molested by a male family member. This just about ruined her for having a friendship with a man, no matter how respectful and considerate the men were (and some of them who tried were very).

For those in these dark places, the obfuscation of gender has shred hope for finding a way to enjoy intimacy. Yet I have watched men counseled with the biblical principles of gender (the material of part 2 of this book) unfold like morning glories in the sun, waking up to being who they are. As they take the gendered trail, they begin to sing about being a man. Similarly, it is marvelous to see women come to enjoy being women, as God looks at them. They bound like Nubian ibexes on the mountains. "O fairest of Creation / last and best / Of all God's works!"[8]

One more thing. The creation narrative makes much of gender. Characterizing it as so fundamental means that much of what follows in the Bible is also about gender. Many passages that we might not immediately recognize as being about gender are in fact about gender. In other words, if gender shows us the image of God, then a book about the image of God (the Bible) will often show us gender.

"Oh, God!" Augustine allegedly once prayed. "Make us hungry to learn what Your love makes You so ardent to teach!" God is ardent to teach us about gender in relationship. We can again rejoice by learning what it means to be God's image together. And the first point to consider about that is what is not different in the genders. It is a point the biblical authors have staunchly and uniquely argued throughout history.

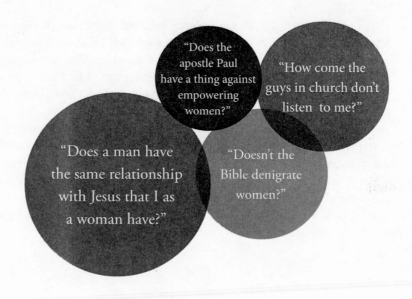

CHAPTER 4

They Are Equal in Power and Glory

Pundits, popular novels, and casual commentators all enjoy pegging the Bible as misogynist. Sometimes they take extraordinary liberties in doing so. One bestselling novel, *The Red Tent*, by Anita Diamant,[1] represents the ancient Hebrew matriarchs as hopelessly oppressed, freed only by secretly embracing Canaanite religion. Such representation betrays a very poor understanding of the ancient Near East and the second millennium BCE Canaanite religions. I find myself wondering how life-affirming Diamant would find the goddess Asherah, (and her lord, the god Baal) if the author actually lived under the religion she so romanticizes. Would she enjoy life as a temple prostitute? Would she feel life-affirmed as she performed child sacrifice?

Diamant may only sustain the novel's fantasy by ignoring one simple fact. When the biblical author first put reed to papyrus or vellum and wrote down the words of Genesis 1:27 ("in the image of God he created . . . female . . ."), it was big news in the ancient world. There was a clear hierarchy. Kings were made in the image of God. Nobles were a little lower. And at the bottom of the cosmological order were slaves and women.[2] To say that a woman was equally an image-bearer of God grated on the ears of the ancients. Nonetheless, the Bible, from its very first chapter and its patriarchs' earliest books, consistently asserted it. For example, in Job, a book conservative scholars date in its original form to the patriarchal age (ca. 2000 BCE), righteous Job, an exhibition of virtue (Job 1:8), gives inheritance to his daughters as well as his sons (Job 42:15). That is, he makes no difference in the inheritance. That says a lot. Job's daughters, in fact, feature prominently in the narrative bookends of Job's story, even being named where his sons are not (Job 42:14). His sons, obviously well trained by their father, make a point of paying attention to and including their sisters (Job 1:4). This is Job the righteous, making his daughters and sons equal.

Contrast the message of equality with other ancient philosophers, cultures, or even sacred writings, which either denigrate women or ignore them. Plato, for example, locates the origin of women in men who had previously led cowardly or unrighteous lives,[3] and his pupil Aristotle nonchalantly suggests woman's inferiority.[4] Whatever the color of their tent, women in the Greece of these philosophers did not fare well, and little better in societies competing with ancient Israel. Perhaps the uniqueness of the Old Testament's stand on equality is best seen in its sanctity of sexual relations. Babylonian and Assyrian legal codes made specific provision for the regulation of prostitutes for men;[5] women were to be treated as men pleased. But Mosaic law unilaterally forbade both secular and sacred prostitution (Lev. 19:29; 21:9; Deut. 23:17–18). At times, Jewish society declined from these precepts, but there is only one reason for Scripture's unique stand. The God of the Bible is as concerned with women's honor and glory as bearers of the divine image as it is with men's.

The Old Testament preaches the equality of women in many ways. For example, in both forms of the great Sabbath commandment (Exod. 20:8–11; Deut. 5:12–15), God instructs the Israelites to keep members of their households from working, and then lists those household members: servants, children, sojourners, etc. In the list of those one should keep from working on the Sabbath, wives are not included. Why? It is simply because they comprise those being commanded. Women are being equally charged with the responsibility of preventing work in their households. They are equivalent to the men in receiving the commands. The Old Testament upholds this equality from beginning to end.[6]

The New Testament emphatically reasserts women as equally bearing the image of God, and its authors do so, again, amidst contradiction from the surrounding culture, be it Jewish or Roman. In speaking about believers, Colossians 3:10 states that "the new self . . . is being renewed . . . after the image of its creator," which statement was written to both men and women, as the letter's greeting, Colossians 1:2, shows.[7]

In contrast, much of Second Temple period Jewish thought seems to have degenerated from the Bible, judging from the prominent men's writings of the time.[8] Philo of Alexandria (20 BCE–50 CE) is typical: "[T]he mind occupies the rank of the man, the sensations that of the woman"; or Josephus (37–100 CE): "The woman, says the Law, is in all things inferior to the man," or the Talmudic rabbi's prayer: "Blessed art Thou who has not made me a woman. . . ."[9] Other texts in the Wisdom Literature, such as the *Wisdom of Jesus ben Sira* (aka Sirach or Ecclesiasticus; second century BCE) and *The Sentences of Pseudo-Phocylides* (probably first century CE), as well as many of the Qumran scrolls (first century CE), contain virulent misogynist language.[10]

Turning to the first-century Greco-Roman attitudes offers little consolation. While the Romans valued the virtuous mother, somewhat elevating matrons, and wealth expanded the posts to which elite women could attain, Romans still took the Greeks as their teachers on the order of things, which understood women to occupy a lower place in the cosmos. Lower-class women were often used for sexual encounters and even upper-class Roman women, because of their supposed inferiority, generally required a legal guardian in property matters.[11] In his humorous piece *The Art of Love*, Ovid describes how to have a mistress, encouraging us to practice deceit on women. He advises deception against only women, because they deserve it: to "deceive the deceivers," as they are a perfidious race.[12] Civilized Roman society would not even mention women by name in public unless they were of shady reputation or dead.[13]

The New Testament raises a cry of resolute opposition to such opinions. Roman citizens, Luke and Paul, who taken together wrote over half of the New Testament,[14] proudly name various women, in obviously positive references and in a variety of contexts. Swimming against his cultural context, Luke teaches, for example, of the business-woman Lydia (Act 16:14), the teacher Priscilla (Act 18:26), and the disciple Tabitha (or Dorcas; Acts 9:36). Paul's public letters to churches, intended for oral recitation, hold forth, for example, Phoebe and Mary and Tryphaena for praise (Rom. 16:1–2, 6, 12), specified together with the worthy men.

Even more telling is that in the empire, women were prevented from posts involving public speaking, as they were to be seen but not heard.[15] Christianity brashly contradicted this sensibility with its women prophets (Acts 2:17–18; 21:9, 1 Cor. 11:5).

Besides explicit statement and cultural contradiction, Scripture conveys gender equality even more powerfully through its portrayal of women's spirituality, correcting these cultures concerning gender with its many passages preaching women as bearing God's image.[16] The following sampling is not an exhaustive list.

Women's Equal Spirituality Conveyed in the Bible

- Women pray to God. Their prayers are heard, answered, and preserved: Genesis 25:22–23; 30:6, 22; 1 Samuel 1:9–12; 2:1–10
- Women receive appearances of God: Genesis 16:7–14; Judges 13:3, 9
- Female servants are equally valued under the law: Exodus 20:17; 21:26, 27, 32, as are women in general: Exodus 20:10; 21:22–23, 28–29; 22:22
- Women are healed: Luke 4:38–39; 8:43–48; 13:10–17
- Women bring sacrifices: Leviticus 12:6; 15:29; 1 Samuel 1:24
- Women become Nazirites and vow to God: Numbers 6:2; 1 Corinthians 7:5
- Women parent children with equal standing and honor: Exodus 20:12; 21:17; Leviticus 19:3; Proverbs 1:8; 31:26; Ephesians 6:1; 2 Timothy 3:15 (after 1:5)
- Women are educated by the rabbi: Luke 10:39, 42; 1 Corinthians 14:34–35; 1 Timothy 2:11
- Women receive salvation, equally "clothed in Christ": Matthew 15:28; John 4:5–30; Acts 5:14; 8:12; 16:15; Galatians 3:27–28; 1 Peter 3:7
- Women participate in Jesus' ministry: Luke 8:1–3; Matthew 12:49–50;[17] Acts 1:14

- A woman in the early church is referred to as a disciple of Jesus: Acts 9:36
- Women serve as Jesus' parable illustrations: Matthew 13:33; 25:1–13; Luke 15:8–10; 18:1–8; Mark 12:38–44
- Women, as prophetesses, receive and deliver divine revelation: Genesis 25:22–23; Exodus 15:20; Judges 4:4–7; 2 Kings 22:13–20 and 2 Chronicles 34:21–28; Luke 2:36–38; Acts 2:1–4 with verses 17–18, after Joel 2:28–29; Acts 21:9; 1 Corinthians 11:5
- Women receive God's gifts in worship: 2 Samuel 6:19; 1 Chronicles 16:3; Romans 12:6–13; 1 Corinthians 7:7; 12:7–11; 1 Peter 4:10
- Women serve in the public worship: Exodus 38:8; Psalm 148:7 with verses 12–14; 2 Chronicles 35:25; Ezra 2:65; 1 Corinthians 11:5
- Women serve as the first witnesses to the resurrection of Christ: Luke 24:22–24
- Women are vital in ministry in the church, sometimes "fellow workers," e.g., Phoebe, Priscilla, Euodia, and Syntyche: Acts 16:15; 18:2, 26; 21:9; Romans 16:1–3; Philippians 4:2–3; Colossians 4:15
- Women are tested regarding some official church positions,[18] requiring similar qualifications to men: 1 Timothy 3:11

Far removed from the cultural context, we might miss the activism behind these privileges. The New Testament recording of women as first witnesses to the resurrection is shocking, as Jewish law of the time did not recognize women as legal witnesses. One should also not gloss over the invitation to education by Rabbi Jesus when He welcomes Mary to "sit at His feet" along with His other disciples. The phrase "sit at the feet of" was sometimes a technical term for admitting a student to formal spiritual training. Again, Jesus' policy on teaching women, while in line with Old Testament principles, stands in contradistinction to the Jewish norm of His time. As Catherine Hezser, an expert in Jewish social history of late antiquity at the University of London, points out, "For rabbis, education means Torah scholarship, and more than once it is stated categorically that women are exempt from it."[19] In fact, according to the Jerusalem Talmud, Rabbi Eliezer the Great (Eliezer ben Hercanus), one of the greatest rabbis of the first century (which is why he was called, "the Great"), angrily told his son that he would rather burn the Torah than teach it to a woman.[20] Not in Rabbi Jesus' school. He was all for giving Mary "the good portion" (Luke 10:42).

So the God of the New Testament is as concerned with women's gifts and involvement in His affairs as with men's. Consequently, the resulting Christian community departed radically from their source cultures in regard to certain rights of women. Against contemporary Jewish law,[21] as well as against almost every other world religion,[22] the Christians preached the right of divorce for women as well as men.[23] Besides denial of right to divorce, easy, husband-initiated divorce contributes a great deal to the plight of women historically. The early church was adamant against this and Christian emperors tried very hard to limit it.[24] Early Christians were also unpopular because they unequivocally condemned polygamy.[25]

Even earlier, the apostle Paul shows his high regard for women, not only in his letters' greetings to them, but in comparing himself to a nursemaid or nursing mother (1 Thess. 2:7). The apostle's imagery speaks volumes. He has no qualms about identifying his role with a peculiarly womanly task, for women are equally important to the biblical worldview. This was two thousand years ago, when his culture was affirming the exact opposite.

As Rutgers professor of ancient Jewish history Gary A. Rendsburg aptly summarizes:

> Open your Bible at random and you will notice something striking: Female characters abound. And it's not simply a lot of women, it's a lot of strong women. These women are the antithesis of what we might expect from a patriarchal society. They are not passive, demure, timid and submissive, but active, bold, fearless and assertive. They are also not what we would expect based on contemporaneous Near Eastern literature, in which women generally do not play leading roles in the narrative.[26]

In other words, women in the Bible seem to know their equality. The alleged misogyny of the Good Book seems utterly lost on them. Because it is not there. Descriptions of women's mistreatment in its pages there certainly is, but the biblical women described recognize the abuse as a contradiction of God's will, not a following of it.

Any conception of gender derived from the Bible must then, first of all, staunchly affirm men and women as equal before God, having the same Spirit (1 Cor. 12:4–6). There is a reason the Bible stubbornly insists on this ontological equality. It is critical for the intimacy God has in store for the woman and the man. It connects them. It allows them to relate to each other. It is the basis for relationship, as it is within God. The Trinity's Members are the same in substance, equal in power and glory.[27] It is the Word's *being* God that allowed Him to be with God in the beginning (John 1:1). It is the Second's equality with the First (Phil. 2:5–6) that allows the two to be filled with each other (Col. 2:9). So a man's best friend really cannot be a dog, however much they may share in tromping through the underbrush. Not the kind of best friend that God wants for him (Gen. 2:20). It is image-bearing that allows two to strike out for the deep woods arm in arm.

You may diminish or ignore one of the gender's equality and still be a theologically sound Muslim (or Arian). But not a sound Christian. Trinitarian understanding demands its practice. Practically, this means that the church has work to do. The proclamation of equality demands women's full participation in the work and worship of God and bars excluding their voice in the operation of families and churches. Unfortunately, though church history displays some shining examples of social elevation of women, it also shows participation in cultural gender oppression, through men's domination and immaturity in cultivating the feminine of the divine image in their sisters. For example, with a few exceptions, reading early church theologians' thoughts on women can be depressing.[28]

Women have always prophesied in the covenant community (as documented in the list above), which makes the point that God desires to testify through them. Richard Bauckham, senior scholar at Ridley Hall, Cambridge, found that ancient authors often substantiated their historical accounts by bringing in their sources at the beginning and end of the events to which the sources testified. Bauckham notes that Luke does this with the apostles. But Luke also names Mary Magdalene and Joanna in this way, as witnesses from Galilee (Luke 8:2–3; 24:6) to Jesus' empty tomb (Luke 23:55; 24:1–10).[29] More than saying that these women are among the eyewitnesses of the Gospel events, Luke is using them as sources, which means that much of what we are getting in the intervening chapters is, in fact, a woman's perspective. That is why we probably have the passages of Jesus involving, interacting with, and teaching about women that are unique to Luke's Gospel. Those interactions are what Mary Magdalene and Joanna would remember. So Luke itself is a testimony to the importance of a woman's perspective in the ongoing ministry of Jesus Christ in the world. The voice of women must be heard.

Sadly, many church and family traditions defeat the Bible's message here, and consequently, lose the relationships that should support us. Here are two tests to measure women's status in your setting: (1) If a woman feels the need to self-censor any female issues or feminine attitudes in order to be taken seriously, your practice is skewed and unbiblical in how it distinguishes gender. (2) If women are marginalized by the structures of operation, we have a great deal to answer for to God, since we are disobeying the very first chapter of the Bible. And not just the first chapter. The first thing to take away from the famous New Testament passage on head coverings (1 Cor. 11:1–16) is that women must be active in the local church. Verse 5 of that passage is unquestionable: women were to be publicly praying and prophesying. The only reason the passage exists is because women's voices were heard in the early church. They were fully participating in its life. If we really want the wooded beauty of intimacy God wishes for us, the path must be made large enough to walk arm in arm.

There are ways of addressing inequality in the vast number of cases of women's under-inclusion. But the way in which equality is championed, as the 1 Corinthians head coverings teaching also emphasizes, makes a big difference in whether we see the image of God. It is often our larger culture's mistake to erase gender distinction, a move that does not incorporate women as intended. Actually, it contributes to their exclusion by failing to illuminate woman's value. Equality, important as it is, is not the end of the story. There is more to the Bible's teaching on gender. Difference must be discerned in men and women, in addition to their sameness, to achieve God's glory. To appreciate this further wisdom, we must first grasp when gender matters.

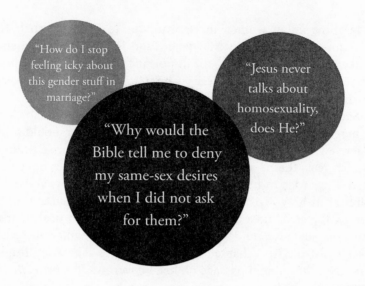

"How do I stop feeling icky about this gender stuff in marriage?"

"Jesus never talks about homosexuality, does He?"

"Why would the Bible tell me to deny my same-sex desires when I did not ask for them?"

CHAPTER 5

Gender Matters in Relationship

W hat I've experienced with Laura," Nick said to me, "I could never have had that, and didn't have that with a man." Nick was among those husbands with same-sex attraction (SSA) that I interviewed. They had been happily married to women for years now, but most had previous relationships with men. I figured that these men could speak authoritatively and informatively on the difference. I got to speak in depth about their experiences. The conversations were enthralling.

Intergendered marital bliss *is* achievable by a husband with a homosexual past. Those concerned with the right of monogendered couples to marry may find this hard to acknowledge. But I found it critical to listen and not to deny what these husbands say that they feel. During the interviews, the subjects showed no sign of painting a rosy picture of their lives because they had become invested in a certain lifestyle, or of simply feigning happiness with their wives to justify the life choices they had made. Rather, authenticity characterized the discussions. The men were frank about the shortcomings of their intergendered relationships. They conveyed little bitterness toward previous partners. They chatted honestly about their temptations and personal foibles. Their answers also reflected years of contemplation and comparison between their intergendered relationships and their monogendered ones. To appreciate this research, one must grant them credence, allowing that these husbands really experienced what they say they did.

And Nick's words above were not atypical. None of the husbands I spoke to would trade what they had now for a relationship with a man, in spite of being subject, at times, to a visual pull to check out other guys. The more I spoke to them, the more I began to understand why.

In considering what constitutes the image of God in people,[1] several theologians of the twentieth century have recognized human relationship to be principal. God disapproved of man living alone. So the second origin story of Genesis 2 portrays the divine image creation by the distinguishing of Eve from Adam, and their subsequent union (Gen. 2:7, 18–23). In Genesis 1:27, the statement "in the image of God he created him; male and female he created them" may be read in this light to mean that He created them in the divine image, in large part, to be in relationship with each other. That is, God is a community of love, inside Themself, and the image of God is unfolded in the individual image-bearers when they enter into intimacy. As Karl Barth put it, "God is in relationship and so too is the man created by him. This is his divine likeness."[2] This would explain why the Bible's gender-specific passages always concern the practices of individuals toward each other, rather than inherent qualities in isolation. If the divine image fundamentally involves relationship, and gender is a critical part of that image, then relationship is where we should look for the meaning of gender.

In Mark 10, Jesus takes His final trek to Jerusalem, heading for the climax of His ministry and necessarily clashing with the religious leaders. In verse 2, the Pharisees test Him with a question about divorce.

> [2]And Pharisees came up and in order to test him asked, "Is it lawful for a man to divorce his wife?" [3]He answered them, "What did Moses command you?" [4]They said, "Moses allowed a man to write a certificate of divorce and to send her

away." [5]And Jesus said to them, "Because of your hardness of heart he wrote you this commandment. [6]But from the beginning of creation, 'God made them male and female.' [7]'Therefore a man shall leave his father and mother and hold fast to his wife, [8]and the two shall become one flesh.' So they are no longer two but one flesh. [9]What therefore God has joined together, let not man separate."

[10]And in the house the disciples asked him again about this matter. [11]And he said to them, "Whoever divorces his wife and marries another commits adultery against her, [12]and if she divorces her husband and marries another, she commits adultery." (Mark 10:2–12)

We may note again the contrast between Jesus' teaching and the rabbis' of His day. Jewish law recognized adultery only as an offence against a husband.[3] But Jesus clearly teaches in verse 12 of this passage that either the man or woman may be guilty of adultery against each other. In addition, the exchange leads Jesus to define marriage. He reaches back all the way to "the beginning" (v. 6) and quotes Genesis 2:24, where marriage is instituted: "Therefore a man shall leave his father and mother and hold fast to his wife, and the two shall become one flesh" (vv. 7–8). But because that Genesis verse begins with a "therefore" (*'al-khen*), Jesus needs to supply a prior statement. He needs to summarize the reason for the distinctive closeness of the marriage relationship, to explain the seriousness of rupture by divorce.

In the original Genesis account, that 2:24 "one flesh" verse follows the story of the creation of Eve and Adam's discovery of her, that is, the story originally distinguishing masculinity from femininity. Jesus summarizes this story by reaching even further back, to Genesis 1:27, to the act of creation of the gendered image of God: "God made them male and female" (Mark 10:6). Jesus joins this separate passage of Genesis 1 to the marriage institution passage of Genesis 2 in order to explain why people marry: "'God made them male and female.' 'Therefore . . . the two shall become one flesh'" (Mark 10:6–8). The Greek behind the "therefore" (*heneken toutou*[4]) denotes cause: "for this reason."[5] Thus, according to Jesus, God's creation of gender is the necessary cause of marriage. Marriage happens as an expression of gender distinction.

Note that to say, with Jesus, that gender causes marriage is not to say that marriage is the only expression of gender or that someone with gender should always get married. It is only to say that gender is the reason marriage exists. If people do marry, gender distinction is why it happens. (We take up the part of gender in a single person's life in chapter 17, "The Continuum of Closeness: When Gender Does and Doesn't Matter.") This does mean, however, that monogendered unions are not God's way for us. Jesus' definition of marriage, so wrapped up as it is in gender distinction, excludes the practice of homosexuality. If our desires go in that direction, something is wrong. Differing gender is the cause of marriage because gender matters in relationship.

So it should not surprise us that the places where the Bible brings up gender are in instructions for relationship with the mysterious other. This is where gender particularly matters. Indeed, it is hard to find New Testament instruction to, or description of, one gender without instruction to, and description of, the other. We cannot find commands to men as men without finding commands to women nearby. There is a reciprocal character to the Bible's gender lessons. Consider, for example, the mold of Paul's instruction to the Corinthians about marriage and divorce (1 Corinthians 7). There is never a statement to the woman without a reciprocal statement to the man:

- Verse 2: "Each man should have his own wife and each woman her own husband."
- Verse 3: "The husband should give to his wife her conjugal rights, and likewise the wife to her husband."
- Verse 4: "The wife does not have authority over her own body, but the husband does. Likewise the husband does not have authority over his own body, but the wife does."
- Verses 10–11: "The wife should not separate from her husband . . . and the husband should not divorce his wife."
- Verses 12–13: "If any brother has a wife who is an unbeliever, and she consents to live with him, he should not divorce her. If any woman has a husband who is an unbeliever, and he consents to live with her, she should not divorce him."
- Verse 14: "For the unbelieving husband is made holy because of his wife, and the unbelieving wife is made holy because of her husband."
- Verse 16: "For how do you know, wife, whether you will save your husband? Or how do you know, husband, whether you will save your wife?"

- Verses 25–26, 27: (addressed to virgins, that is, women)
  "I give my judgment. . . . I think that in view of the present
  distress it is good for a person to remain as he [she] is";
  (addressed to men) "Are you bound to a wife? Do not seek
  to be free. Are you free from a wife? Do not seek a wife."
- Verse 28: "But if you do marry, you have not sinned, and if
  a betrothed woman marries, she has not sinned."

Reading all these, you might be tempted to advise Paul to stop the
singsong and save some space. Just say it to one or the other. But he
cannot because any instruction to men as men is in terms of women.
Any instruction to women as women is in terms of men. The other is
already included in the thought. In other words, gender is defined in
relationship. This is not just Paul's prototype. Everybody in the Bible
adopts this model of speaking. Even God. When He uses parenting
imagery in speaking to Job, He says,

> Has the rain a father,
>   or who has begotten the drops of dew?
> From whose womb did the ice come forth,
>   and who has given birth to the frost of heaven?
> (Job 38:28–29)

Do you notice how God gives the separate parents equal time?
You cannot have the yang without the yin.

Taking this pattern to another major gender passage, 1 Timothy 2:8–15, easily the most commented on passage in Paul's letter to
Timothy since the nineteenth century,[6] recommends a helpful overall
reading. Near the beginning of Paul's teaching for how people ought
to conduct themselves in God's household (chapters 2–3), the apostle
instructs on gender distinction. People tend to focus on the instruction
to women about refraining from teaching men. This is not unreason-
able, since, unusual for such a passage, more is spoken to women here
than to men. It is normally the other way around. But this gender passage, just like the others, still begins with corresponding instruction to
men, conforming to the reciprocal pattern of not having one without
the other.

The manly instruction is to representative prayer, "lifting holy
hands without anger or quarreling" (v. 8). When people do pay attention
to this part of the passage, it is usually thought that the arguing against

which Paul speaks is with other men. Though that could be included in Paul's prohibition, given the subject of the passage, it is more likely, primarily, that the men are arguing angrily with the women. I would paraphrase Paul's sentence as, "I desire that, in every situation of life (or in every local church), the men should pray for the women in their lives, lifting their hands to bless them, not strike them. Men should not be insisting on their own way but be setting apart women to benefit them, that is, the men's hands should be sanctifying instruments, not tools of angry domination, causing quarrels." Likewise, instruction to the women about dressing modestly (v. 9) is for . . . who? You guessed it, the men. Paul's gender-specific instruction to the women concerns their treatment of the men and, to men, their treatment of the women.

As might be expected, if gender is closely tied to relationship, it is most intensely expressed in intense relationships. Remember how, as pointed out in chapter 2, "The God of Closeness Has Shown Himself," relationships fall along a continuum? Depth of relationship brings gender into play. Therefore, the closer the relationship, the more gender matters. So the Bible distinguishes gender most forcefully in the context of marriage, as shown in this list:

The Distinguishing of Gender in Scriptures about Marriage

- Genesis 2:18–24—In prefacing the creation of woman with, "It is not good that the man should be alone," God makes the new gender enterprise about relationship, leading to marriage.
- Proverbs 31:10–31—The distinct work of the wife makes the success of the husband in their marriage.
- Colossians 3:18–19 (as well in Eph. 5:22–33)—The household table instruction on marriage distinguishes wives and husbands in its direction.
- 1 Peter 3:5–7 (referring to Gen. 18:12)—Husband and wife must consider gender as they conduct their marriage in the home.
- 1 Corinthians 11:3–16—Husband and wife must consider gender as they enter the communal intimacy of worship together.
- Titus 2:3–5—Older women are to train the younger women to be "husband-lovers," gender-specific instruction focusing on the marriage relationship, while older men are to remain sound in love toward their wives.

Gender is a gift, a specialty, for developing another person in relationship. In a passage like Ephesians 5:22–33, the major marriage address in the New Testament, this is certainly the case. The husband takes on his masculinity in order to beautify his wife with attention and likewise the wife takes on her femininity in order to empower the husband with honor. In the Bible's view, the definition of manhood is a very feminine affair—its cultivation concerns and requires relationship with women. One DSM ("Does She Matter?" study) husband put it quite simply: "Her femininity has very much enhanced my masculinity." Similarly, the definition and cultivation of womanliness is a masculine affair.

"Icky," and "It doesn't make any sense," complained Audrey. Like many young women I counseled for their upcoming marriages, Audrey found the New Testament instruction to her as a wife, explained in part 2 of this book, distasteful and incomprehensible. Several months later, her words for that teaching were, "It's beautiful." What accounted for this transformation? It wasn't the brilliance of my counsel. It was her growing relationship with her fiancé. Audrey had never really gotten close enough to a man, or cared enough about a man, to see the point of the teaching. But the trust she had with Norman changed everything. The things the Bible said didn't make sense until she was applying it with a particular guy. A woman finds what it is to be a woman in the company of other women and then, especially, of men. A man cannot understand himself as a man apart from his relationship to other men and, then, especially to women in his life. William Ickes, professor of psychology at the University of Texas, in a now classic 1983 study,[7] got unacquainted male-female pairs to talk to each other. Girls with older brothers and boys with older sisters much more easily conversed across the genders, and were more likely to see the other in a favorable light. They were given a head start in the gendered game of life.

This explains why Christians find less agreement on what "makes a man" or "makes a woman" than on what they should be doing for one another. Their Bible does not say, "A man is this" and "A woman is that," but rather "Man, do this for her." "Woman, do that for him." It is clearer on action than on essence. The Bible does not insist on men or women having certain characteristics. It allows for different characteristics, but these differences are hidden. In the man's action for the woman, he finds out what it is to be a man. And in the woman's doing for him, she becomes a woman.

In addition to doing something to themselves, they are doing something to each other. Masculine compounds catalyze her femininity. Womanly power ignites his manhood. This is why, again, the Bible makes a big deal about marriage being intergendered, directing a man to reserve his most intimate relationship for woman, and vice versa.[8] The display of God's image, and our individual growth into that image, are at stake.

I'm not a man, and you're not a woman, because we split up at the movies and you see *Pride and Prejudice* while I watch *The Terminator*. Movie preference is not what makes me a man. Gender is a matter of missing ribs. As Paul puts it, "in the Lord woman is not independent of man nor man of woman; for as woman was made from man, so man is now born of woman" (1 Cor. 11:11–12). Our English versions frame it as "dependence." Literally, verse 11 says, "Woman is not apart from man. Man is not apart from woman." Manhood is defined in relation to woman and womanliness in relation to man.

Adam could not really know himself without Eve. Or, look at it this way: the church was not the church until Christ died for her. Similarly, the Son of God could not be the Christ until there was a people for whom He would be anointed for His mission of salvation. Likewise, gender is something we are, but something we *are* for the purpose of loving involvement with others. How we *are* that thing that we are for one another, we are almost ready to explore. But first, we need to distinguish between the biology and the theology of the matter.

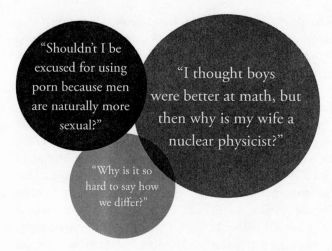

CHAPTER 6

Sex Differences Form the Platform of God's Gift

Throughout the world, in every geographic area, in every country measured, more males than females are conceived. As health and medical writer Carol Ann Rinszler points out in her popular writing, the ratio may be 120 boys for every 100 girls, or even 200 for every 100.[1] But the male-flavored sperm, that is the Y chromosome–bearing kind, are more successful at reaching and penetrating the human egg. At the same time, around the world, women live longer than men. Boys are more likely to be born early. Girls are more likely to be born late.[2] From conception on, there are differences between males and females, based on significant differences in their genomes. The now well-publicized eighth week testosterone brain bath in preborn male babies means that even the brains of the sexes are built differently. Her corpus callosum, that connection between her right hemisphere and left hemisphere, is forged bigger and stronger even before she sees the light of day. That may be the reason she will use more areas of her brain to define vocabulary words and judge rhymes, while her brother's thinking will be more localized.[3]

When those little babies grow up, they have different body types and even some different organs. Over the last half century, studies upon studies have been done on all ages, delineating female-male differences,[4] often theorized to be the result of neural or hormonal differences. Women tend to react sooner with motion sickness. Male skin is thicker than female skin. Women complain of insomnia twice as frequently as men do. Men are more likely to sleepwalk than women.[5] The list can now be multiplied far beyond anyone's interest in paying attention.

Of course, people do pay attention when physical differences bleed into emotional and mental differences affecting abilities. Now, what goes into human thinking is hard to understand, much less to measure. So psychology professors such as Janet Shibley Hyde and Nita M. McKinley of the University of Wisconsin–Madison and the University of Washington, respectively, do "meta-research" on the whole host of sex difference studies, trying to carefully account for bias, sample size, and changing social attitudes. Even after removing all the hype and bias, they find that women still tend to be better at verbal fluency while men are much better at rotating a three-dimensional object in their minds, a result hinting at some big mental differences. Reading and speech disorders are far less common for young girls, while boys generally, starting in high school, more easily solve math problems.[6] Of all the psychological variables that get measured, about 13 percent of them show large female-male differences.[7]

Emotional experiences and expressions are also highly complex, so differences there expose deep distinctions between the sexes. It is not just that most people with anorexia nervosa are women, or that men are more likely to commit suicide, both of which are true.[8] It is the far more significant and repeated finding that men, in their automatic reactions, are less able than women to recognize sadness or happiness in another's face.[9] Women refer to emotions more often in conversation and writing than men do.[10]

Some scientists question the cause of these patterns. Is it biology or the long-standing expectations and tasks women and men have been socialized to take on?[11] It is a fair question. Social factors can affect the way the brain develops or what hormones get produced. So which is cause and which is result in links between emotion and brain structure or hormone levels?[12] Yet some differences may not be explained as socialization. Northeastern University scientist Judith A. Hall and University of Neuchatel scientist Marianne Schmid Mast recently measured interpersonal sensitivity among men and women, making every effort to remove bias toward female relevance in the testing, designing the experiment to favor scenarios that would engage men. But even for male-stereotypic content and for tasks framed to favor men's motivation to perform well, the men's sensitivity never exceeded the women's.[13] Even researchers who downplay sex differences report that men are typically more sexually active and more sexually permissive than women, a fact easily tied to testosterone, flowing through men's bodies at ten times the level of women's. University of Wisconsin–Whitewater professor Jennifer L. Peterson and her Madison colleague Janet Shibley Hyde performed a meta-analysis of research in pornography use, casual sex, and positive attitude toward casual sex, which admitted a medium size difference in males.[14]

So some sex differences are quite real, even reaching the complex systems of our thinking, emoting, and sexuality. But two very important caveats become apparent if we look at a typical graph of the distribution of a sex trait. Take the height of women and men in the United States. The following graph lines trace the number of women who reach sixty inches tall, sixty-two inches tall, etc., as well as the number of men of different heights. The graph tells us that most women are around sixty-four inches tall, and most men are sixty-nine inches tall:

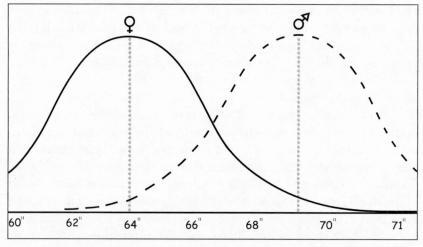

Count of Heights of Women and Men in the United States[15]

There are two things of note about this graph. First, the difference between women and men, though distinct, is quite small. This permits some whose foremost concern is equality to say, "See! Men and women are not very different at all. They both average between five and six feet,"[16] while permitting others, who value gender distinction, to say, "See! Men are taller. They are definitely different." Both are right, aren't they? Women and men are not very different in tallness compared to penguins. But men as a whole do have an edge in height, which can mean many things for life.

Yet more confusing, most sex characteristics, while numerous and definite, express themselves as overlapping statistical distributions, not absolute dichotomies.[17] The above graph shows this clearly. To say that more men tend to be taller does not mean that you will never find a seven foot woman (on the high end of the female distribution for height) or a five foot man (on the low end of the male distribution for height). These graphs of biological traits speak less of absolutes and more of potential specialties. God made maleness and femaleness to include a great variety and overlap.

So right after you declare, "Men are taller," you can probably find a couple where the wife tops the husband in height. Viewing them side by side, you may be tempted to eschew the science, swing your fist down on the pub bar, and shout, "See! Sexual differences are all a bunch of hogwash!" Perhaps more important than your winning a bet in the pub is your asking yourself if you should form your beliefs of what husbands and wives do based on statistical sex differences. Wouldn't it be a shame, and for some people quite harmful, to teach that a man should always change the lightbulbs in a marriage because men are taller? What about the man who is not taller? Is he out of luck in obeying God? Or in being a man? How about the far more complex trait of being a nurturing person? In light of the distribution of all male-female traits, do you really want to say that that is what a woman is? Do you really want to say that men should lead because they are naturally more aggressive? Many advice books do just this, advocating roles or policy based on essential sex differences without realizing these complexities.

Let us rather applaud the wisdom of the Bible's teaching, not defining gender in terms of essential characteristics. Doing that will always exclude some people and fail to account for the rich variety of male-female expression. The Bible does not insist on men or women having certain characteristics. Instead, in defining gender in one's relationship to the other gender, the biblical account shows savvy and sensitivity.

What then of these biological sex differences like height and math or verbal distributions? Are they meaningless? No. These lower-order sex differences are also God's work. Recall the male and female versus masculine and feminine dichotomy of the Scriptures. I argued, in chapter 3, "Gender Is Hard to Talk About for Good Reason," that the singularity of human gender reflecting God's image is something above and beyond the biological male and female, the "male and female" found also in the plant and animal kingdoms. Our own biology is rooted in these lower kingdoms. First God called for the earth to bring forth the creatures of the earth (Gen. 1:24), suggesting that He used His creation thus far to bring about living animals. Then He made humanity from the dust of the earth (Gen. 2:7), indicating a kinship, even of us, with the lower-order creation. Looking at the beasts of the earth and their physical sex differences, we can see Him developing sexuality, literally, from the ground up. It was a dusty effort with a determined direction to support the gift of gender that the image of God would then confer.

Gender was the goal of His earlier creative distinctions, and human sex differences, arising from the dust of the earthly creation, became the receptacles for the more profound gender reality. Or, one might say, these sex differences provide the platform for the gift of masculine and feminine. But the former do not determine the meaning of gender nor is gender entirely constrained by them. God will make a unique mixture of traits in each man and woman's platform, as He sees fit for them, both to encourage and to challenge them in relationship growth.

In seeing sex differences with overlap as God's platform for gender, the Bible comports with gender theorists who distinguish between physical sex and gender.[18] Our maleness and femaleness, given by God, are not the same as our masculinity and femininity, also from God. But the Bible parts ways with the theorists in not treating the first as evolutionary happenstance from which to free ourselves nor the latter as a malleable product of how we are raised. Both are real and both are works of God. Christians who understand this dichotomy can avoid the error of using biological distinctions as a guide to behavior while at the same time build, according to God's intentions, on the platform of those distinctions.

"Let's be realistic," said Jack, a single young man, to me. "Shouldn't I be excused for using porn? After all, men are naturally more sexual. It almost feels like I am denying my nature to forego this." Pornography, ubiquitous as it now is, efficiently denigrates God's gift of sex given for marriage. The urge to drool over pornography usually comes to young men right along with the thought that it is natural for them to do because they are men. Men supposedly want sex more, right? Even if this were strictly true (and things are more complex than that), it fails to recognize that the increased testosterone in a man's body can take more than one direction. Testosterone-fueled drive can as easily power self-sacrifice as sexual gratification. This discovery comes of being not just male, but man. Your gender, bearing the image of God, makes you more than a sex engine. Though we are often told otherwise today, we are never at the mercy of our biology or neurology to act immorally. To believe that testosterone positively demands sexual variety is to slip into the fashionable amoral worldview, which reduces you from the whole reality of what you are. The man bearing God's image will discern that masculinity has more to do with lusting after righteousness than answering moral urges in immoral ways. Consider Paul's admonition in Romans 12:11 to "get hot [*zeō*] with the Spirit." Fortunately, Jack, bearing God's image, could feel how using porn harmed his relationship to the women in his life, and to God. That is why he was speaking to me. Instead of justifying his habit, we could focus on one of the larger issues to which Jack's porn problem drove him: what he needed to do in his life to get ready for marriage.

But the platform matters. When I asked the DSM ("Does She Matter?" study) husbands how they thought of their monogendered unions, they portrayed them with terms of limitation. The question, "How would this be different if you were with a man?" elicited Fred's term "reasonable facsimile" to say that they could achieve some level of closeness, but ultimately for him love was limited. Nick explained, "That's not to say there . . . isn't an ability to be compatible [with a man. But] I think in the deepest way . . . to be compatible, what I've experienced with Laura . . . I could never have had that, and didn't have that [with a man]." Or, as Ted reflected, "I mean, I learned things . . . about people. There are certain things you can take with you I've learned . . . but . . . looking back on it now, I think that it [was] . . . shallow." As Toseph described it, monogendered unions felt for him like trying to thread a metric screw through an English nut: it seemed to work when you first started, but eventually resulted in a bind. Pressing them about the importance they were ascribing to the platform of sexual difference revealed a variety of reasons that we discuss in chapter 15, "Deeper Still: Dynamics of Intergendered Intimacy." For these men, physical forms made a foundational difference to the depth of relationship.

Though the platform of sexual difference for expressing gender confuses us at times, God has done a good job. The brilliance of the creation's difference with overlap is apparent in how (a) it makes connecting possible, (b) it displays God's love of variety, and (c) it directs us in how to include the exceptional person among us.

If sex traits were inviolable dichotomies, we could enjoy little possibility of friendship between the genders. Women wouldn't just be from Venus and men from Mars. Women would be from Venus and men would be from MACS0647-JD, the farthest known galaxy in the universe. The situation would be far worse than the bafflement that we often feel at each other. We could not even comprehend each other. The overlap preaches to us our equality and yet hints at mystery more. Biblical gender is a call to use the various sex differences, regardless of where one falls on the distribution curve, to serve one another. Gender is not just something we are, but something we do.[19]

In addition, overlapping sex trait distributions as a platform for God's image should tell us one thing for sure: the Lord of this galaxy loves variety. He definitely does not want all marriages to look the same. When a man and a woman love, a unique combination of differences, some pronounced, some minimal, some opposite to the norm, some stereotypical, emerge as we fulfill God's directives to us in relationship. In the variations on the themes, the image of God glistens. His commands to each couple may be the same, but the way they are obeyed must be as diverse as the image-bearers and their receptacles. God wants each unique arrangement to bring out a different hue of Their rich, rich Self. The platform reveals relationships to be the adventures that He intends them to be.

In one couple I admire, Doug is short, shorter than his beautiful wife, Nora. Back when they first considered dating, Nora was hesitant partly because she had always thought of men as tall, taller than she was. At first, it was doubtful that it was going to work. What Nora didn't know back then, was that Doug's shortness had worked an amazing depth of leadership in him. Keenly aware of his height, as well as another physical difference that made him stand out—a lack of hair—he had to go to God repeatedly for his confidence. God responded by giving him an exceptional sensitivity to others who feel insecure about their own shortcomings, and a patience with people that engenders their trust.

What Doug didn't know back then about Nora, was that her past had greatly confused her about what a man was. She had had experiences with men that left her unable to trust them, and she needed a great deal of patience in a man to overcome that. The process of challenging this stereotype about height caused Nora to grow in ways that she had not known before. As she rethought manhood, she opened up to Doug's sensitive patience and found that she craved what he had. So it was the gift of his shortness that bonded them. He helped her to love deeply. And when this beautiful woman came to love him, he seemed to grow a few inches. This story could not be told if God had not decided to play around with maleness in one of His children. It is fun to hear Nora speak of Doug now. She once remarked about his great stature as a man. I remarked, "Vive la différence!"

Finally, we are led by this understanding to respect limits in sexual traits, appreciating them but not confusing them with gender. A woman who excels in mixed martial arts is not less of a woman, any less than a man with an eye for decorating or who cannot grow a mustache is less of a man. It is essential for the church of Jesus Christ to realize this and embrace the exceptional, for the group's benefit as well as the individual's. When the exceptional young are excluded, be it from family or church, developmental problems hinder them long into their lives, but the excluders themselves are also stunted. Instead, we should understand that God gave us the exceptional for the growth of us all. When we encounter a woman who loves rugby and video games, we should happily watch to see how femininity is expressed in her ties with others. When we meet an emotionally sensitive man, or one who excels at learning languages and follows directions by landmark instead of compass, we should espy God's image in how he obeys the Lord in relationship. This is the garden of God's gendered work.

"Fine," you may say. "There are some insights here to ponder. But I am still confused about what a man should be. I still am not hearing what a true woman is." Well, good news. We have now traveled a good distance into the forest. Having explored the first biblical principles, we are ready to enter the groves of gendered intimacy, to see what makes a man and woman what they are.

Recall the ground we have traversed. God loves variety, so what a true man or woman is must be broad enough to encompass the myriad combinations wrought by male-female statistical distributions. Sexual or biological differences are a platform for gender, but gender, created to express as God's relational image, is something that plays on the platform, something that parades what goes on in God's own Triune Self. Gender matters and is defined in relationship with the other equal gender.

There is one more principle that we need to reach a definition, to be able to say what a true man is and what makes a real woman. And that principle is the most mysterious. Pursuing it can lead us into a dense thicket or a verdant private clearing. Thorny dangers threaten even discussing it. But for intimacy, our guide tells us, it is absolutely necessary, as necessary as equality. It can be summed up in one geometrical word: asymmetry.

PART 2
The Trail Markers
Embracing Asymmetry for the Other

The New Bride and the General

She was from the high country and she was a prize. Many had secretly desired her, but didn't dare go beyond that. They would need to go through her formidable father, the laconic and battle-hardened general, and who would venture that? As she sat astride her donkey now, on her way to see the great man himself, she wondered at her dramatic betrothal and recent wedding. Her father had always sought out the best for her— the best sandals, the best training, even fussing over the best donkey . . . so why not the best husband, she laughed to herself. For that is just what her father had done.

She remembered back to that extraordinary day. The tribe of Judah had been scoring amazing victories against the dreaded Canaanites, defeating Sheshai and Ahiman. Even Talmai fell to them. The Israelites could hardly believe it. Would the land, so long polluted by human sacrifice and the sacred prostitution of Baal, finally be theirs to start the world's new redemption? Had God's word been true all along? But there remained Kiriath-sepher, the unconquerable town, with its towering walls and a skilled army to match. Even atop all their heady victories, the Judahites quavered before it. Not really possible, they reasoned.

That is when her father had done it. He called an assembly and stood up there on that makeshift platform. He had told her what he planned to do, but she was still shocked when she heard it uttered. She wasn't sure anyone else could have pulled this off. But this was the great general. Revered. Wise. People always moved aside when he walked by. And when he spoke, the rest of the army always grew silent to listen, even Joshua. They sure listened now. His old face, lined with untold experiences, commanded their attention. His old voice, full of a lifetime of joys and sorrows, hung in the air. He shouted the offer: "To the man who attacks Kiriath-sepher and takes it, my daughter shall be his!"

That had done it, all right. Changed the tide of morale. That night, several different men had begun to strategize and plan an attack. She could hardly believe it—she, little Achsah, mere Achsah, the motivation for the Lord's mission! She was just a girl. She hardly slept because every time she thought of it, her heart beat too fast so she couldn't stay lying down. Would they do it? And who would be the first? Yes, who would it be? Three days later, when it turned out to be Othniel, the son of Kenaz, she had smiled. She knew that some people did not hold him of much account, but she knew better. Her father had done it. Once again, he had gotten her the best.

Now, here she was, months later, married and motherly, trying to make their future work, trying to make their home. She had urged Othniel to speak to her father about this issue, strongly urged him, had her first fight with him about it even.

The donkey had stopped. Achsah was roused from her thoughts. There was her father, Caleb, right there before her. The moment had come. She alighted from the donkey he had given her so long ago to make her request. She began, "You've always given me the best..."

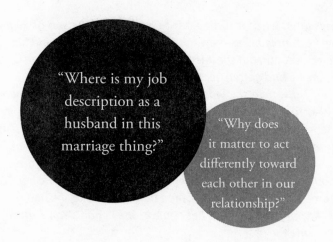

"Where is my job description as a husband in this marriage thing?"

"Why does it matter to act differently toward each other in our relationship?"

CHAPTER 7

The Grand Asymmetries of Gender Give Us Specialties

It was a hit. The weekend the movie *Wall Street* opened back in December 1987, it grossed $4 million at the box office. Michael Douglas won the year's Oscar for best actor in the leading role. Many people who worked on Wall Street found a hero in Gordon Gekko, the powerful stock trader who made money by shady practices. His proudly proclaimed proverb, "Greed . . . is good," became a mantra in many downtown offices of New York City. The funny thing was that the moviemaker, Oliver Stone, meant the film as a cautionary tale. He had meant to show the moral vacuum and degradation that came of bottom-line thinking, thinking that disregarded the effects of the moneymaking on people's lives. How did some viewers walk away with such an opposite interpretation of the movie?

It all came down to what details you focused on while watching. The Wall Street brokers saw the power and glamour gathered by the characters. They didn't notice as significant certain other details, such as the people's lives that were destroyed when a company was bought and broken up for profit, or when insider trading shredded trust and friendship. They did not give attention to those cues of the moviemaker. The movie's misinterpretation was a lesson in hermeneutics.

Interpreting the seminal passage, Genesis 2, about the creation of Adam and Eve,[1] has always proven controversial because people argue over which details are significant. Much of the church's debate about gender directives in the Bible amounts to the question, when the author utters in ink some sentence or phrase (or word!), is it all important or inconsequential? What should stand out to us and what needn't?

Interpretation is always easier when another biblical author cites and explains which details matter. That author stands much, much closer to the source writing than we do. And probably is a whole lot wiser, seeing as how his or her explanation has made it into the Bible (has yours ever?). Such intertextuality, as it is sometimes called, allows us to let the Bible interpret itself. Fortunately—praise the Lord!—we have just that circumstance with Genesis 2.

The apostle Paul gave us almost a quarter of the New Testament.[2] His authoritative writings shape the Christian worldview and largely define our faith. His writings also grant us three comments of gender distinction in his reading of Genesis 2. Citing three details of the narrative as important[3] in his extant letters, Paul reads the Genesis 2 creation narrative as purposely introducing readers to three asymmetries of gender significance. In the account of the beginnings of the equal image-bearers, these three differences teach how to carry out God's call in close relationships. Unlike the misinterpreters of the *Wall Street* movie, Paul reads the narrative with a literary sensitivity and an attunement to the Genesis author's concerns and setting. In fact, not just Paul but other biblical writers also use the differences Paul cites to show men and women how to serve each other in close quarters. Part 2 of this book is about these three distinctions, how to lean into our genders. Understanding them opens up for us true womanliness and real manhood.

One asymmetry of Genesis 2 is found in the order of creating. God creates the man before the woman (v. 7, 21–23) and commissions him first alone to the work of humanity (v. 15). As writer C. S. Lewis once poeticized, the man is "always older."[4] Paul points to this genesis of Eve after Adam to argue for asymmetrical behavior in church relationships: "I do not permit a woman to . . . exercise authority over a man . . . . for Adam was formed first, then Eve" (1 Tim. 2:12–13). The priority translates into authority and representation on his part, and promotion on her part. Equal before God, and equal in the charge of taking dominion, yet *in relationship* the man is to take charge and representation for her sake, the woman to promote him to that place of responsibility for his sake.

This detail may, at first, appear arbitrary. Why does Paul make an issue of who came first? Because he recognizes the Genesis author's cultural analogy to how the firstborn of a family was supposed to function as its head (Gen. 27:19 with v. 29; 49:3–4, continued in Deut. 21:15–17). In the author's day, the firstborn son had the responsibility to take care of the family, and he was afforded authority and resources to do it. Paul uses this same reasoning to explain Jesus Christ's authority. Christ, being prior and "firstborn" to everything and everybody, has authority over all (Col. 1:15–18). It's a theme.

We can imagine the first pair originally delighting in this arrangement. It intoxicated her to see him rouse himself to take responsibility for her—for her!—it made her different. He exulted that she would extend to him—to him!—prerogative for them. This enjoyment gave them each a place in the other's heart and bound them together.

The apostle Peter points out how many subsequent women, in pursuit of holiness, embraced Eve's asymmetry (1 Peter 3:5). And the masculine specialty of governing and representing them, we see immediately in the next few chapters of the Genesis narrative. From Genesis 1 to Genesis 5, the masculine term "man" (*'adam*) is used exclusively for the individual man twenty-seven times. Yet, bracketing those times, the same Hebrew word is also used for the name of the race, inclusive of both women and men, twice in Genesis 1:26–27 and twice again in Genesis 5:1–2. The masculine representative purpose is thus inserted into the name itself. In the biblical narrative, the Hebrew word functions just as it once did in English, meaning "mankind." This semantic asymmetry is evidenced in the way contemporary people object to using the word "man" to stand for all humanity and so substitute other terms for it.

Speaking of objections, my reader no doubt notes that many today find such an asymmetry distasteful and offensive to the cause of equality, so we should think about it carefully. It behooves us to ask if equality actually suffers under this distinction. And are there indeed benefits in becoming to one another the Firstborn and the Promoter? These questions we explore in chapters 9 and 10.

Genesis 2 also pictures the woman as created differently than the man. Adam was formed from the dust (v. 7), and Eve from Adam's rib (vv. 21–22). Surely the account preaches the equality of women and men. But Eve is not born equally from the dust as Adam is, suggesting that equality is not the only point to be made. The conditions of this second creative act are crucial:

> [18] Then the LORD God said, "It is not good that the man should be alone; I will make him a helper fit for him." [19] Now out of the ground the LORD God had formed every beast of the field and every bird of the heavens and brought them to the man to see what he would call them. And whatever the man called every living creature, that was its name. [20] The man gave names to all livestock and to the birds of the heavens and to every beast of the field. But for Adam there was not found a helper fit for him. [21] So the LORD God caused a deep sleep to fall upon the man, and while he slept took one of his ribs and closed up its place with flesh. [22] And the rib that the LORD God had taken from the man he made into a woman and brought her to the man. [23] Then the man said,
>
> > "This at last is bone of my bones
> > and flesh of my flesh;
> > she shall be called Woman,
> > because she was taken out of Man." (Gen. 2:18–23)

Let us consider the creation experiences of the two characters in this story, obviously key to its meaning. Adam's response to Eve at the end of the story recalls the beginning difficulty, which started the whole thing: It is not good that the man is alone, so God eventually surmises (v. 18). There must be an unrest to Adam's life during this earlier time, and he knows it. He wanders from animal to animal, petting their fur, getting nuzzled. Some of them are quite responsive, and mirror parts of him. They are enjoyable, but then the ache returns. It is not good. God responds by giving him other important work. In naming the beasts, Adam begins to take intellectual dominion over the creation. To do taxonomy well requires not only scientific talent but also creative skill with language. This job brings together science and humanities thinking, engrossing and fulfilling employment. Along with tilling the garden, the physical dominion-taking, this second task, the intellectual dominion-taking, renders his days absorbing. God's kingdom progresses all right, but still . . . the man's restless nights pondering the moon or taking a swim to clear his head intensifies with time. There's no fit. Eventually God feels that enough is enough.

God brings Adam into a state of divine sleep, *thardhemah*[5] (v. 21), a term denoting an unusually deep place of rest.[6] In Hebrew thought, this respite comes directly from God, and the sleeper is in God's hands.[7] The ancient Greek Septuagint translators saw a profound emotional state in this word and translated it with *ekstasis*, from which comes our English word, "ecstasy." Obviously, the medium of Eve's genesis is one of profound relief. Adam approached absolute zero here.

But then anguish yanks the sleep. The familiarity of the story should not shield us from the wounding in God's operation on the man. The rib, along with the deep rest, is wrenched from him. He now misses both. This scene helps us to comprehend the eventual reunion's effect on Adam.

Eve, meanwhile, entered this brave new world without much of a runway. She may have had a lot of time, or just a little, to wonder about where she was, what she was there for, and . . . most of all, *who* she was. But, wonder she must have. Yes, that was the pressing question for her: who she was. Of course God was there. She had her own relationship with Him first. Indeed, He led her to meet Adam, or maybe, she was brought to the man by the Lord's providence, allowing her to find him on her own. Perhaps God explained some things to her, but I imagine on many points He said what He so often seems to say to people, "Wait and see."

And then she did see, across the clearing, this wondrous being. And her new heart skipped a few beats. That was all right. It would catch up. This was not a moment for mundane things like hearts beating or let alone even breathing. She was suspended in the knowledge that the instant for answers had arrived. And, marvel of marvels, she could understand him! She comprehended his full and rich words, through the precious gift of image-bearing language. What did he have for her, this fabulous creature, this exciting animal? Or wait, maybe not an animal, no, something much more. What did he have for her when he found his own voice again, after his loud sigh, his ecstatic interjection? It was the thing that she needed from him. It was the burning question. It was the means of securing her in the newness of this land of blossoms. Yes, the one made of solid ground grounded her with a name (v. 23). Or, in terms of the other Hebrew words for woman and man, the *'ishshah* (woman) unearthed her root in the *'ish* (man). And so much then opened up to her. Where she was from, what she was, who she was in relation to him. And the understanding raged up in her as overwhelming confidence.

Adam's response to Eve upon their meeting announces the unrest he had been experiencing before she shows up. He exhales, "At last!" (v. 23). In other words, their connection resolves the unrest he has suffered. Adam exclaims in recognition, specifies her, and their resulting relationship brings him back to the place of rest. He pined for what had been missing from him, wrenched from him in his deepest rest. So he expresses, when they meet, that she was taken out of him. The climax portrays the dynamic of their union: while she restores to him a divine rest, a respite from animal and toil, he secures her with a name. While Adam secures Eve, Eve is home to Adam.

This asymmetry comprises Paul's gender reasoning in 1 Corinthians 11 about how a husband and wife bring what is in their home into the worship service. There the apostle is at pains to explain that it matters how they bring their relationship public. Recalling this Genesis 2 account, he says that a wife gives something to her husband that is different than vice versa: "Woman is the glory of man. For man was not made from woman, but woman from man" (1 Cor. 11:7–8). The way this works for intimacy is explored in chapter 8.

Adam would further name her later on (Gen 3:20), but for now, this was enough for Eve. And as this Man of the Solid Earth perhaps lay down his stone hand axe and took his first step toward her to . . . what? shake hands? embrace? He knew it was finished. This Woman of the Resting Rib brings him to ease. As he tread towards her and his last doubts flew away, he knew, finally and completely, the deep and profound peace. He was home.

Yet there is more. In terms of the most important feature of their life together—God's mission for them—there is distinction. They are both to carry out the mandate of Genesis 1. Yet the woman in this work is also made to supply something that the man does not give to her. His aid to her is likewise not what she gives to him. The Genesis distinguishing text is explicit: the man and the woman are created for expressly different purposes for one another. Once more, the apostle Paul recalls this very asymmetry when he speaks about how the glory that a woman gives to a man is different than vice versa (1 Cor. 11:9–10).

What difference does the Genesis narrative declare? Whereas God specifically makes the man to set up shop and till the garden (Gen. 2:15), to work the new environment, God expressly states that He creates the woman to be the unique, strong helper to the man in these callings (vv. 18, 20). Now we should be careful. It is clear, recalling Genesis 1, that both man and woman are called to the filling of the earth, the multiplication of the image, the ruling of God's creation. There is no distinguishing there. But, in their relationship, the second account tells us that this work together takes on separate contours.

First, Adam was expected to get in there and apprehend God's mission for them. In fact, if he had not, he would never have progressed to the point of getting Eve. It was through his mission-mindedness, taking up the work of actually encountering and studying the animals, that his need was revealed: no helper fit for him. Then God could move him forward with the invasive surgery that yielded his rest. So Adam had to be about God's purposes, discovering them and leading in them.

Eve is expressly stated to be something else. As has been frequently recognized about the narrative, God uses the same word, "helper" (*'ezer*, v. 18), for Eve that in other places is enthusiastically applied to God Himself in His great strength (Exod. 18:4; Deut. 33:7, 29; Ps. 115:9–11, 121:2; 124:8; 146:5). Often these uses appear in a climax of proclamation of God's power. Thus its use here means that the woman possesses a divine power and ability to enable the man in mission. Adam later describes her to God as the one "whom you gave to be with me" (Gen. 3:12). The third asymmetry consists in her bringing divine empowerment for the enterprise of God's call to them, and his assuming that call's lead. Again, they should both be about God's purposes. But in the relationship, there is this difference. What that means practically is the subject of chapter 11.

These three, then, are the gender significant details of Genesis 2, identified with Paul's help. How the man and woman are made for each other, the temporal order of their origin, and their purposeful intent in the work, form the grand asymmetry of gender specialties. The great theme of asymmetrical callings in a relationship of equality continues in each of the Bible's covenants and genres. These blend and overlap, but bearing in mind the Genesis 2 themes can tease out what is going on. These, according to apostles Paul and Peter, as well as other biblical writers, have implications for how the woman and man fulfill their representation of God together in relationship. Together, as equals, they share the common creation calls, such as to "be fruitful" and to "subdue [the earth]" (Gen. 1:28). And, as women and men, they are to be different toward one another in carrying out the call. Their distinctive services provide structure for the close relationships of life.

Of course, this beatific vision of godly harmony did not last. The great fall of humanity distorted the gender asymmetry. The fallen wife, it is said in Genesis 3:16, would consequently "desire" her husband, but he, also fallen, would "rule over" her. The description "ruling over" (*mashal*) can mean ruling by force, harshly and selfishly, a corrupting of the job of authority, which should instead provide securing, cultivating, and leading in God's call. Just such corruption the New Testament identifies as a husband's now sinful tendency toward his wife (Col. 3:19; 1 Tim. 2:8). At the same time, the woman's "desire" (*teshuqah*) forms a remarkably parallel sentence with Genesis 4:7, where sin "desires" Cain, that is, desires to master him.[8] No longer strong helper, deferrer, or giver of rest, Eve will seek to control Adam, by defiance or manipulation, again, indicated in apostolic teaching as a now sinful tendency for women. At least, in Corinth. The two separate verses, 1 Corinthians 11:16 and 1 Corinthians 14:36, which form the conclusions of two of Paul's arguments on gender differentiation, both anticipate opposition: "If anyone is inclined to be contentious . . ." and "Or was it from you that the word of God came? . . ."[9]

I know the shattered harmony. In these verses I recall my many failings with women close to me. I remember the look in my sister's pleading eyes, when we were growing up and I left her to deal with the stranger at the door, or how, when we were grown, she turned away when I dismissed her opinion. Instances of disdaining condescension from me that made even mature women feel patronized rather than honored and prized. Backing away when I should have stepped forward to represent amidst confusion. Assertiveness as self-assertion rather than self-giving. All these I have done. They happen when the gender specialties are rejected or taken selfishly rather than as a call to paint within the lines of Christ. And they, hand in hand, with wandering steps and slow, through Eden took their solitary way.[10]

Hope still lives. The New Testament, while pointing out these sinful tendencies in men and women, also pronounces the undoing of them through Christ, reaffirming the proper entrusting, enabling, self-giving asymmetry. Paul calls this restoration of relationships "fitting in the Lord":

Wives, submit to your husbands, as is fitting in the Lord. Husbands, love your wives, and do not be harsh with them. (Col. 3:18–19)

Note that Paul's statements do not indicate a progression from Old Testament to New Testament, but a re-creation of the original creation's gender project.[11] Just as equality continues between covenants, so does asymmetry. In fact, most instances of New Testament instruction on gender distinction look back to the Hebrew Scriptures for justification. First Peter 3:1–7 looks back to Genesis 18, calling for direct imitation of, not improvement upon, the women of old (v. 5). First Corinthians 14:33–36 looks back to "the law," most likely Numbers 30:1–16.[12] The quintessential New Testament marriage teaching, Ephesians 5:22–33, the mystery of husband and wife illustrating Christ and the church, looks all the way back to Genesis 2 in its explication of marriage asymmetry (Eph. 5:31). Mark 10:2–12 (and Matt. 19:3–9) look back even further to Genesis 1. The New Testament authors see a unity to the teaching found in earlier covenants. They portray, in various ways, how the ancient gift of gender asymmetry prevails.

The heading under which the apostle Paul expresses different specialties toward one another for one another is headship (1 Cor. 11:3). In a marriage, a husband is to specialize in taking prerogative for his wife, and the wife is to work at promoting her husband to that position of headship. He is to provide security for her as she gives him rest. He is to help her discern God's call to them, and she is to divinely enable them for their task. It is not insignificant that when the DSM study husbands were asked in what ways they saw their wives acting as a woman towards them according to the Bible, they thought about feminine gendered activity in these three categories. Though expressed variously, their recipes of esteeming gender boiled down to these three. If any progression from Old Testament to New can be perceived, it is that the New Covenant writings promise a greater intimacy through gender to those remade in Christ's image. But is that not like God? The greater the problem, the greater His solution.

The Weightlifting Woman and the Despot

He was coming. She pushed down the stairs, through the bodies of men and women scrambling upwards. That was all she could think as she fought the crowd: He was coming. She could hear the zings and zips of bows and slings coming from the roof, where the men were emptying their supply of projectiles. She broke through and found herself on the storage level.

He was coming. She looked up, alarmed at the sight. Lining the stairway and hanging off the ladders, people pressed tightly against one another, a mass of limbs. She looked down, to the levels below, even more bodies, with nowhere to go. There must be hundreds of people in here, she thought. Then she remembered the Tower of Shechem and shuddered. They had heard what happened there. The false safety. The barbarity. The screams.

He was coming. But she had reached the room she wanted. She knew this level like no man here, because of her "women's work" she smirked to herself. It was the community mill storage, where spare stones and supplies were kept for all the townspeople to use. It was a great system, so long as someone minded the place. And, as the storage matron, she had been the one to do it. She fumbled for the foot-long key hanging from her sash and stuck it in, flinging open the closet and gliding swiftly to the item she wanted. This is our chance, she thought. When she pushed to come out, she found a cluster of townspeople had surged to the door, looking for room to avoid the crush. "The stones!" she cried to them. She didn't know if they paid any attention to her, but she was already back at the stairs, heaving forward with the "rider," a rounded upper millstone balanced on her shoulder. Some of the men recognized what she was doing and began clearing the way of people before her.

He was coming! As she climbed the stairs, the people inside the tower had fallen deathly silent. They were listening to a long speech he was shouting at them from outside, chastising them for their lack of support. With every stairstep she mounted, his voice seemed to grow more raspy and crazed. "Why do men always get so silent when you wish they'd say something . . ." she thought, "and always talk so much when you wish they'd shut up?" "Ah well," she reasoned, "just keep talking till I get there."

The "there" was a lonely opening between the stones, an eye of a window in the tower wall, forty feet directly above the only door. This is where he'll end up, she knew.

He was here. Then so was she. She could smell the smoke as she reached the window. There were precious few moments left. He had waited until the defenders on the roof had exhausted their supply of arrows and stones, and then had ordered his men forward. She peeked through the unobtrusive opening and saw the massive piles of wood surrounding the base of their soon-to-be funeral pyre. He had finished his speech, or more likely exhausted himself with it, and was sidling up to the tower door with torch in hand. For the fire would be started at the tower door to prevent any from escaping, she knew, and he would insist on lighting the fire himself. He would let none rob him of that grisly honor. As Abimelech reached the door, the woman of Thebez gave one last heave of her millstone through the crack. It tumbled out into space . . .

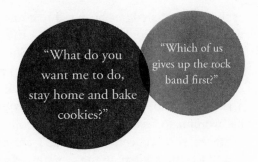

"What do you want me to do, stay home and bake cookies?"

"Which of us gives up the rock band first?"

CHAPTER 8

The Asymmetry of Origin: The Man of the Solid Ground and the Woman of the Resting Rib

I used to live in an SRO on the Upper West Side of Manhattan. That stands for "Single Room Occupancy," which means a roach- and rat-infested excuse for an apartment building where the landlord got whatever he could from people who had very little to give. As we were hard up financially, in order to survive, we sunk to occupations of the gutter, the world's most disreputable jobs, like prostitution and telemarketing. I chose the latter. It was where life was basic and I learned a lot there about basic life.

Like when Millie's "husband" had to have a word with me. I doubt that they were actually married, but it was close enough for our building. I forget his name, but I will never forget his definite tone, informing me that I could not wear just a towel to the bath. The floor had to share a bathroom, with one toilet with crevasses running through its seat, one sink with a shard of mirror perched on a shelf above, and one rusted shower. I used to walk to it in my flip-flops and towel, to avoid spending any more time in there than I needed to, such as dressing and undressing. Millie, from across the hall, got very upset at this and enlisted her husband to come tell me I had to wear clothes when I was in the hallway. I found this ridiculous—considering the other things that went on in that hallway. The place did not exactly cry out for modest manners. Besides, there was no clean place to put clean clothes. Even though I was put out by it, I came to see how, in a situation with little security, Millie's guy was creating a space for his woman to feel secure. He was doing what he could. I saw there a movement between them that I am sure accounted for why they stayed together when, in the statistics of a place like that, the odds were against it. He was securing her.

As with each of the asymmetries, Adam and Eve's securing and giving rest can be traced through the Bible's other genres, beginning with the law of Moses. The book of Deuteronomy, giving direction to the second generation of Israelites out of Egypt on how to live in the land they are entering, prescribes a one-year leave from military service or any public service for that matter, for all new husbands, that they would use their newlywed time to "bring happiness [*vesimmach*[1]] to" their new wives (Deut. 24:5 NIV). Here the commandment codifies the masculine securing specialty of Genesis 2:23. The words used for man and woman here are *'ish* and *'ishshah*, creating a poetic beauty. The man stays home to root his wife in his love. The Mosaic laws go on to unilaterally forbid prostitution (Lev. 19:29; Deut. 23:17; 23:18), quite unusual for an ancient Near East where using women in this manner was routinely legal. Such gender statutes practically preserved the community's women. They kept the home a refuge by forbidding women from selling the gift of sex outside of it. And they kept the men securing their wives and daughters by disallowing a society where men could bed women without commitment. A land without the possibility of prostitution is a land where women sense safety.

The call of men to securing continues through the Old Testament narrative. I opened part 2 of the book with the story of Achsah and Othniel (Josh. 15:16–17; Judg. 1:11–15). It begins thus:

> From there they went against the inhabitants of Debir. The name of Debir was formerly Kiriath-sepher. And Caleb said, "He who attacks Kiriath-sepher and captures it, I will give him Achsah my daughter for a wife." And Othniel the son of Kenaz, Caleb's younger brother, captured it. And he gave him Achsah his daughter for a wife. (Judg. 1:11–13)

Readers often skip over this passage as incidental. But it actually introduces a main theme in the book of Judges: the view and place of women in the mission of God. The book, in its apologetic for a monarchy for ancient Israel, develops the theme of ineffective rulership of charismatic but uncommitted and covenantally unfaithful leaders. The author means to show how poorly things go when "there was no king in Israel" (Judg. 18:1; 19:1), when "everyone did what was right in his own eyes" (17:6; 21:25). The book develops its themes of leadership through a brilliant arrangement, what scholars call a "chiasm" (or "chiasmus"), which pairs matched events, and several levels of the chiasm feature women characters. Appendix 2 lays out this structure, showing how Judges's chiastic design contrasts the beginning period of the era (chapter 1), when the situation was hopeful and the society good, to the end of the era (chapters 19–21), when luridly brutal atrocities exhibit an Israel that is worse than Canaan (lines B/B' and C/C' in appendix 2).

The biblical author thereby teaches how to gauge a society: measure it by how the women in it are treated. The opening chapters' Achsah and Othniel story demonstrates that, in the beginning, while the leader Joshua lived, women are treasured, the secret resource for how and why things get done. Othniel secures the woman by taking the city for her. By the end, we witness the opposite of women secured: they are raped and ravaged and ultimately treated like disposable objects.

These are some examples of how the Bible preaches the asymmetry of origin. What does it mean for men today? To translate the message, consider that when Adam gave Eve her name, it helped her know that she had a place. She had a context for her identity to unfold. This wisdom of God gives us a broad directive, which can be fulfilled in both traditional and nontraditional ways. Securing may mean massacring marauding dragons or making calming coffee. It is going to vary with the woman. It will also change with the cultural context. Every husband needs to ask the question, "What makes my wife secure?" If, for her, amassing a gun collection or learning kickboxing would do it, then perfect your roundhouse kicks. If it is earning a steady income, then do that. It might be heroic or mundane. It might seem familiar to you or strange. But it is surely God's call to you in this relationship. The main point is to answer the question, how can you make her secure? Have you asked her?

Pastoring in Greenwich Village, downtown New York City, I counseled many couples made up of young artists. Many talented young people come to New York City with a dream to succeed in dance, music, theatre, film, TV, painting, sculpture, opera, writing, illustration, or animation. However, all of these are tough to break into and usually do not pay a lot unless you reach the very top of the profession. I usually advise a five-year plan, to test if God would bless their aspirations. But something often interferes before the five years are up—another artist. Artists attract one another with their countercultural attitudes. They look into each other's eyes and feel understood. They fall in love. Then they try to begin a life together. Gender comes into play. What does being a man mean in that situation? Being a man often means that he gives up art as a vocation first to get a job that provides some income. Because one of them has to. Young guys would give up the rock band to secure their women.

On the other hand, a husband should not assume that making as much money as possible is what will make his wife secure. Often, attentiveness to her situation mixes much stronger cement for her foundation. Carl's wife, Penny, was beside herself. Like many women with a young child, her life was frazzled. Her apartment was a mess. There was barely time to get some semblance of a meal on the table. She never got anything done, was constantly overwhelmed, and often felt like a failure when Carl walked through the door after work. What had transpired since when he had left in the morning? She couldn't even remember. How come nobody told her how much work a little girl required? Or did someone tell her and she wasn't listening? It didn't matter, Penny thought, as nothing would make her less of a failure at this mothering thing.

This situation continued until Carl and Penny sat down and talked about what life was like. Carl listened and at last told her that all he really wanted, to feel at rest in their home, was to have the toys off the floor. That was it. The discussion helped Penny see that her life was feasible. She was not a failure because she was not super-housewife. Carl's sensitivity secured her like nothing else could. Or as Peter puts it, "Husbands, live with your wives in an understanding way . . ." (1 Peter 3:7).

A husband's securing work changes with his phase of life. As a marriage progresses into the family stage, probably one of the biggest things a husband can do to give his wife security is to raise her children. His attendance to them does something for her that nothing else does. Thus the Bible consistently instructs fathers to take a leading part in child-rearing. Its pages call men away from leaving the kids' spiritual formation to their wives, which husbands tend to do. From the beginning, when God says that the forefather Abraham will secure the covenant community by how he directs his children (Gen. 18:18–19), to the New Testament's gender-specific direction to fathers to bring up their children "in . . . the Lord" (Eph. 6:4; cf. Col. 3:21), the call upon men in this phase of life is to shepherd their wives' kids.

And women? How do they lean into this asymmetry? Judges's chiastic design also contrasts Achsah, the godly wife of the first and best judge, Othniel (Judg. 3:7–11, along with 1:11–15), with Delilah, the ungodly "wife" of the last and worst judge, Samson (Judges 16) (Lines E/E′ in appendix 2). The contrast highlights the importance of women in accomplishing God's purposes in the land. Delilah is the epitome of how much damage a woman can do to God's purposes for a man. Achsah is the model of the best, an example of how powerful and influential a woman can be.

Giving rest can find both conventional and nonconventional expression, but the simplest way for a wife to give rest to a husband is by making a physical home for him.

> When she [Achsah] came to him, she urged him to ask her father for a field. And she dismounted from her donkey, and Caleb said to her, "What do you want?" She said to him, "Give me a blessing. Since you have set me in the land of the Negeb, give me also springs of water." And Caleb gave her the upper springs and the lower springs. (Judg. 1:14–15)

Achsah and Othniel, the future great judge, are making their home in the Negev. When you hear "Negev," you should think dry. Very dry. Desert dry. The word Negev (or Negeb) in Hebrew means both "south" and "dry." Barely sufficient rainfall to support agriculture. Uninhabitable unless there is a water supply nearby. Water is what Achsah sets out to get, land that would give her and her husband water. Achsah first approaches Othniel to solve their need. She is asking him to secure her. Achsah then attempts to provide for her covenant family-to-be with the request to her father. Caleb gives them "the upper springs and the lower springs," a merism meaning he is granting them full rights to all the water in the area.[2] By rolling up her sleeves and pioneering a viable residence for her husband and future children, she is being womanly. She is making a home for him.

In contrast, Delilah from the lowlands (Judges 16) does everything to take rest away from foolish Samson. She finds her security in the bounty price on his head. He has no refuge in her house—he is constantly attacked there. His sleep is often interrupted—by people she invites in to capture him! And, as their relationship of suspicion unravels, he gets tired "to death" (v. 16), the opposite of Adam's rest. In the end, the only home she leaves him is a dungeon (v. 21).

The womanly quest to give rest may find expression outside of conventional homemaking, but we must allow homemaking as one form of it. Let us first speak of that way. Evangelical women are employed at rates similar to that of the general population, and their median household income mirrors that of other Americans.[3] Yet there persists among them a conviction that the wife should focus on the home. Their wives' practice in this area was the second most talked about category of distinction among the DSM study group. Why? Because they find it in the Scriptures as a way to give rest to their husbands.

In the Bible's poetic or "writings" genre, we find perhaps the most famous passage about wives, Proverbs 31:10–31. An acrostic poem lauds the industrious woman for making a place of rest and base of operations, that is, a home. Though her businesses—she has several!—bring her outside the home, her goal, achieved through her raiment making (vv. 13, 19, 22, 24), her bed covering (v. 22), her food work (vv. 14–15), her home help management (v. 15), her agriculture (v. 16), her sales (vv. 18, 24), her teaching (v. 26), her charity (v. 20), and even her real estate deals (v. 16), solidifies a fruitful dwelling for her husband and family (vv. 11–12, 21, 27–28). As the text concludes, "she looks well to the ways of her household" (v. 27). Her husband secures her value with superlative praise, both privately (vv. 28–29) and publicly (v. 23, 31), cherishing her, à la Ephesians 5:29, so that she knows the value of what she does (v. 18). This passage of exalted poetry came up more than once in the DSM interviews. Fred's wife, Denise, would quote Proverbs 31 to him to explain her to-do list. Or, as Edwin stated bluntly of Sandra, "She's very Proverbs 31." Denise and Sandra pressed into this passage, resulting in husbands of profound peace.

Paul's New Testament gendered advice to Titus for running the church on Crete runs along the same lines. The apostle directs older women, who have seen what goes into relationships, to teach younger women to focus on the home (Titus 2:3–5).[4] The uncommon Greek word he uses connotes not so much staying at home[5] but carrying out household responsibilities.[6] In other words, placing emphasis on the home is a way the wives of Crete could give husbands rest. Clement of Rome, the first-century Christian writer, in probably the earliest preserved noncanonical writing of a Christian community, repeats this advice of Paul to Titus, using the same word as a verb, in the first chapter of his epistle to the Corinthians (*1 Clement* 1): "They [wives] should manage their household affairs becomingly...."[7]

Women measuring themselves by these Scriptures sometimes feel discouraged, but the real point of the passages is to create a vision for their work, a means to make decisions about their priorities. Practically, just as with men making their women secure, home-emphasis will change with a woman's phase of life. A woman who is single or without a household with young children may not carry the same physical home focus to fulfill her gendered call as her motherly counterpart. But small children, when they come, usually demand specialization from one of the partners. The wife's household in Proverbs 31 includes children (vv. 15, 27–28), but the vision there does not seem to be of the baby-bearing or small children phase. If it did, her husband would not yet likely be an elder (v. 23) or have the intimacy of complete trust that they share (v. 11). She would also have little time for all her cottage industries. The Old Testament author, then, is likely describing the blossoming of an older woman's life in a mature household, or the whole of her life over time, through many seasons. In contrast, in Titus 2, the women being taught to home-make are definitively young, married, and with children (v. 4). Perhaps the Titus 2 wife matures into the Proverbs 31 matron.

If we are reading the Scriptures well, something counts in a wife's work to create a home in some way. Because of its value in providing rest, we should not be too quick to dismiss feminine home-emphasis as merely retrograde or a vestige of bourgeois tradition. This might explain the division of household labor studies that have long puzzled researchers: Wives tend to perceive, as fair, chore arrangements that are not equitable.[8] Even when women bring home equal salaries, they will judge a chore division as fair when it really is not an equal split. Why might this complexity underlie the chores? The simplest answer is that her aspiration to make a place of rest may color her judgment on what is fair. Results from sociological studies on gendered housework division and marital quality are conflicting, but some studies do suggest the counterintuitive result that embracing gender distinction in housework improves marriages.[9]

DSM husband Fred's wife, Denise, took "a step back from her business career for the family," which deeply moved Fred in his experience of the marriage. The act of giving up immediate career advancement, of not doing what she could do, in order to make a home for him, carried the makings of intimacy. Denise's service to Fred and his children made a place for him to "at last find his rib," to use the language of Genesis 2. As Theo offered, "[Melanie sees it as] that she has a really powerful role to play in what kind of environment she creates for me to live in."

All of this can be beautiful for some but hard to pursue for others. Many writers have observed how drastically the Industrial Revolution changed Western social structure of the home.[10] Writer-scholar Nancy Pearcey, for example, of the Francis Schaeffer Center for Worldview and Culture, helpfully analyzes how the late-nineteenth-century fragmentation of the family into private and public spheres disrupted the household. Although both men and women lost under this fragmentation, women suffered more because of their confinement to the private sphere. The split removed women from economic production. The values they were supposed to embody were no longer considered as important as happenings in the business world. The women's sphere was devalued and so were they.[11] It may be feared that associating women with the home in a unique way perpetuates this separate spheres doctrine that fragments the household and denies women meaningful work. Does this kind of teaching keep women down?

The Bible answers this objection by showing us examples of women and men pursuing these goals when economic obstacles block the avenues of gender, or when cultural conditions are unkind to the truths of gender equality and asymmetry. Because the Bible's gender principles are made to mesh with God's creational and providential variety, they hold out a vision to pursue and principles to apply even amidst cultural contradiction. It is rest-making, not domesticity, that is always womanly in the Bible, so sometimes true femininity turns domesticity on its head, especially in a world where values are skewed. The book of Judges showcases this vision. It first shows some spectacular examples of masculinity—by counterexample! The men of Judges repeatedly fail to secure the women around them. Meanwhile, the women, while not stepping away from being women, act bravely in a gendered way. As providence plays ironically with domesticity, the women use the feminine asymmetry to forge ahead with God's purposes.

In Judges 4:17–21, the housewife Jael plays a critical part in God's history. It is a time when a decisive war is being waged for the future of the kingdom of God on earth. While her husband, Heber, aligns himself with the Israelites' enemy (vv. 11, 17), holding himself aloof from the covenant community and failing to secure her, Jael shines in her femininity nonetheless. She is the original Girl with the Dragon Tattoo, ready for anything. Jael bravely beckons the fleeing enemy general to her tent; she invites Sisera into her home. She ostensibly provides a place of rest for him, just as Eve did for Adam. She gives him milk, a symbol of motherhood. In fact, he is so taken in, he goes to sleep. But, actually, she is using her homemaking for God's mission, to save Israel from Sisera's clutches. We know from Bedouin practices that it was the woman's job to set up and break down the tent. So the mallet and tent peg are her domestic tools and she would be handy with them.[12] Ironically, "while he was lying fast asleep from weariness" (v. 21), she uses these domestic tools to kill him.

The chiastic match of this story in Judges 9 (lines H/H′ in appendix 2) calls for action similar to Jael's for the community. The usurper, Abimelech, is out of control and no one can stop him. No one, that is, except the brave woman stuck in the tower of Thebez, with whom we began this chapter. Abimelech has vengefully surrounded the tower, locking the town's innocent inhabitants inside, showing us what awful leadership looks like: the opposite of securing. He draws near to burn it down. Once again in Judges, as the man fails, the woman shines. Similar to Jael, the Thebez woman uses a millstone, a domestic tool, to deadly use. She heaves her homemaking tool from the tower and cracks Abimelech's skull. In so doing, she accomplishes God's purpose, ending Abimelech's awful siege on the people of God (Judg. 9:52–55). The text is hilarious in summing up the action. The attackers stand there, looking at the dead Abimelech, and then decide there is nothing else to do. So "they went home" (v. 55 NIV). In other words, the Thebez woman returned everybody to their homes.

These brave women, in creative ways, brought rest to their homes, as well as the covenant community. In the process, they teach us that the way in which we do gender is not limited to one narrow job. The biblical word is a far cry from saying, "A woman's place is only in the home." Its wise counsel can encourage the many women who are feeling guilty about working outside the home, as well as the many women who now feel guilty for staying at home. But both conventional and nonconventional means of homemaking can be valid ways to fulfill our femininity. On what does it depend? The men! Again, our genders are for the sake of the other in relationship. The way in which a woman provides rest can be as various as men are. For example, what is it but rest-giving that the apostle Peter gets at in directing wives to a quiet manner of behavior (1 Peter 3:1–4)? Be creative. While an essence of womanhood is to give rest in relationship, the way she does it will vary with the positions of providence, the people involved, and the purposes of God.

Likewise for men, God-made masculinity is not always providing for, but making secure. Familiar roles like bringing home the bacon may be part of the job, or may not, but they are not the job. In the book of Ruth, righteous Boaz goes outside of norms to make sure the women of his concern, Naomi and Ruth, are secure in their greatest needs. To keep her from being molested was the first matter of security (Ruth 2:9, 22). His discreet solution to their financial insecurity is to instruct his men to let Ruth glean among the sheaves and even to pull out some barley from the bundles to leave for her to find (2:15–16). But Boaz provided things for them far more important than money. After Ruth makes her pass at him, Boaz protects her reputation (3:14) and makes both daughter and mother-in-law secure as their kinsman-redeemer (3:9, 12–13).

One may still object that couples find it unfeasible these days to sustain a household on one income, so how can the wife focus on the home? Or how can the long hours of a husband's job allow active engagement with the children? Both of these realities of modern industrialized life provide challenges. But again, the biblical gender goals are resilient enough to pursue even in contrary circumstances.

Roxanne, a woman in my church, needed to be the breadwinner in her marriage. Steve, her husband had much more limited work possibilities. They were without children, which allowed flexibility, and I encouraged them to think along the biblical categories we are discussing. Roxanne felt that these categories were too abstract to be useful, but I saw them played out in their love anyway. Because her position subjected her to severe criticism, Roxanne often found herself insecure about her worth and abilities. I watched her husband repeatedly value her, cheering her through a year that might have crushed her otherwise. The irreplaceable securing that Steve did for Roxanne illustrates the range of the job. It reminded me of the story of

Hannah and Eli, in the account of the conception of the prophet Samuel (1 Sam. 1:9–20). Hannah was a woman in deep distress. Eli, the priest in the temple at Shiloh, at first mistook her anguish for drunkenness. But he made the effort to repent of his false first impression, to affirm her with a kind and promising word (v. 17). That simple affirmation put her on solid ground (v. 18). She was ready to worship (v. 19). Making secure, for men, may mean marrying (Ruth 4:13), moving heavy objects (Gen. 29:10; Exod. 2:16–17), or merely making love (2 Sam. 12:24; 1 Sam. 1:19). And, for a woman, in whatever way she can, gendered work is enacting Proverbs 14:1: "The wisest of women builds her house, but folly with her own hands tears it down."[13]

So there is no rigid dichotomy of spheres here. The Bible does not teach that women should never have careers or that men have nothing to do with home chores. Evolving economic storms periodically change what men and women do in society,[14] blanketing us with arrangements, sometimes hostile and sometimes favorable, to God's holistic intentions for us. But the principles of rest-giving and secure-making are the roadway underneath the snow of cultural practices. The Triune God of closeness calls us to lean into these specialties, whatever the weather.

Certainly we should resist the culture where it crosses God's purposes. We should welcome opportunities to bring income production back into the household when it allows a wifely focus on rest-making and a husbandly focus on child-rearing. We should roundly reject the devaluing of work in the home that generates no pay. Couples should also willingly limit material wealth to live a happier life in close relationships, and stand ready to refuse an employer who demands heart and soul, inhibiting genderly practice. When we do, we find what God has for us in our relationships. When my children were toddlers, I earnestly begged God to help me fulfill the command He gave me as a father to raise my children by bringing my income production into the home. He did. Unusual for those times, I suddenly became able, as a computer programmer, to work from a home office. And I was able to continue for most of the next sixteen years, those crucial for the children. I no longer do, but it left me with a sense that God is serious about these things if we are. Not all work can be done from home so this cannot be everyone's story, but God will back you up if you pursue His goals for your family.

Curiously, though Proverbs 31 is about the wife and her part in building God's kingdom in the land, the passage cannot help but talk about the husband. Why? Because of her enormous effect on his status in life. It is no accident that the husband in Proverbs 31 comes to be a member of the esteemed elders in the gate: "The heart of her husband trusts in her, and he will have no lack of gain. . . . Her husband is known in the gates when he sits among the elders of the land" (vv. 11, 23). The woman was the source of his gain.

Similarly, the latter half of Ruth is supposed to be about the covenant faithfulness of Boaz and Ruth (providing the pedigree for their offspring David as king). But the narrative cannot help but show how Boaz's securing work transformed Ruth's mother-in-law Naomi from bitter widow to famous woman thoroughly blessed (Ruth 4:14, 16, 17). The man was a "restorer of life" to her (v. 15).[15]

The Approaching Daughters and the Old Man

They were angry. These sisters were women with a mission, and no one—certainly no man, they were part of the problem—was going to stop them. When they reached the guards, men whose job it was to kill on sight anyone who approached improperly, a charge they took very, very seriously, the tension in the air was electric. The five young women slowed down a little, as caution cried out in their minds. The youngest glanced at her third older sister, who was not stopping, which gave her courage. No! They would keep going. For their cause was righteous, was it not? The women's march took the guards by surprise. After an initial hesitant tussle, the Levites let the women pass without bloodshed.

So approached the five sisters to the revered seat. The hoary head lifted, and one eyebrow of the sharpest eyes you might ever see rose in slight surprise. He knew Mahlah, and a glance at the others told him who they were. In fact, he made a good guess at why they were here. And he honestly didn't know what he was going to do about it. But now the women froze before him, as if they had forgotten why they were angry. He motioned them forward. Eleazar came and stood behind him in attendance. The sisters shuffled into the great presence.

When no one said anything for what seemed like a long time, he spoke to reassure them, "The daughters of Zelophehad are welcome. What is your case?" Mahlah, who had been so brave up to this point, seemed to have lost her nerve. So Hoglah stepped forward. She tried not to look at him, but then his words reminded her of why they were here: Yes! Her father's name! She raised her face and, now in confidence, her voice rang out.

Hoglah began, "Our father died in the wilderness . . ."
Moses nodded.

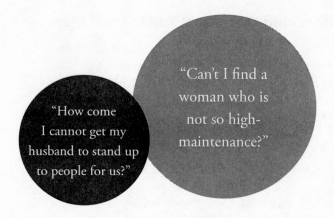

"How come I cannot get my husband to stand up to people for us?"

"Can't I find a woman who is not so high-maintenance?"

CHAPTER 9

The Asymmetry of Order (Part 1): The Firstborn

The details of the story recounted above from Numbers 27:1–11 convey the respectful treatment of women in the ancient covenant community. The daughters of a now-deceased man who had no sons had come to argue their case for keeping their father's land in their family. They have no masculine voice to argue for them so they have to make the case themselves. The women challenge accepted practice and Moses takes them seriously. Seriously enough to make sure he gets the Lord's answer. In their audience with Moses and Eleazar, which garnered the attention of all the people and then expanded into a nationwide issue of legislation, the women's complaint stumps Moses. So he wisely brings this one to the very top, asking God Himself for righteous judgment in the matter. These women meet no dismissive air in the address of their concerns.

In matters of complaint such as this, it is essential to note that in ancient Israel the women's access is equal to men's. This story (Num. 27:1–11), along with the book's closing story regarding the women again

(Num. 36:1–12), form the bookends of the final section of the book of Numbers. They open and close part 3, wherein the final laws of the second generation are formed to prepare to take the Promised Land. That land was the significant issue. These two stories emphasize preserving the assigned territories in the respective tribes to maintain the twelve-tribe identity. These passages about the Israelites' identity, interestingly, are also passages about gender. As the chapter 36 story is a coda to this one in chapter 27, it should be read together with it. The scenes described in 27:2 and 36:1 directly compare: in the first, the women come with a challenge, and in the second, the men. Same procedure. Same privilege.

The daughters of Zelophehad, furthermore, are held up as faithful and theologically astute. They come asking for their father's inheritance to be passed to them, in the absence of any sons. Again note, as women, they are trying to make a home for their covenant families. Verse 3, where they make their argument, shows they have understood and internalized the way Moses has taught the community to understand their lives:

> Our father died in the wilderness. He was not among the company of those who gathered themselves together against the LORD in the company of Korah, but died for his own sin. And he had no sons.

There was this problem of sin. The reason the older generation hadn't made it here was because of just that problem. And there were relative degrees of heinousness of sin—all of these notions the women's reasoning contains. They are with it. They are part of the community's theological conversation. And they are faithful. Their request for land, following in verse 4, is being made before the land of the other tribes is actually won. So they are trusting in God's promises to be fulfilled.

But the real statement of equality comes from God Himself. He answers Moses without fuss: "The daughters of Zelophehad are right" (v. 7)! In other words, yes, women are quite capable of handling property and in this case should do so. In fact, He goes on, their case should serve as a precedent (vv. 8–11). As God then gives the ordering of inheritance, daughters come before any other extended relatives.

It could have been simpler. Just have the land pass to the nearest male relative, which was apparently the usual practice.[1] That would have easily kept the land in the tribe. But, no, God wanted the women involved in preserving the inheritance. His legal precedent proclaimed ontological equality of women and their involvement with the Promised Land program.

Similar to Genesis, Numbers makes statements of both equality and asymmetry. We find the latter in the bookend story, chapter 36's account of the complaint brought to Moses by the sons of Gilead (of the tribe of Joseph). This time the men come, pointing out how the previous ruling for the daughters of Zelophehad had the repercussion, if they married out-of-tribe, of separating the land from the tribe to which it was originally assigned. Over time, this could lead to large tribal inequities that would, in turn, lead to strife and disunity. This time God said, "The tribe of the sons of Joseph is right" (Num. 36:5 RSV)! His solution is to restrict who the property-bearing women could marry. The Lord ruled, "Let them marry whom they think best, only they shall marry within the clan of the tribe of their father" (v. 6).

And so was introduced a gender asymmetry in the law, in the form of this restriction on whom certain women, but not men, could marry. Once again, as in the first case in chapter 27, there was a simpler solution. Intertribal couples could have been limited to one land or the other. They could simply decide which property (and which tribe) they wanted to go with. The Gadite man who married into Manasseh could make a choice to become part of that tribe just as the women did. If the tribe is the greater identity, with its land, it would be simpler to say, "If you marry the woman with the land, you can switch tribes and take on her land instead of your own." Women were already switching tribes by marriage all over the place. That would be a sensible and equitable way of keeping the lands within the tribe. Moreover, here is an opportunity to really put women on an equal landowning standing in the covenant community. Moses could say, "Let's make sure that they are fully equal partners in establishing the kingdom of God on earth."

Instead, Moses, and presumably God, wanted to make a different point with this ruling, one of asymmetry. The women must marry within the tribe. Why the complexity? Because the married women, if they have sons, will bequeath the ownership of the property to them. Practically, within a generation or two, this second law will transfer property back to primarily men. There will always be situations of women handling the property, which is fine, since women are perfectly capable of doing so, but this solution, rather than the simpler one, will guide the property back to the guys.

Not needing to preserve tribal identities, we do not need these laws today. The Bible is not teaching us that women should eschew property ownership in our time. But it is teaching us something about gender in the covenant community: these two laws made them need each other. The men were required to steward the land for the women to make their homes in. And any women in the situation of the sisters, Mahlah, Noah, Hoglah, Milcah, and Tirzah, were required to preserve the land for the men to steward. In other words, the laws kept them communally dependent on one another. The husbands of the daughters of Zelophehad are not named here. The women really were managing the property, which made the men of future generations dependent on them. This is what the asymmetry of order is about.

I almost began this chapter with the sentence: "Of all the points of gender dynamics I am discussing, this is probably the most controversial." Then I realized that that sentence could introduce any chapter in the book. It seems that any point of gender may be contentious and is liable to be difficult in our times. Such is the density of the relationship thicket into which we have wandered.

Nonetheless, the issue of firstborn authority, who should be in charge in close relationship, might indeed be the most difficult biblical gender topic. For many today feel that the gender asymmetry of authority/promotion denigrates women. For example, the late University of Chicago political philosopher Iris Marion Young identified wifely submission as a central harm of marriage itself and that which dooms the entire institution as unjust.[2] The concern of equality and fairness is a serious one and deserves careful consideration in any discussion of relationship quality. Why does anyone need to be over another person in any way? Why, if ours is a religion of love, would one person have to exert his will over another? Why can't they just work things out as equals? Does not Ephesians 5:21, "Submit to one another" (NIV), encourage mutual submission as the more perfect path of Christ?

Those questions are worth answering. To start with, the pattern of relationships between men and women, throughout Scripture, beginning, middle and end, is definite: equality and asymmetry. It might be helpful to give a brief tour. As noted above, the firstborn man is given the place of naming the woman, affording her security in the identification. After naming her "Woman," sort of like a surname (Gen. 2:23), Adam goes on to name his wife, "Eve," further securing her with a first name (Gen. 3:20). But that naming also serves, to the Genesis author, as an ancient symbol of exercising authority (Gen. 1:28 with 2:19; 2:23; 17:5, 15).[3] When that pair becomes a nation, the same pattern held. Just as with the daughters of Zelophehad, the other laws of the book of Numbers assert equality and asymmetry in relationship. The law of the jealous husband protects a wife from abuse while upholding a husband's limited authority over her (Num. 5:11–31). The laws of vows, while no longer directly applicable outside of their theocracy, assert equality of privilege in community to women in making vows (Num. 30:3–4, 6, 9, 11). Women should be encouraged to speak on matters of import to them. Yet, the book's statutes also call women to welcome husbandly or fatherly override of those vows (Num. 30:5, 7–8, 12, 13, 16). God commands the husbands and fathers, correspondingly, to proactively engage with their wives' and daughters' concerns (Num. 30:4, 7, 11, 14, 15). The woman's words matter very much—fathers must seriously heed them on a daily basis (vv. 13–14). The men are also to attend to the preservation and security of the whole community (Numbers 36). Levitical law captures the asymmetry even in the symbolism of the sacrifices. For everyone's unintentional sins, the sin offering was a female goat (Lev. 4:27–31). Except for a leader. In their cases, the sacrifice had to be a male goat (Lev. 4:22–26).

The same pattern continues throughout biblical history. As shown in chapter 4, women have always prophesied in the covenant community, making the point that God equally speaks through them. At the same time, in all parts of the Old Testament and its history, the offices of king and priest, the institutionalized leadership and representation of the covenant community, are asymmetrically reserved for men. Jesus continues this pattern in welcoming women to travel with Him, an extraordinary act for a rabbi, but then choosing all twelve of His apostles, the leadership of the New Israel, to be men.

In the rest of the New Testament, it is the same. Women are fully participating in worship by publically praying and prophesying (1 Cor. 11:5, 13) but are not among the elders who judge the prophets (1 Cor. 14:29–35).[4] The apostle Paul asserts the asymmetry in relationship, after noting it, along with the equality they practiced, to be the sacred tradition:

> [2]I commend you because you remember me in everything
> and maintain the traditions even as I delivered them to you.
> [3]But I want you to understand that the head of every man

> is Christ, the head of a wife is her husband, and the head of
> Christ is God. (1 Cor. 11:2–3)

In this passage about their worship service, Paul begins by commending what they are doing (v. 2). What is he affirming? In light of how the Corinthian service tradition is contradicting Jewish and Greco-Roman custom, Paul must be praising them for holding to his teaching of including women appropriately, that is treating them as equals and also maintaining gender asymmetries. In this context of their steadfastness, he goes on to help them handle a current trend among the elite of removing head coverings. Chapter 13, "Culture: The Clothes of Gender," explains more fully how the Corinthians were practicing gender in the use of head coverings, but we need to be clear about the first point the apostle is making.

Paul's parallel of husband/wife and God the Father/Christ in verse 3 hinges on the meaning of the word "head." I know it is hard, but we have to get the idea out of our mind that "head of the body" here means skull of the trunk of a human body, because Paul does not mean that. Several times in his writings Paul uses this metaphorical image in ways that make it clear that he does not mean the skull above the shoulders, but rather another meaning of "head," namely, the chief member, representative, or leader. He talks about how, nourished by the head, we are to grow up into the head (Eph. 4:15–16; Col. 2:19), which, if he were picturing a human trunk and skull, is not physiologically possible. Also, even when he calls the church the body of Christ, he represents it as a whole human body, not just the trunk, because it has eyes and ears (Eph. 4:16; 1 Cor. 12:16). But the biggest reason we know Paul does not intend us to think of head as a physical skull is because he says "the head of Christ is God" and "the head of every man is Christ" (1 Cor. 11:3). This cannot mean that Christ is the body of the Father or that every man is a trunk with Christ as the head.[5] Nor is Paul pointing out that the man is the source of the woman, like Gish Abay is the head of the Nile River.[6] No, Paul uses "head," as he explains rather clearly in verse 10, to mean "authority": "That is why a wife ought to have a symbol of authority on her head . . . ," that is, her physical head. His use of the word "authority" in the discussion clarifies for us that the metaphorical head he means is more like the leader of a regiment. Although some in recent years have expended enormous energy to get around them or explain them away, these statements cannot really be circumvented. They are the New Testament expression of the Old

Testament theme. They simply convey that the husband is in charge, and expressions of such should be taken public. A husband should take that charge for his wife's sake, first in the marriage, but in the family as well. First Timothy 3:4–5, 12, for example, calls a man, through elder or deacon qualifications, to govern his whole household.

Some feel that this somehow contradicts the Bible's teaching of women's equality. But it does not have to, and Paul recognizes this. In 1 Corinthians 11, which as we have just read is one of his most pronounced gender distinction passages, the apostle states forthrightly that the husband is the wife's authority (head). Yet, continuing in the chapter, he also makes statements of equality:

> Nevertheless, in the Lord woman is not independent of man, nor is man independent of woman. For as woman came from man, so also man is born of woman. But everything comes from God. (vv. 11–12 NIV)

Paul felt quite confident that equality and asymmetry in relationship could be kissing cousins, as they are in the Trinity of God. Apparently the people who read him think so too. Most Christians consider the equality of being and the asymmetry of headship to be noncontradictory tenets of family life.[7] Sociologist Sally K. Gallagher found, for example, that 87.4 percent of evangelicals believe that "marriage should be an equal partnership" while, at the same time, 90.4 percent believe that the "husband should be head of the family."[8]

So the Bible is clear and consistent. But it is still worth asking how authority is supposed to be exercised among equals. In the equal Trinity of God, how do the Members live out their asymmetry? In this chapter and the next, we shall explore what it means to say that the husband is the head. What is the substance of his firstborn authority (this chapter)? What is the meaning of her promotion (next chapter)? It is worth taking a few pages to give a picture of what this firstbornness looks like. For I find the asymmetry many Christian couples practice[9] to foster a kind of equality that matters more to them than equal authority.

Anyone who has ever been in charge as God wants him to be in charge knows that it is not all it is cracked up to be. To become responsible for another person or group is a strenuous task. Jesus once revealed the greatest expression of love that a person could produce. In a moment of intense emotion, He declared, "Greater love has no man than this, that a man lay down his life for his friends" (John 15:13 RSV). A pretty dramatic statement, no? He was at dinner with His friends, on the night before His own death. He was explaining how what was going to happen tomorrow was happening because He loved them so much. Later New Testament writers, knowing what a difficult path Jesus walked, were not eager to repeat this phrasing in their call to follow Him. We are supposed to become like Him in all things, but there is only one chapter in all of the New Testament in which this formula for love is brought up again as something to imitate. It is none other than Ephesians 5—you remember, that passage to which we keep returning? Paul says, "Be imitators of God, as beloved children. And walk in love, as Christ loved us and gave himself up for us . . ." (vv. 1–2). Fine. But then there is one group to whom he specifically applies this call. One group he commands to "lay down their lives . . ." for another. That group is husbands: "Husbands, love your wives, as Christ loved the church and gave himself up for her" (v. 25). Authority, properly understood, involves a death to self every day for those we love. This is what it means to be in charge.

In Peter's teaching about gender in marriage, remarkably similar to Paul's, he lays out the same dichotomous instruction to women and men:

> Wives, be subject to your own husbands. . . . Likewise, husbands, live with your wives in an understanding way, showing honor to the woman as the weaker vessel, since they are heirs with you of the grace of life. (1 Peter 3:1, 7)

The first apostle explains the husband's proper attitude with what might at first seem to be puzzling words, calling the woman "the weaker vessel." Several different readings have been advanced here through history. Many commentators read Peter to be making a statement about the essential qualities of some women, emotionally or physically. But given the biblical authors' aversion, including Peter, to speaking in essentialist terms, I would recommend a reading more in line with Peter's concerns in the passage. Does Peter have any reason to bring up essential qualities? Also, women were not terribly different in Peter's day. We can be confident that he knew strong women and weak women, athletic women and frail women. Do we really think that the apostle, in his circular letter here, was issuing instructions that some couples could not keep, because, for them, the wife was not the weaker vessel? Should we think that this is the one place where the Bible talks about essential male-female qualities? I suggest rather that the best reading follows the thrust of gender: it is about relationship. In this passage, Peter is not speaking about women in general but about wives in relationship. He is not speaking about essential qualities but about submission.

The vessel Peter is thinking of is a container, that is, a dish or jar or vase.[10] The jar would hold something, perhaps a valuable, in a protected place. One way of looking at being under someone's authority is to be contained, which could very well be why Peter uses this image. Peter's idea may be similar to Paul's discussion of different kinds of vessels in a household, some with higher status and some with lower (2 Tim. 2:20). You limit yourself by receiving an authority over you. If the containers Peter cites are expensive, decorated ceramics, then one would need to be careful handling them—they are vulnerable to breaking if you drop them. You wouldn't throw those vulnerable vessels around in common use. Likewise, people submitting in relationship are vulnerable, dependent upon the careful and righteous stewardship of the one in authority. Wives have so allowed themselves to be contained. They have made themselves weaker.

So the "weakness" of the womanly "vessel" is better understood as the position of submission. Her position of containment, or vessel, is indeed weaker. Her husband, recognizing that weakness, should stress their equality before the Lord, that they are "joint heirs of the grace of life" (v. 7 RSV). Understanding just how vulnerable someone is in surrendering prerogative to you should make you careful for her in your authority. Just as Paul urges more honor for the less honorable body parts (1 Cor. 12:23), so the same principle of Christ's teaching that "the last will be first" (Matt. 20:16; cf. 19:30; Mark 10:31; Luke 13:30) applies here. As she lowers herself, you should raise her with attention. In fact, you should treat her as your treasure. This is the Triune love of God. As the Second (Christ) did not grasp His equality with the First but "emptied himself," made himself the weaker before the First (Phil. 2:5–7), the First treasured the Second to the moon (Phil. 2:9–10).

Firstborn authority means being engaged every day. Of course, in striving to be the husbands Christ wants us to be, we often fail. But there is grace there, direct from the Lord, for husbands who take up the charge. We must be receiving Christ laying down His life for us to do the same for her. Like Christ for you, you lay down your life specifically for her sanctification (Eph. 5:25–26). In this passage, Paul gives an important way of carrying out this death to a husband's self. He pictures it as washing her. The apostle John describes how out from Christ's wounded side flowed blood and water (John 19:34), blood to purchase His bride, water to purify her. Paul says that Christ cleansed the church "by the washing with water through the word" (v. 26 NIV). So the Christian husband should be continually sacrificing, not to make his wife a Persian kitten on a pillow, but for her growth. That will make your daily routine different than the pursuit of the American Dream.

The washing in verse 26 is literally "through word." There is no article in the Greek. That is to say, words are the way to wash. If you tend to be uncommunicative, the strong silent type, you need to change. It does not have to be a lot of words, if they are well and timely spoken, if they wash her with the truths that God has given us. But you need to talk to her, to be ready to concentrate in conversation with her, even when you do not feel like it. That is largely how the sanctification happens.

If you have trouble with being interrupted, being in charge means setting up a regular time to address her concerns. One time I over-heard two church guys talking. George was speaking with his friend Sal about how George's wife sometimes just goes on a complaining ti-rade. "Does yours?" George asked. "No," said Sal. "Well that's the dif-ference between your wife and mine," George said. When I heard this I knew, knowing both couples, that George was wrong. Sal's wife was not different. She never went on a tirade because she never needed to. Sal had set up a regular time to solicit his wife about her concerns. That's what it means to be in charge.

These things may seem tough. Experienced husbands who are honest will confess that they sometimes feel like they married some-one who is too much trouble. When you feel like your woman is high maintenance, recognize that as God's call to you to follow Jesus in His life-giving. This is what being in charge principally involves: being engaged with her issues when you have enough to worry about for yourself; taking on her student loans as your own costs to pay back; entering into her strains with her parents as something you need to ad-dress; in short, approaching her problems as your own. True masculine strength bears other's problems even while burdened itself. Probably the most masculine act Jesus performed during His earthly life was turning to minister to the daughters of Jerusalem while He, physically half-dead already, trudged to His own execution (Luke 23:27–31). This is the function of the authority a woman gives a man. He needs a certain amount of elbow room to take responsibility. He needs to feel the charge from God. He needs allowance from her to do it for them. And he needs her trust that he is trying to do right.

When a husband thinks about being a head, he should also think about representation. Other parts of Scripture flesh out this representational assignment. Seth is born in the "likeness" and "image" of representative Adam, rather than Eve or both of them together, even though she gave birth to the son (Gen. 5:3; 4:25). Furthermore, even though the woman is first to sin (3:6), it is the man, Adam, whom God first calls and comes to question (3:9). Adam is held accountable first as their representative. And while consequences afflict both the man and the woman, the repercussions of their sin for the kingdom work fall upon him (3:17). In the New Testament, Paul makes a similar determination about the representative responsibility of the man, Adam (1 Cor. 15:22, 45–49; Rom. 5:12–21). Likewise, when Job must answer to God, the Almighty cites Job's masculinity—"gird up your loins like a man." For what does Job have to be a man? For God calling him to account (Job 38:3; 40:7 RSV).

One time, earlier in our marriage, a man came by our house while Mary K. was outside. She had wanted the branches over our garage cut down for a long time, and he talked her into having him cut them down. The price the man suggested was exorbitant, but she just said, "Okay." Some women are shrewd negotiators but Mary K. is not. While the branch-trimmer was at work, I came home and she told me the price. Mary K. had been taken. It was a moment for me to step forward as the family's representative and insist on negotiating a fair price. But I was ashamed and did nothing. I failed to cherish her as a representative head. The man walked away with our branches and our money.

The husband should see himself as the representative. This not only means uniquely representing his family's interest over his own. It also means that he is responsible for the family's communal sin, their collective failings, the ways that they are falling short. He should imagine himself one day standing before God to be held accountable for his marriage, his family, his church. We tend to blame one another for problems, just as Adam does when confronted with their first sin. He blames his wife, saying "The woman whom you gave to be with me, she gave me fruit of the tree . . ." (Gen. 3:12). Such is our now responsibility-avoiding nature. Rather the husband bearing the image of Christ in his representative role should feel it incumbent upon himself to own their wrongs before God, as well as to see that errors get fixed. That is, again, precisely Jesus' work in taking up the cross, representing us, His bride, in our sins (2 Cor. 5:21). That is a man in relationship. This is what authority is for.

Understanding firstborn representation also clarifies some Scriptures that, on the face of it, simply seem sexist. When Leviticus 12, for example, proclaims a new mother's ritual uncleanness after giving birth, the time period is twice as long if the baby born is a girl. If the woman has a boy, she is unclean for one week. If a girl, two weeks. Many readers wonder, is it because there is something wrong with girls? Do girl babies make a mother more unclean? But the principle of masculine representation explains the meaning of this law.[11] The uncleanness of all babies bespeaks our original sin. We cause uncleanness to our mothers simply by coming into the world. But, under that old covenant, the man is appointed to represent the community by circumcision, to be cut as a sign of the sacrifice needed to cleanse from sin (v. 3). That circumcision is performed when the boy is one week old. The baby boy's circumcision on the eighth day prematurely ends the mother's uncleanness, providing a picture of how the sacrifice prescribed by God will end sin. So the law is not attributing a greater uncleanness to girls, but rather illustrating how boys bear sin as their family's representative.

When a man fully grasps what it is to be a man—and how far short he falls in being one as a husband or brother or son—he is liable to despair. The road runs through rough territory. But the rewards are ravishing. In his Ephesians 5 passage, Paul knows the utter extravagance of his husbandly instruction so in the next verses he goes on to try to convince us that living this way is really for our benefit as well (vv. 27–29). He reassures you that laying down your life for your wife generates a life of great enjoyment. The peripheral issues of this passage should not keep us from wondering at the momentous claim Paul makes: the power of your gendered behavior can actually change a woman.

There are a number of aspects of Christ and the changing church that Paul could go into, but what he talks about is Christ presenting the church to Himself as a beautiful bride. That is, Christ enjoys the church. The apostle is contending, "Honest, guys, the sacrifice of yourself for your wife is for your benefit." You and your wife are so connected that your sanctifying headship is like exercising and feeding your own body. Your bodybuilding shapes great benefits for you from her muscular faith. The actions of engagement in taking responsibility for her convey just how cherished she is. Paying attention to her on matters of import to her, "her vows" for instance, does something very deep in her. It makes her a woman confident in her words and capable in her endeavors. It builds her trust in God. Your attentiveness validates her and her goals to a depth that not even Oprah can reach. Or a hundred women's magazines. Your authority makes her confident. A confident woman is a stunning woman. So "He who loves his wife loves himself" (v. 28).

I have known, and loved, many high-achieving women. They had shattered glass ceilings, reached pinnacles in their companies, and reduced their body fat to 6 percent. But some of them were a mess. I would not take away from their workplace achievements, because some had gotten very good at what they did. But their achievements did not do for them personally what had been promised. My friends, it turns out, are not isolated cases. Betsey Stevenson, a professor of public policy at the University of Michigan and former chief economist of the U.S. Department of Labor, and her U-M colleague Justin Wolfers, professor of economics and public policy, say that despite all the objective improvements to their lives over the past four decades, especially in the workplace, women today appear to be less happy than they were in 1972.[12] I was skeptical when I read this because it is difficult to gage happiness, but based on a large number of self-reported survey answers from many different sources, the researchers conclude that "women's subjective well-being has declined" over most of the industrialized world. Their study is not the only one to show declining feminine happiness since the 1970s, a fact that suggests that women's happiness might be related to things other than their ability to work outside the home, the area in which women have made great gains. Do you want to see a truly empowered and attractive woman? It is not an independent woman. It is a woman whose men in her life handle authority well. This is what the firstborn will do for her.

I conclude with a contrasting example that takes us a little afield of the marriage relationship. I must defer the discussion of more distant relationships where gender *doesn't* matter to chapter 17, "Continuum of Closeness," but suffice it to say here that these gender principles have great force in close ties, such as with Chloe and her Christian brothers. Chloe was a published writer, a fashionable and street-smart New Yorker, and generally an over-competent person. But these were not what I saw when I looked at her as her pastor. I saw someone whose walk with God I admired. Chloe had confidence and poise that many around her found arresting. She had what I would call a softness toward the Spirit that grounded her in life. You might look at her and think, "Here is the quintessential independent and liberated woman, self-reliant and needing no man," but you would be wrong in thinking that. Because, as her pastor, I was privy to how she acted and reacted toward the men close to her, and how she embraced the asymmetries we are discussing. What is most surprising of all, she did so while single. Many women have trouble making sense of the firstborn-promoter asymmetry before they are married. But not Chloe. In fact, when she was present in groups of women where these things were plainly unpopular, I witnessed Chloe vocally defending them. So I once took her aside and asked her, what did she actually get from the firstborn authority of the men in her life? How did those with whom she was in relationship—family and brothers and church—help or hinder her? Her striking answers are worth quoting at length.

Chloe told me that a large part of her happiness was the men being men in her life: "I'd probably be more depressed, more uncomfortable with being a woman without them," she said. She spoke of the guys— in family and church—"taking charge in a way that sees me." The masculinity she appreciated was not superficial: "I'd rather have a guy take responsibility in a situation than open a door for me." "When he tries to bring me back to a place that is good, I feel cared for."

I realized, as she elaborated, that Chloe was surrounded by men in close respectful relationship, none of them yet romantic (yes, really), yet all of them in subtle ways helping to make her a woman of faith. Example after example came forth of how one rendered thoughtful care for her recreation or took care of something or paid attention to her appearance or changed his attitude when he saw her feelings, as if it were this Christian brother's responsibility to fix. Whether the particular guy could fix it was immaterial—she was touched by the brother trying to help with pain. One time, when she was infuriated with a relative, a brother's response was, "Come to this ice curling–watching event. . . ." He got her to watch a sport to redirect her to a better place.

These men, in relationships that were safe and appropriate, have helped her to avoid mistakes with men by setting a high standard: "I see when guys avoid responsibility. I see the contrast. I see the need to be patient with some guys, but I feel like I see where they need to go."

She used remarkable terminology in describing what she got from these men "not shirking," as she put it. Their taking brotherly initiative in her life made her "relaxed" and "comfortable." She spoke of feeling "satisfied," "uplifted," "OK." Chloe was not without personal difficulties—I know them—but she said that these close men have "made room for lots of different kinds of pains. . . . I don't feel crisis in the painful parts of my life."

Chloe went further than I expected. She spoke comfortably of being "identified by these caring men, having an identity as a woman from men in her life." As she gave place to their voices in her life, she said, "They have given me liberty to be a woman." These men have a part "to establish my own self. . . . They establish me as a woman." "I have an identity as a woman because my guys establish the reference point." She described peers without what she has as having "a deep, deep hole in their lives." Chloe is becoming a master of faith. She was one of those I look at as a pastor and sigh happily. Whatever life throws at her, she will triumph. Of that, I have no doubt.

Some women cannot imagine stepping into Chloe's experience, or speaking in her terms, chiefly because their experience with men has been anything but helpful. Almost of necessity, mistreatment by men has shaped a philosophy of self-sufficiency. They feel they have only one recourse, and that is to rely on themselves. Independence, for men as well as women, is the consolation for living outside of the fellowship of gender that God desires for us. But, surrounded by one another's failure as we are, Christ remains present to teach us how to be different.

When I think of my own husbanding, I feel like a little boy who just got his training wheels taken off his bike. His father runs along behind him, grabbing the back every time he is about to fall to one side or the other. The boy thinks that he is doing it himself, and sometimes, wonder of wonders, he actually is, balancing and doing it right for a few moments, actually doing it by his own learned power. But the ride couldn't happen without the father rushing along behind, extending grace at many moments. I am that boy on the bike. My husbanding often errs by not being engaged with her concerns or over-engaged to get my own way. As I tilt to one side or the other, our Father's grace, through my wife's forgiveness, is there to steady me. And as I lean into these Scriptures, I find that there are moments when I am actually doing it. And they are our Father's moments of greatest joy.

The Jealous Husband and the Accused

It was bad timing. All the people, breaking down their tents, packing up their pottery, turned to stare as he stomped by, leading her. But it could not wait. So many happy faces, so expectant and joyful for the journey about to begin, just made their misery worse. But he was not taking one step through the desert with this, this . . . this bane of his life. He had to know.

He led, gripping her, too hard, by the wrist. We used to hold hands, she thought. They made their way through the deconstructing camp, billowing tent skins and tilting poles. Every so often he sheepishly eyed the enormous pillar-shaped cloud over the tabernacle. The thing had lifted high in the sky in front of them, watching them, he felt. He reached the priests and smacked down the sacrifice: just cheap barley meal, the lowliest sacrifice in the law of Moses, without oil or frankincense. They both stared at it, thinking of their joyless marriage, cheapened by suspicion, unoiled by any mirth or spirit. The priest understood immediately and assembled the elders. He knew that God cared a great deal about faltering marriages and wanted their conflicts addressed. If their family unions broke down, they would never make it across the desert.

By now a crowd had gathered, solemnly awaiting the ordeal. The priest gently released the husband's hold and took the woman from him. There was nothing for him to do now, but wait there, fuming and silent. He witnessed the ceremony standing there in a stupor so that he hardly remembered the details afterward. He recalled her positioned before the tabernacle, hair unbound, holding the barley. The priest speaking to her, she shaking and answering. The priest waving the barley before the altar and taking out a handful for the fire. The dust from the tabernacle floor, along with the ink of written curses washed off papyri, dissolved in the holy water, then in her hands. And she drinking it!

He suddenly came to himself. She was standing in front of him, with the priest. "We find no guilt in her," said the priest. He looked at her recriminating, tear-strewn eyes and could read them clearly: "I told you! Are you satisfied now?" Then he was in a side tent and the priest was counseling the man on his marriage. "What do I do now?" he asked. "Go get ready to leave Mount

Sinai with us all." said the priest, "Break down your home. And rebuild your marriage. Trouble her no longer."

The man was led back to his wife, now feeling the eyes of the crowd upon him—him, the false accuser. He studied the pillar-cloud looming over them for a moment and then knelt down. "I'm sorry," he stammered. She took his hand stiffly, and lifted him up. They walked back, worn out, but somehow hopeful that they could build a new home in a new land . . .

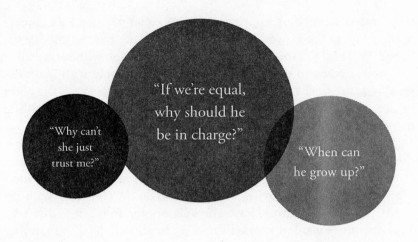

"Why can't she just trust me?"

"If we're equal, why should he be in charge?"

"When can he grow up?"

CHAPTER 10

The Asymmetry of Order (Part 2): The Promoter

The submission of a woman to a man may be explained as three things. First, it is a gift. An often overlooked feature of the Bible's wifely submission commands is how they are addressed to the wives, not the husbands. In contrast to the Qur'an, for example, the Bible never tells husbands to make their wives submit—quite the contrary. Consider the prophet's instruction in the Qur'an: "Men have authority over women because God has made the one superior to the other. . . . As for those from whom you fear disobedience, admonish them, forsake them in beds apart, and beat them."[1] The Bible, in contrast, tells wives to voluntarily surrender prerogative for the sake of the husband (and not to men in general). So the asymmetry the Bible teaches is not subjugation, or even domination, which has so characterized the sad history of men and women in relationship, and which was ominously predicted in Genesis 3:16, saying that the fallen man will dominate the fallen woman. Rather, it is the valued and limited submission appropriate to an equal partner. As Lemuel's mother says of the Proverbs 31 wife's husband: he "has full confidence in her" (v. 11 NIV). You cannot have true submission without equality.

I have come to use "promotion" interchangeably with "submission" because husbandly authority is a gift to be offered for the good of the other. Promotion is the positive work behind all the telling of women to be quiet in church that Paul does (1 Tim. 2:12; 1 Cor. 14:34–35). No inherent benefit lies in women's silence. The marriage, the family, and the church all need to hear their voices. So does Paul. In the same letter to the Corinthians, he commends them for having women publicly praying and prophesying (1 Cor. 11:2 with vv. 5, 13). In another pastoral letter, he tells women to teach (Titus 2:3). Paul obviously wanted women speaking in church. So commanding their silence at a certain time, in this case during teaching or official judging, when "others weigh what is said" (1 Cor. 14:29), is his call to express the gendered gift. Not speaking when they could speak promotes their brothers to grow in taking responsibility. When Paul writes to Timothy about women's silence in authoritative teaching,[2] his mind goes back to Genesis 2 because of Eve's silence before Adam in their story. When they meet, Eve certainly could speak, but the account presents us with no speaking on her part. Instead, she allows Adam to name her.

Women are told to give the gift and men to receive it because of the good that results to both, the way it enables a man to grow out of selfishness and into living for others, and the way it enables a woman to become strong in faith. When women in church refuse to speak in certain contexts, the resulting silence grows louder and louder until the men are roused to represent.

Second, promotion is a feat of strength. Of the valiant Proverbs 31 wife, the author admires, "She dresses herself with strength and makes her arms strong. . . . Strength and dignity are her clothing" (vv. 17, 25). The praise is in the form of heroic poetry, usually used to laud a champion's military exploits.[3] The woman in the Thebez tower, braining Abimelech with a millstone, pictures this strength also. Millstones come in various sizes, but they are all heavy. If she was anything, she was strong. Young girls are not out of line, in the Bible's worldview, feeling invigorated when they hear Katy Perry roar.

Realizing this renders the strange military imagery appearing around the Bible's women as not so strange, as when the Proverbs 31 presents the wife as a champion, akin to Israel's ancient heroes of the battlefield,[4] or as when Jael, in active duty, "went out to meet" Sisera and wins the Lord's war (Judg. 4:18–24; 5:23–27). Mary, the mother of Jesus, breaks out into martial language to express what God is doing through her submission as His handmaid. Her famous song, the Magnificat (Luke 1:46–55), praises "He who is mighty" (v. 49). As Old Testament scholar Tremper Longman III points out, this refers to God's military strength, His might in battle.[5] In addition, she speaks of how the Lord has "shown strength with His arm" (v. 51) and "has brought down the mighty from their thrones . . ." (v. 52). Again, military terms.[6] These last two women, Jael and Mary, are the only two women in Scripture praised by their own gender as "women among women" (Judg. 5:24; Luke 1:41–42). Mary, like Jael, is fighting a battle as a woman with her womanhood, and she knows it.

Similarly, several of the DSM study husbands with especially intimate marriages sought to correct what they considered to be a mischaracterization of wives who voluntarily submit to their husbands. In discussing gender-inspired submission, the men took the opportunity to adamantly assert that their wives are not weak:

> Edwin: "She's a strong leader personality. . . . She's very feminine. She's a very strong woman; a strong feminine . . . Her submission to me is so very strong. . . . If I get angry at anything, it's when people criticize her as being weak or not standing up for herself. Because she is not weak."
>
> Silva: "Her frailty attracted me because it seemed contradictory to her strength. She is a strong character. . . . She won't be curtailed [by others' timetables]. . . . My wife is strong in opinion."
>
> Ted: "But she's not a shrinking violet either at all. She's very outgoing. . . . She gets very . . . can be quite feisty about things. . . ."
>
> Fibeo: "I don't feel like she's trying to take that away from me or put herself on an equal footing with . . . male-hood. . . . Not that she's weak, because she's not at all."

In the discussion of decision-making these interviewees insistently equated feminine surrender of prerogative with strength. Submission marked, not inequality, but might in their wives. Voluntarily showing respect, promoting, and putting forward someone else are practices that take deliberate and sometimes heroic effort, and the men recognized it. This is quite different from the picture of submitting wives as dominated or weak and unable to stand up for themselves. These husbands' attitudes betray a parity of respect in the marriage.

Third, submission or promotion, properly understood, actively engages us with those we love. The submission of an equal does not shrink into the corner and blend in with the violet wallpaper. As Achsah pressed Othniel, God would have women fully engaged in the offering of submission.

Some writers argue that the Christian ideology of husbandly authority and wifely deferral creates a climate of male domination and female subservience that not only discourages men from being expressive with their wives but, worse, promotes domestic violence.[7] In point of fact, however, research indicates no association between conservative Christians (or even religion in general) and domestic violence. Rather, there are indicators that abuse is lower among churchgoers.[8] Nonetheless, abuse is still something to worry about. The Bible worries about it too, which is why God always sets limitations on the authority of the people He puts in charge, from kings and governments, to churches and pastors, and especially to husbands.

Deuteronomy regulated divorce to do just that, limit a husband's authority (Deut. 24:1–4). God gave Scriptures such as these in the old covenants to comfort sufferers in less than perfect home situations. The laws guarded them against hopelessness that there is no solution to their derailed or oppressive relationships. Even before Deuteronomy, as the first-generation Israelites ready their first march from Sinai, there arose the domestic problem envisioned at the beginning of our chapter: a marriage that had spiraled down the vortex of distrust.[9] The resulting law of Numbers, while not in effect today, testifies to God's attentiveness to such pain.

The law (Num. 5:11–31) upheld a husband's limited authority in the marriage while protecting the wife from spousal abuse. The jealous husband suspected, but had no proof, that his wife had been unfaithful. Adultery committed by an ancient Near Eastern woman was a very serious thing. Violence to a suspected wife was a grave danger. A judgmental community, an overwrought husband, or a zealous relative, taking matters into hand could lynch her, as happens even today in the Middle Eastern so-called honor killings. So God instituted a law to protect the suspected woman and give the couple a chance to restore their home. First of all, only the husband could bring a charge of suspicion, not neighbors, nor relatives, nor any meddling third parties. Moreover, God used but modified a familiar cultural practice, by which He removed the sentencing and punishing of an unapprehended adulteress from human hands while making the larger point of jurisprudence: you may not condemn someone, man or woman, without proof. The dust that the woman drank in the trial by ordeal would be harmless apart from divine intervention. So the law transferred her from her husband's authority to stand, by ritual, before her God. A more serious place, but also a place of protection from the faulty judgment of one man.

Such laws, as stated above, should not be followed today, but the principle behind them should. Lauren, a woman in my church, disagreed with Reggie, her ministry leader husband, in his decision to cancel a certain church function. They argued about it, but he could not agree that the advantages she listed outweighed the disadvantages of maintaining the ministry as it was. Seeking to live out this principle of limitation, Reggie shrugged and said, "I do not know what to tell you, Lauren. If you really feel strongly about this, you are welcome to go over my head. Write the session [church elders] and I will wait to submit to them." There was a man who well understood the nature of his authority.

Our quintessential New Testament marriage passage, Ephesians 5, begins[10] by telling the wives in verse 22, "Wives, submit to your own husbands," carefully adding, at the end of the sentence, "as to the Lord," (*hōs tō kuriō*). The phrase "as to the Lord" modifies "submit," not "husband." Paul is not saying, "Obey your husband as if he was God," but rather "Obey your husband as a way of obeying God." The likeness is in the verb, not the object: you imitate your attitude to God (who only asks you to do right) in your attitude to your husband. You should be as willing to do right for your husband as for your God. There should be trust in his leading, and seeking God's will in what your husband says. But if your husband asks you to do something clearly wrong, his authority ends, because then you cannot submit to God in submitting to your husband. This means that submission is an active process of discerning God's will.

One time I was driving Mary K. and our small children through a heavy storm. I was pressing forward to get us to our vacation destination. The storm got so bad that some of the roads we were traveling got flooded. We tried various routes, got blocked, retraced and, as the night wore on, finally reached the one remaining road that had not been closed (yet). But a few inches of standing water covered it. The farther I drove along it, the deeper the water became. We entered into a disagreement about whether to go on. (She tends toward the safe side for the sake of health, I toward the riskier side for the sake of the experience.) The ensuing scenes elucidate how active her submission is in an ambiguous situation.

"Turn back, Sam," Mary K. stated. "It's not worth it."

"We can make it!" I reassured her. "I can see the land rise in the distance." Mary K. did not like my driving down the wet road. She needed to voice her disagreement with my action. She does not like doing this, but for her in that moment to simply remain silent would not be submission "as to the Lord."

I continued driving. She spoke again, respectfully explaining why she thought the situation was an unsafe one in which to have the children. She recounted the unexpected power of flood water to carry off cars. I disagreed that we were in such a situation. These exchanges between us continued as we crept along. This was part of her submission. As the one in charge, I need to hear from her. To deny the value of her voice, I would be a fool. To refrain from talking out her disagreement, explaining concerns and making appeal, she would not be honestly submitting.

Mary K. dropped the subject, while still monitoring the water. She disagreed, but actively decided to continue to leave the matter in my hands. This submission was a conscious choice "as to the Lord," entrusting us to Him. To continually harangue me after she had made herself clear and after it was clear that I heard her would not be to submit.

She continued to do this until she felt the water through her sandals. Then she deemed it a situation to put her foot down (after she lifted it up out of the water in the bottom of the car). She reasoned that we could drive in the other direction and probably find a hotel so that I had no good reason to refuse. She decided that the limits to my authority had been passed and, because my actions were needlessly threatening the safety of the children, righteousness meant precisely not submitting or promoting me. So she openly defied me, threatening to leave the car with the children. The water was not moving so this was a safe alternative. This, too, was part of her submission "as to the Lord."

Disobedience is expected if the husband contradicts the Lord's command. Such disobedience is expected of Sapphira by the apostle Peter in the book of Acts (Acts 5:1–10). When her husband covets position in the community and so lies to the apostles about proceeds they are contributing from the sale of their field, God judges him and actually strikes him dead. Sapphira comes in separately and is faced with the choice to participate in his act of dishonesty or refuse. Peter fully expects her to disobey her husband by refusing. The punishment that falls from heaven upon her when she follows him in lying (v. 10) makes it clear that God fully expected her to also.[11] Christ does not want passive men in His church. But no less does He want passive women.

Mary K. never finds this pleasant to do, but in this case, she judged it appropriate to avoid an unrighteous, endangering action. Recognizing her Lord now meant not recognizing my authority. Our young children found these the most exciting events of our vacation.

All couples err to one side or the other in walking this out, too much or too little, so we should persistently examine how authority works in the Scriptures to keep growing in how to do it right. But the point is that limitations on human authority make submission an energetic endeavor, demanding vigorous engagement. Note the limitations that even Paul, the great apostle, places on his own authority. He says, in the introduction to one of his other gender passages, "Be imitators of me, *as* I am of Christ" (1 Cor. 11:1). He does not claim our imitation in ways that he does not imitate Christ. But Paul's and our ever-remaining tendency to shirk or overstep our responsibilities need not prevent us from envisioning Christ and the church in our relationships.

"I still do not feel it's right," Georgette told me. She wanted to talk to me about this issue of a wife promoting. She was listening, but was unable to understand why, if she felt her husband's decision, though not morally wrong, was not the best, she should submit to his decision. I talked about visualizing the Lord Christ behind her husband, looking past this fallible man to the infallible Lord who assures that she would be cared for even if she did this. But Georgette had a hard time visualizing this, understandably, since she was not a believer in Christ. We wondered together whether this was doable without God in the picture. Finally, she sighed and said, "I guess having God in the picture makes the difference."

Indeed. Obeying or submitting "as to the Lord" is really about trusting the One who tells you to do this. Promoting wives know that you cannot properly surrender prerogative to your husband unless you trust God, nay, unless you are doing it *because* you are trusting God, trusting that God is in this picture, that He will take care of you and your own. Otherwise it is not real submitting but cowing or fawning and you cannot do it right. This is the real point of the Numbers 5 ordinance of the jealous husband. The law doesn't work unless God is real and involved, which the law promises that He is. In the active engaging and ultimate surrender, a woman becomes a master of faith, a real woman. She knows, as the woman in Numbers 5 did, that eventually God will make all things clear.

In counseling engaged couples from Ephesians 5, I speak in these ways, trying to show the man how he is called to lay down his life and the woman how she is to surrender prerogative. Then I usually ask the couple which they think is harder, which they'd rather do? They look at verse 24's "in everything" and at verse 25's "gave himself up." They come to the conclusion that each is equally demanding. Both involve a death of sorts. The asymmetry is not in degree but in kind. How much do we need to do this, they ask? How much, says the wife? How far shall I submit? How much, says the husband? How much life shall I give up for her? And the answer to both, for intimacy, is more than you think should be necessary.

To fulfill such extraordinary commands, it helps the firstborn and the promoter to understand the dictates' extraordinary benefits, the greatest of which lie in fostering intimacy. Teaching a man to take responsibility for his woman and teaching a woman to advance her man compels them both to deal with real issues between them and consequently deepens their relationship.

Many simply presume that gender distinction limits rather than promotes intimacy in marriages.[12] Some contemporary family scholars argue that egalitarian marriages, that is, those that consciously seek to suppress gender distinction in responsibilities in their relationships,[13] should result in greater intimacy and high-quality, stable marriages by building up mutual understanding.[14] But sociological statistical research on this theory is inconclusive,[15] and in my qualitative DSM study, responses to the question, "What would you advise wives to do to foster intimacy in the marriage?" very often concerned submission or respect. Without prompting, much of the advice went along these lines: "Do not emasculate your man in any way. Build him up"; "Want to hear him talk"; "Allow yourself to be vulnerable enough to allow [your husband] to be the man . . . to lead"; "Let them be a man in the relationship"; and "Respect them. Let them know they're respected. Beyond all other things, let them know that you see them very much as a man." Again, these were their answers to the question of how to promote intimacy.

Theo answered, "Embrace 1 Peter 3," notable in being where the apostle Peter makes the extravagant claim that a wife's gendered behavior may actually convert a man's soul to Christ (vv. 1–2)! Such is the power wielded by a knowing woman. This tectonic force rumbled through the life of Silva, who admitted about Alexa: "My wife trusts me [implicitly]. I trust myself not nearly as much as she does. But because of her trust, I trust God more than I once did."

The DSM husbands' answers explain what her active promotion achieves. Wifely deferral and honoring was the largest category of feminine gender distinction brought up in the DSM study interviews, the one that matters most to the interviewed men. The request to "describe a time when she made you feel like a man" drew a similar response from every single interviewee. Each answer contained this idea of respecting. It was expressed variously: "acknowledging [my] decision-making [place]"; "when she said, 'I'm really proud of you [for sacrificing for me]'"; "when she puts her arm in mine"; "when she asks my opinion on things"; "the way she gives me the respect . . . the honor"; "when she entrusts me with something important to her"; "seeing, from the stage, her smiling at me"; "how she really affirms me as a dad, you know, she realizes she can't do for them what I can do for them . . . as a dad, and as a man"; "when she has really affirmed my leadership, where . . . she sees something big, in terms of God's call on my life"; "when she'll brag to her family about stuff that I do"; "when . . . she indicates that she could see me in . . . even a larger [vocational] role than what I am doing now, whether its national or . . . she certainly sees that as something that wouldn't surprise her at all"; and "when she tells her friends how blessed she is to be in our relationship." Always included was the same theme of honoring, showing respect, and putting the husband forward, a huge identity-forming factor in these grateful men's lives. The bond forged with someone instrumental in developing one's identity is not to be underestimated. Reverence is a supremely valuable gift that wives can give. And when it is given, intimacy flourishes.

A woman might ask, why can he not show concern for me without being in charge? Why the need for authority? The answer is that the distinction makes him a man. After infatuation fades in a relationship, a great distraction replaces attentiveness. Promotion trains men out of that. It also thwarts indecisiveness. They learn to make decisions on matters of import, when it is difficult and when one might be wrong. When Mary K. consults me, purposely using me to help make a decision, she not only raises her expectations of me, she raises my expectations of me. I grow up.

We are sometimes tempted to look at other couples and wish that we had a husband like that or a wife like that. But gender distinction supernaturally invigorates our own relationships. Respect of him will give a woman what, perhaps, she really wants—a husband worthy of respect. Taking charge for her concerns will give a man a radiant wife, increasingly beautiful. Be a real man in relationship and you will find yourself married to a real woman. Be a real woman and you will find yourself married to a real man.

The Anointed in the Nick of Time Interrupted

It had been a long time. A long time of dusty desert trails and fearful sprints from danger. He was tired. Tired of running. Tired of not having a home. Most of all, he was tired of maintaining a vision for something that had about as much substance as morning fog. Sometimes, it really seemed possible that he would become king, just as the prophet promised. But then again, there were lots of times, this being one of them, when it just seemed ridiculous. No support base. No political pathway. And no end in sight to the murderous monarch to whom he had sworn his loyalty for life. There was just no way this could work out.

Abishai approached him tentatively. Yes, what was it? His men were hungry again. Paran was a waste. Why did he even come here? He wasn't sure. He had had to get away and think. And pray. But Paran wasn't such a great choice, he now thought. He knew the land. He had managed to get them to water. But they needed to eat too. He allowed his mind to run over the inhabitants in the area. Would there be a friend for them here? There was Nabal, to the North, whose numerous sheep he had protected for many years. Nabal would be shearing his sheep in the hill country now. Still, Nabal was a little iffy. But what was to be done? They needed to eat. He ordered Abishai to send a delegate to Carmel and ask the rich man for assistance.

When the answer came back, a resounding "No," David snapped. "Who is David? Who is the son of Jesse?" Nabal had replied. Who is David, indeed. Well, maybe there were some things he couldn't do—wouldn't allow himself to do—but he could certainly teach this son of an ass who David was. David ordered the entire company to arm. He told them they were going to fight. They were happy about that. Maybe he would never lift his hand against Saul, but by God this ungrateful worm would feel his wrath. Then he would know who David was. And others would too.

Four hundred mounted and rode toward Carmel behind him. David's mind was hot. The tendrils of revenge, so long pruned, he now well watered with his thoughts. Riding always gave time to think. And when he was riding to war, his thoughts always sped up. What he was thinking, honestly, was that this sparing of "God's anointed" was getting old. There had been a hope because of Samuel. He was supposed to be a prophet, but

David liked to think of him more as a friend. That guy had been so sure. So many times, when David was losing the vision, faltering in his resolve to stay in Israel, despairing sometimes even of life, Samuel was there, so confident in David's coronation. The Lord's plan, Samuel had called it. He had been so sure! But now he was dead. And maybe the vision of David's rule should die with him. Who was David, anyway? Nothing. Nobody. And as such, why couldn't he arrange his own relief?

His thoughts were abruptly interrupted by a small caravan that had blocked the path. His company pulled up short. Who could this be? And why were they in the way? David opened his mouth to order them aside but he never got it out. It was a woman in the lead! And she was not moving. What on earth ... ? "My Lord!" she cried, as she fell at his feet, her face to the ground, but he had seen her face. "Let the guilt fall entirely on me!" It stopped him in his tracks. He was listening then.

And she began. And as she spoke and kept speaking, David's grip loosened on his sword hilt. Then his hand dropped to his side. Then his head fell forward. And he remembered. He remembered Yahweh, hidden in his heart. She was speaking the vision. The picture of righteousness that Yahweh required, of forgiveness as he had been forgiven, of waiting for Yahweh's deliverance instead of striving for it himself, of faith and love, of the sureness that Yahweh would fulfill His word to David. David let his eyes glide over the long train of donkeys stretched out behind her, laden with food, and the sheep she was offering to be slaughtered instead of her husband's men.

Finally, David stepped forward and lifted her to her feet. He had almost thrown it away, the whole kingdom project. For Yahweh, he knew, wanted a king after His own heart and, in killing Nabal in revenge, David would no longer have been that. So much would have been lost, not just for him, but for the nation to be. Now he remembered who David was. As he looked into her eyes, he could see that she understood this. That is why she had come. She had hurried to prevent his hands from being bloodied with guilt. She had come for God's kingdom. How did she know all this? Who was this heavenly queen?

"Abigail," she said. And she asked him to remember her when God made him king. Remember her? How could he ever forget that face?

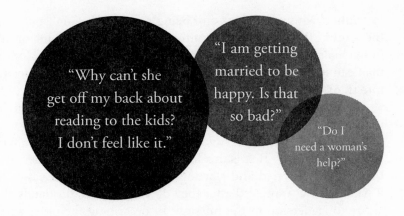

"Why can't she get off my back about reading to the kids? I don't feel like it."

"I am getting married to be happy. Is that so bad?"

"Do I need a woman's help?"

CHAPTER 11

The Asymmetry of Intent: The Commissioned and the Empowerer

I like to meet with couples that I marry one year after the wedding. It is something of a checkup, to see how they are doing. I mainly want to ask them one question. It is a seemingly straightforward question, but hardly anyone is ready with an answer. The question is simply this: What is the point of your marriage? Why are you two together?

An answer is not forthcoming because they, like all of us, look at marriage as a way to be happy. We get married to pursue a contented life. But that is not how God looks at marriage. Marriage has a greater purpose, to accomplish His kingdom on the earth. From the beginning, close relationships were there to further the beautifying and productive reign of the King. God put the man in the first garden to till and develop it, and He put woman there to empower that mission with her strong help. Oh, our happiness is His concern also, and is to come as a consequence of union. But the happiest marriages are about something larger than themselves. And gender cannot come to fruition without relationship being directed to God's purposes in the world. This, the third asymmetry, is most important of all. As individuals, we are each about the work of God. But in relationship, a man can lead a woman into sacrifice and a woman can propel a man into transformative engagement.

A husband's call is to find the larger picture that encompasses them both. Proverbs 24:27 says to young men, "Prepare your work outside; get everything ready for yourself in the field, and after that build your house." That is, his life calling should take higher priority than getting married and starting a family. It is always easier when it happens that way. And after they do get married, husbands should aspire to leadership in the mission. In describing the other apostles' marriages and what apostles have a right to do, Paul allows the privilege to "lead around" (*periagō*) a wife in fulfilling the call (1 Cor. 9:5). Paul is not specifically teaching on gender distinction in this verse, but the word choice shows that, in his mind, the godly apostle is leading his wife in the mission. Masculinity is distinguished in marriage by getting an answer to the question, "What is the purpose of our home?" A man steps forward to be commissioned by God in that.

In our times, this asymmetry has been misunderstood as its parody: "Men go off to work" or "The man's is the professional realm," and this misunderstanding of work apart from God's call leads to a battle of the genders. Because understanding employment as a way to advance God's kingdom is largely forgotten today,[1] a man's distinction of purpose is usually invisible and unvalued. The image-bearers devolve into pursuing material wealth or fighting over whose career is more important. At best, husbands and wives find an arrangement of pursuing their own ends, maybe good ends, but their jobs separate them and do not forward the intimacy to power the progress of Christ's kingdom. On the contrary, image-bearers do not simply have jobs. They have vocational ways to advance God's purposes. Who is the breadwinner is never God's question. It is rather whether the two together have a call. Can the man assume responsibility for apprehending it, whatever their relative salaries?

The tendency of many men to define themselves by their work gives us a glimmer of masculine commissioning, but also a twisting of it. Joanne Lipman, former deputy managing editor at the *Wall Street Journal*, tried to make sense in 2009 of the severe loss of jobs she beheld around her in New York City. She wrote, "I'm in the unfortunate position of witnessing many friends and colleagues laid off over the past year." But in the midst of the crisis, she observed that "the women are less apt to fall apart—and this goes even for the primary breadwinners[2]—because they are less likely to define themselves by their job in the first place."[3] The inclination of the men that Lipman knew to define themselves by their jobs reflects the tragedy of men conceiving of their work without God.

Meanwhile, women do not go unaffected by the men's tragedy. Feminism's mistake is to think that equality will finally be achieved by women taking up the same idols of materialism and success that many men have taken and making them theirs. So some women are climbing this mistaken ladder to nowhere. Other women are simply frustrated with their husbands' inattention to matters of the family, another expression of the forgotten work of the commissioned. When children come he does not take up the lead in their spiritual education, as part of their home's vision. So he does not tell the children bedtime stories. These are all losses proceeding from the burial of God's masculine commissioning mandate.

The diminishing of gender severely inhibits a man's ability to find God's work for him because he is not looking for it. As writer Henry Miller put it, "The loss of sex polarity is part and parcel of the larger disintegration, the reflex of the soul's death, and coincident with the disappearance of great men, great deeds, great causes. . . ."[4] and, I would add, great women. When a man realizes his gender distinction, and grasps the responsibility to God in his manhood, it quickens him. There is securing and developing, where before there was selfishness or lethargy. And he sees woman with new eyes.

Doing God's work on earth is not easy. It is a thorny job requiring divine help, which the feminine delivers. Woman, the helper divine, assures the mission will succeed. The empowerment can take many forms. The DSM interviews expressed it variously as "giving her thoughts," "taking things off my shoulders," "challenging me," "questioning me," "praying for me," or "encouraging me," among other expressions. When I probed as to whether this venue was a true distinction between husband and wife, rather than a mutual practice, I repeatedly heard that it was truly distinct. That is, the interviewees felt that their wives really did something for them in these things that they did not do for their wives, or at least not in the same way. What are some of these things?

Sometimes the help is in the very finding of God's call to the husband. Although Proverbs 24:27 (about attending to field before house building) should be the man's goal, for many men it seems always just out of reach. In these cases a woman helps a man find the mission that he cannot get to on his own. In our model married couple of Judges, Achsah and Othniel, her femininity empowered Othniel to take Kiriath-Sepher. As judge, he goes on to defeat what is probably the most powerful enemy that appears in the book (Judg. 3:8–10).[5] She was the motivation for Othniel to move forward for God's purposes and thereby move God's purposes forward. Because of her they found their place in history. This is womanhood at work. In contrast, Delilah led Samson away from God's purposes for him. He had a hard time focusing on what God wanted of him anyway. And she, with the power to caretake his call, instead trampled it.

Another example, outside of marriage, can be seen in the prophetess Deborah[6] and her help of the reluctant general Barak. Deborah set up her place under a (then) central tree in the hill country, what came to be called the "palm of Deborah" (Judg. 4:5). She makes herself available to the covenant people there. Heber, the noncommittal husband of Jael is contrasted[7] with the fully engaged Deborah. He stands aloof from the covenant community at "the oak of Zaanannim" (v. 11). Heber surrenders masculinity by refusing to seek God's kingdom, while Deborah exudes femininity giving herself to aid God's purposes. Her heart is in the mission. So she sends for General Barak, the deliverer, to come and lead the nation. In Judges 4, the author's chiasm focuses us on the central exchange between Deborah and Barak (see next page; vv. 6–10, indentation and emphasis added to show the chiastic matchings).

Deborah, in her femininity, tries to promote her covenant brother Barak. Barak refuses the leadership to which he is promoted by Deborah. He goes, but only if she will go with him, instead relinquishing the ultimate victory—for God will have His victory—to the hand of a woman (v. 9), as it turns out, Jael (vv. 17–22). Deborah also composes a judiciously encouraging song about it (Judges 5). While the prophetess is doing all she can to make the land a home for the people, Barak only reluctantly secures the women of the land with his leadership. But, because of her, he does go. For a woman a man rises to heights to which he would not otherwise rise.

Chiasm in Judges 4

⁶*She* sent and summoned *Barak* the son of Abinoam from *Kedesh*-naphtali and said to him, "Has not *the* LORD, the God of Israel, commanded you, 'Go, gather your men at Mount Tabor, taking *10,000* from the people of *Naphtali and* the people of *Zebulun*.

⁷And *I* will draw out *Sisera*, the general of Jabin's army, to meet *you* by the river Kishon with his chariots and his troops.

And I will give him into *your hand*'?"

⁸Barak said to her, "*If you will go with me, I will go,*

but *if you will not go with me, I will not go*."

⁹And she said, "I will surely go with you. Nevertheless, the road on which *you* are going will not lead to your glory,

for *the* LORD will sell *Sisera* into *the hand of a woman*."

Then *Deborah* arose and went with *Barak* to *Kedesh*. ¹⁰And Barak called out *Zebulun and Naphtali* to Kedesh. And *10,000* men went up at his heels, and Deborah went up with him.

The divine help of femininity can thus take many different forms. In his gendered instruction, Paul calls the power "good works," with which women are to adorn themselves (1 Tim. 2:10). It may be motivating, as in the case of Achsah, or partnering, as with Deborah. It may be explaining covenant faithfulness, as does the noble wife, who "opens her mouth with wisdom" (Prov. 31:26). As DSM interviewee Silva said of his wife, "[A] woman who knows who she is has tremendous innate power."

Or, the feminine divine help may consist in calling back from error. First Samuel 25 tells the story of David's interaction with Nabal, a rich man of the land of Carmel, before God gave David the kingship. The rich man was a shortsighted and base person who failed to see God's purposes, specifically in raising David up, so Nabal disrespected the future king by turning down David's request for supplies. In response, David arms his men for revenge and sets off to kill Nabal and his entire company. Abigail, Nabal's wife, discerns what is happening and quickly moves to intercept David. Her husband's company was saved, but her greater victory was keeping the future king on course. She helps David to keep himself clean from bloodguilt. She reminds him of the mission—to walk before God in faith to be a true king. This is woman in motion.

The Bible is chock-full of instances of wives and mothers making the difference, or almost making the difference, in the mission of the men in their lives. Whether it be the cruel materialism of Sisera's mother egging him on to pillage God's people (Judg. 5:28–30), the fierce bigotry of Naaman's wife convincing him to plot righteous Mordecai's death (Esther 5:10–14), the implied affirmation of Artaxerxes's wife in granting Nehemiah the key approval to reconstruct the Holy City (Neh. 2:6–9), or the holy trepidation of Pilate's wife nearly staying the governor's sentence on Jesus (Matt. 27:14–26), one only need to have this pointed out to begin to see it all throughout the Sacred Writ. The entire two-volume book of Kings is a continuous testimony to the effects of a mother, either Yahweh-worshiping or foreign-god-importing, on the reign of her son in the kingdom of God on earth.[8]

If the marriage is about the advancement of God's kingdom, then in some cases the call on a marriage may even center on the woman's talents rather than the man's. A familiar name to many Christians, Joni Eareckson is a woman with a powerful ministry to the disabled, herself a quadriplegic. When she was thirty-two, already with a successful career as an author and advocate, she married schoolteacher Ken Tada, who became her caregiver. Her daily work is speaking and writing. His daily work involves a two-hour routine of care just to enable his wife to get up in the morning and then the same routine again, in reverse, to go to bed. As her influence continued to increase, Ken stepped on to the board of directors for the Joni and Friends International Disability Center.[9] Ken is a man who recognized what God was doing in bringing them together and pursued that purpose.

As we realize these distinctions in our close relationships—he identifying and pursuing the mission and she empowering it—we flourish. Ironically, the full happiness of marriage will elude us otherwise. You cannot be happy in life if your life is about you. You cannot be happy in a relationship if your relationship is about itself.

Many men would like to open their Bibles and read how to be a man. They would like a verse that says, "Be a man!" and then tells them what that means. Well, there actually is one place where the Bible does that. One verse where a biblical character says, "Be a man!" It is King David, nearing the end of his life. He is speaking to his son Solomon when the perspective of death comes upon him. Then the greatest Israelite king explains what he means by being a man. His words call to mind the lessons he learned long ago from Abigail:

> [1]When David's time to die drew near, he commanded Solomon his son, saying, [2]"I am about to go the way of all the earth. Be strong, and [be] a man. [3]Keep the charge of the LORD your God, walking in his ways and keeping his statutes, his commandments, his rules, and his testimonies, as it is written in the Law of Moses, that you may prosper in all that you do and wherever you turn, [4]that the LORD may establish his word that he spoke concerning me, saying, 'If your sons pay close attention to their way, to walk before me in faithfulness with all their heart and with all their soul, you shall not lack a man on the throne of Israel.'" (1 Kings 2:1–4)

(Translations may say, in verse 2, "show yourself" a man, but the verb is "to be"). In expounding upon his call to manhood, David does not tell his son, "Go and lift weights," "Play basketball," or "Score a lot of chicks." He does not tell him, "Be successful" or "Be famous," "Go fight a lot of wars" or "Make a lot of money." No. Being a man, according to David, is to apprehend and keep God's charge. Fulfill God's testimonies to you. Walk in faithfulness to the office or purpose God is giving you. In other words, being a man is about carrying out the mission. It is no easy thing to do God's work in this world. It is very rare that a man can do such a thing alone. That is why divine help, in the form of woman's power, makes all the difference.

The Undefeatable and His Promoter

He had never felt so energized. At last, a way of understanding so many of those Bible verses he had memorized as a kid. It had happened a year ago. That moment when he felt like he had gotten it. He felt then like he had grasped the keys to the universe.

It had all started with some innocent conversations with those travelers who had come to the big city from Jerusalem. Their talk about a Christ had seemed strange at the time. Then, slowly, it had begun to make sense. At one point after one of those discussions, while he was walking from the Jewish quarter, the Spirit of Jesus had entered him. He remembered the exact moment, halfway between the library and the amphitheater, while he was looking up at the great lighthouse of Pharos. He knew because, for the first time in his life, it really did all make sense. Christ was the greater light, the most wondrous of any of the Seven Wonders of the World. And his brothers, the Jews, were going to know about it.

Now, here he was in the Ephesus synagogue, down the street from the towering temple of Artemis, one of the other seven wonders, but its unassailable pillars were also not comparable to Christ. This place had a reputation for down-to-earth debate. He had come on business, but he couldn't keep himself from entering the synagogue and talking about Jesus. Many had been convinced but some had resisted. Why all this baptism they see among the followers of this Christ? "For repentance," he had replied, but his answer only made him realize that he didn't understand this part himself.

Then he saw her, standing there next to a man obviously her husband, watching him. After the debate, they approached him. "You don't understand baptism very well," she had said. How did she know? But it was true. "We're followers of Jesus the Christ," she said, "and we can help you." "Yes," he said to her, "I could use your help."

So help she did. The three of them, this woman, her husband, and he, spent the next day on the shore not far from their home, looking out over the sea, reviewing signs of the covenant, and Jesus' words about the meaning of baptism. The newcomer's eyes burned brightly as the three of them, walking down the harbor road from the amphitheater, debated and figured and finally agreed. Of course, he thought. Jesus would have had to introduce a new sign of initiation, to go along with the new covenant He forged with His blood. More pieces had fallen into place. The man raised his arms to the sunset on the beach and praised the great God of signs. But then, the next morning, along with the joy and the sunrise, doubt arose about his actions. He obviously was inferior to these two, especially the woman, in their understanding of things. Maybe she should be preaching, not he.

He voiced his doubts to her. If there were things he was wrong about, he asked, should he really be the one to bring the message of Christ to the synagogues? "What should I do now?" he asked her. "Get out there and do what you were called to do." She said smiling. "Go and preach the gospel of Christ. You are the man for the hour." And so he did. And again, no one seemed able to refute him. But how could they? The Scriptures were so clear on the Christ.

The time came for him to leave Ephesus. They walked him to the boat. Her husband, kindly, went to arrange for the passage. He watched him warmly, his new stalwart friend, Aquila, saunter off down the dock. Then he turned to her. "You have been just wonderful." Apollos sighed. "I wonder if I could be doing this without you." "Of course you could." Priscilla laughed. "Just not as well."

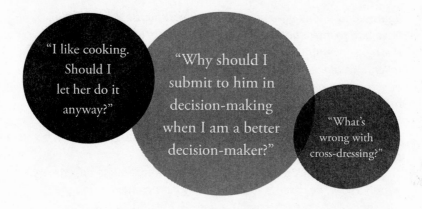

"I like cooking. Should I let her do it anyway?"

"Why should I submit to him in decision-making when I am a better decision-maker?"

"What's wrong with cross-dressing?"

CHAPTER 12

Gender Specialties: Banishing Independence

Gender comes in specialties. Specialties are things we all might do sometimes, but the specialist focuses on especially doing them. We may do many things for each other that are the same, but the gender magic happens when we lean into the asymmetries. Just as, physically, both males and females need both androgen and estrogen hormones, and it is the relative amounts that differ in the sexes, so the gender distinctives are things that both men and women may be able to do, and *do* do, but when done as specialties to one another, they propel relationship. This makes Ephesians 5:21 with 5:22 understandable: ". . . submitting to one another out of reverence for Christ. Wives, submit to your own husbands, as to the Lord." We are called, as fellow believers, to submit to one another (v. 21). But there is also a distinct practice of submitting for a woman in relationship to her husband (v. 22). It's a specialty.

Let's be clear about what I read the Bible to be telling us. If a husband submits to a wife's judgment on what house to buy or stands under her authority in choosing their health plan, the sky will not fall on them. If a woman discerns in prayer God's direction on whether they should relocate and tells the husband, and he, agreeing, assists her in packing, no lightning bolts of God's displeasure will strike them down. A godly woman does not creep around the house, fearful of ever leading her husband. A godly husband does not feel his manhood challenged by doing household chores. None of what I have said precludes husbands cooking or changing diapers or submitting to their wives or wives getting promoted in some way. Specialties mean that we may perform many of these applications for one another whether in sickness or in health. But the logic of asymmetry operates, and the relationship is profoundly advanced, when partners differentiate: namely, the man by responsibility-assuming and secure-making and mission-defining, and the woman by promoting and strong-helping and rest-giving.

My daughter, Veronica, recently submitted an article she wrote to a magazine for publication. I did all I could to support her endeavor, taking time out of my schedule to help her with comments and proofreading. When the article was published, it was a great achievement for her. Now, is this inconsistent with how I think of gender in a family? No. In this episode, I was being the strong helper, empowering her project, yes. But in taking up the project she was following the vision for cultural engagement I set for the household. In the great stream of our family, she was being the strong help, getting done that into which I had led us. Though in this smaller publishing eddy, she took the lead. Veronica and I do other things that are gendered that actually deepen our relationship. When we are out alone, she will surrender prerogative for the trip, or when at home, she will look for ways to give me rest.

The principle of specialties might, by itself, lead us to minimize gender. So we also must remember how passionately God feels about gender distinction:

> A woman shall not wear a man's garment, nor shall a man
> put on a woman's cloak, for whoever does these things is an
> abomination to the LORD your God. (Deut. 22:5)

Some speculate that this law is not a universal moral requirement but just a word spoken against what other religions were doing at that time. Yet this is the earliest reference to transvestitism in the ancient Near East. There is no evidence until centuries later of any cross-dressing going on, a fact that directs us to understand this prohibition as not just a temporal command addressing some situation the Israelites found themselves in, but part of God's continual moral order.

The word "abomination" in this verse tells us that we are dealing with not a rule but a Person. If gender were just a rule, we might break it. Why not? Why not experiment? Why not color outside the lines? But it is not just a line. There is a Person who stands behind the rule who feels passionately about distinguishing our genders. Gender distinction is a personal matter to God. His passion for goodness and health in His creation determines the wrongness of cross-dressing. Why He cares so much about it is the subject of this book. God's ardor would spare us a sad lifetime of trying to make up for ourselves lines that subtract from our humanity. But honoring the distinctions God makes will make us come to feel alive again.

Still, sometimes women are good at exercising authority and sometimes men are good at being strong helpers. Can't people just do what they are good at and like doing? Why bother with this gender stuff? Again, we bother with gender for relationship. The Brooklyn Botanical Garden in New York City cultivates gardens in the woods. Following their paths, you happen on especially colorful areas, where anemones and portulacas lace the landscape. The yarrow and salvia shout exuberance. You see something you didn't see in the common and similar greenery of pachysandra and ivy. Gender is like those cultivations of color. Yes, we should all be growing in the common greenery of faith. Yes, we should all be submitting one to another and leading in goodness. But in close relationships, there is a special beauty that God wants to cultivate to shout out His Triune image.

This leads men and women, sometimes, to allow gender to trump gifting. The husbands and wives in the DSM study were able to do certain chores well, and they often did do them for one another. Most interviewees qualified their answers about their wives' giving rest through home chores, saying that they, the guys, do some of the work of the home also. At times the husbands are better at some of the home chores than the wives. Although some expressed amazement at what their wives can do with very young children that they themselves felt they could not, in some cases the wife also works outside the home. They were describing the general greenery of the wood.

But the couples still also divided responsibilities to make gender distinction, even in spite of giftedness, in order to speak something to each other about a deeper reality, the special beauty. For example, Edwin, a great cook, limited himself to allow Sandra to be distinguished in giving him rest: "we felt like we needed to do that [his breadwinning, her cooking] in those early days, as part of us growing into who we were as men and women. But over time it's come to . . . something [else]." They have since found other ways to express securing and giving rest, even more deeply, but they continue to lean into their genders with one another. Thus, the import of their distinction in chores lay in something other than the chores themselves.

The Bible's focus on action by variously different image-bearers, rather than innate abilities, means that there might be some divergence between what we feel we are gifted to do and what we are called to do. Would there be times when God would ask us to limit ourselves in our gifting for gender purposes? The Bible answers with pictures of limitation for a greater goal, like Mahlah, Noah, Hoglah, Milcah, and Tirzah, the daughters of Zelophehad, limiting their marriage choices to serve the tribal land identities; or Jacob, stifling his intense desire to return home in order to spend seven more years securing his wife, Rachel; or the able women teachers of Ephesus, who limited their teaching to promote the men of the church into responsibility-taking (1 Tim. 2:12); or David, limiting his military might for Abigail and her own; or Priscilla, described in our last vignette, who chose to use her knowledge to equip and advance Apollos, fresh from Alexandria (Acts 18:24–28).[1] Or, for that matter, Jesus, not saying all He could to the disciples, His bride, because it wouldn't be helpful for them (John 16:12).

So gender might trump gifting, but when *should* gender trump gifting? When that trumping would move the relationship forward. Barney, a friend of ours, would identify himself as gay. But one fateful day, Barney met Daryl, a "boi," which means that Daryl was a woman but preferred to dress as a man. Barney and Daryl fell in love. As their relationship progressed, Daryl found a growing desire to somehow express femininity for Barney, which Barney welcomed. But she knew nothing about how to do such things, having assumed manly manners for such a long time. Barney, in turn, had an eye for women's fashion, and had even dressed up as a woman at times for fun. Consequently, he was more gifted in the cultural expressions of femininity than Daryl was. They took a momentous step on that evening when they stood together before the bathroom mirror and Barney taught Daryl how to apply makeup. He limited himself to let her explore specialization for him. (He drew the line at encouraging high heels since, he told her speaking from experience, they would just murder her feet.) Not all of us begin from such extreme starting lines, but the principle is the same. For the sake of moving a relationship to a new level, these kinds of decisions that involve limiting ourselves may be made. As a woman and a man focus on their individual specialties for the sake of the dance, the beauty of the dance overshadows both.

When we limit ourselves for things that matter to Him, God finds ways to use our giftedness. Fred's wife, Denise, we recall, took a step back from her business career for the family. Now she could not be more content. She finds her gifts are still very much needed and used. He who loses his life for things that matter to Christ will find it.

Dan came to me after a sermon commenting that what I preached about gender was not useful to him because he wanted to know how to be a man at work. He wanted to know about masculinity, but just in general, not with all this fuss regarding women. I replied that, from a manly standpoint, it didn't matter what he did at work, since that is not where he was a man. Danielle then strolled up to reason with me: "I don't need a man to do those things for me . . . I am a single woman who has survived on her own for quite a while, thank you very much." I knew that she spoke truly. Danielle was an able individual who could indeed do quite well on her own. Who was I, really, to tell her that she needed men—not marriage, but men—in complement to define her womanhood? Well, I could filter this through the other side of the complement for Danielle because I had just talked to Dan. "Dan doesn't feel like he needs women to sacrifice his life and time for to be a man. You don't think you need men to promote to be a woman. What do you think your relationships will be like?" Both Dan's and Danielle's feelings on this point, and sometimes my own, are misleading. I do need women. I cannot be a man without adopting a responsible attitude toward the women close to me. If I do not have that distinction, I am left with my own self-centeredness. We both miss the picture. In short, independence has no place in gender. As the daughters of Zelophehad and the sons of Joseph were made to depend on each other by the Numbers laws, so God's commands forcefully direct us to interdependence. As Chloe (from chapter 9, "The Asymmetry of Order") put it, "We need the other side. Men put women in their place (in a good way). . . . Without men, I am sure I would not be able to have an identity in my gender." And without women, the same could be said for a man.

Independence is the foe Paul fights in penning an oft-argued passage in the Pastoral Epistles about women not doing authoritative teaching in the corporate worship or in discipling men. The apostle opens by declaring his gendered instruction pertinent to the churches "in every place" (1 Tim. 2:8), that is, he is not just addressing a problem in Ephesus. After giving the men instruction, Paul turns to the women. After discussing their clothing, he instructs:

> [12]I do not permit a woman to teach or to exercise authority over a man; rather, she is to remain quiet. [13]For Adam was formed first, then Eve; [14]and Adam was not deceived, but the woman was deceived and became a transgressor. [15]Yet she will be saved through childbearing—if they continue in faith and love and holiness, with self-control. (1 Tim. 2:12–15)

Verse 15 has been called "certainly one of the strangest verses in the New Testament."[2] Does Paul mean that women are eternally saved by having babies? That would be absurd, not only in Paul's theology, but merely in the theology of the letter taken by itself, which situates ability to save squarely on God through Christ (1 Tim. 1:1, 15; 2:3; 4:10). So it cannot mean that. What then? Well, it is not so strange when understood as the words of a Pharisee by training who steps into the Old Testament passages he explicates.

The key question is this: To whom does Paul refer when he speaks of childbirth? Let us look back. In verses 13–14, Paul is talking about Adam and Eve. By calling Eve "the woman," he is intentionally stepping into the Genesis narrative—where she is not named Eve yet. In saying the woman transgressed, is he saying that the man did not? No. It is clear from Paul's other statements on Adam and Eve that he does not consider Eve alone to have sinned. In fact, the representative guilt he lays on Adam (Rom. 5:14; 1 Cor. 15:22). As he is addressing himself to the Ephesian women at the moment, he simply highlights Eve's part in it, including the error of leaving off dependence on Adam.

Is Paul saying that women are more easily deceived than men? No. He is saying that Eve caused problems by stepping out of right relationship to Adam. If she had brought the serious choice to Adam, the deception might have been counteracted. God had created a bulwark against evil in their unified image-bearing. Adam, for his part, transgressed in the relationship also, knowingly following her voice to do the evil. When both of them departed from the gendered way established for them, their defense broke down.

To whom does he refer in verse 13? Adam and Eve, recounting the creation of gender in Genesis 2:21–22. To whom does he refer in verse 14? Again, Eve and Adam, recounting the tragic departure from the gendered lines of relationship (transgressing) of Genesis 3:1–7. Now then, when we move to verse 15, to whom is Paul referring? The simplest answer is still, Adam and Eve, this time recounting the next part of the story:

> [The LORD God said to the serpent,] . . . "I will put enmity between you and the woman, and between your offspring and hers; he will crush your head, and you will strike his heel." To the woman he said, "I will make your pains in childbearing very severe; with painful labor you will give birth to children . . ." (Gen. 3:14–16 NIV)

It makes the most sense to understand the "she" of the first part of 1 Timothy 2:15, the one being saved by childbearing, to be Eve, and the "they" of the second part of the verse, those continuing "in faith and love," to be the first couple.[3] The tenses may throw us off, but Paul has stepped into the story and, from the standpoint of the transgression, looks forward to what God so graciously promises them. A more literal translation, "she will be saved through the childbirth,"[4] makes this meaning even clearer.

Eve hears that, even in this sad pronouncement, God is promising them salvation through her seed. The head of evil will be crushed through the One the woman will bear in her childbearing. This is why, when Eve actually has another baby, she sees it as God not abandoning her. She exclaims, "I have gotten a man with the help of the LORD"! (Gen. 4:1). She is anticipating the promise of release from their judgment. God would restore her, save her, through a man that came out of her. If this is indeed Paul's train of thought, then the critical following phrase, "if they continue in faith and love and holiness, with self-control" (1 Tim. 2:15b), drives the point of gendered relationships home. Again, who is Paul talking about now? Still, Adam and Eve.

It really does not make sense to read the apostle as speaking in verse 15 about the Ephesian married couples having children because the passage is about gender in church folk, not wives having children with husbands. Rather, what the apostle is explaining is that for salvation to come to Eve, it had to come through Eve. She and Adam needed to stay together in order to continue to procreate and bring forth the Savior. Eve will bring forth salvation in Seth only if she and Adam keep together and maintain their intimacy.

Please realize that their continued union was not a done deal. Not after what God says in the narrative's next sentence about their relationship: you will desire to master him and he will dominate you. That is, their relationship was going to be characterized by strife and power struggles. Besides the trauma of expulsion from the garden, and adjustment to a whole new world of sinfulness in each other, they would soon lose one of their sons to murder. Often, no matter what era they live in, when a couple loses a child, they split up.

Salvation, first Eve's and then the rest of ours, depended on Eve continuing in faith, Adam persevering in love, both continuing in holiness in their gendered relationship. They had to grow in intimacy and continue to have relations for God's plan for them to unfold. Thankfully, that is what happened. Adam and Eve did continue in faith and love and had the holy seed: Seth, and through him Noah, Abraham, Moses, David, and then the son of David and son of Adam, Jesus Christ. Jesus was the eventual salvation that came forth by childbirth, the one Mediator whom Paul had just mentioned in verse 5, the "one mediator between God and men, the man Christ Jesus." By men and women of the covenant becoming interdependent with one another, God worked out his plan of redemption.

This reading not only makes sense of these verses, but also explains why Paul brought up the Genesis story in the first place. The Christians of Ephesus (where Timothy was stationed) needed to respect gender lines to see God's salvation worked out among them. Their gendered behavior wouldn't bring the Savior, since He had already come. But, just as for Eve, it would allow Christ's redemption, reversing the consequences of Eve and Adam's fall, to unfold between them. Christ's salvation, for them also, would spread out, not through their independence, but in their interdependence. This is what should keep us as men and women coming back to each other in our hearts, men praying for our sisters, women promoting our brothers.

Our discussion has now brought us deep into the woods of relationship. I have no doubt stumbled in these weighty topics, and the path I have hacked may be more crooked than straight. I pray that even through this journey of error-prone words and inferior thought, true manhood and what makes a woman have become recognizable through the trees. I feel we have come far enough to reach a definition.

A definition of gender, I proffer, will appreciate God's love of variety and be broad enough to acknowledge the outliers always among us. It will realize that no formulation can be accurate except one in terms of relationship to each other. It must flow from God's nature Themself and take on the contours of Christian godliness. It will simultaneously insist on the equality of the image-bearers and celebrate their profound asymmetry.

Do you want to know what a man, a real man, is? A real man is someone who, consistently and with joy, lays down his life for the close women in his life. He ties himself to their growth through taking charge for them, securing them, and finding God's purpose in their relationship. And a woman, a true one? Someone who, consistently and with joy, advances the close men in her life. She ties herself to their promotion through granting them authority, giving them rest, and divinely empowering their mission together.

This is what man and woman are. Which means, of course, that there are things that they are not.

"Should we have a knitting group ministry for gals in our church?"

"Should I be worried that my friend Peggy spends all her spare time on football?"

"Do clothes really make the man?"

"Does the Bible really tell women to wear head coverings to church?"

CHAPTER 13

Culture: The Clothes of Gender

Some men might protest this book's definition of masculinity—finding its terms as it does in women and their growth. Such a definition robs them of feeling manly while frequenting a barber shop, watching football, or winning video games, but the truth is that those things are not being a man. A real man is someone who lays down his life for the women in his life. Defining gender in terms of relationship to the other gender means that many of the things that we may think are masculine- or feminine-defining really are not. You might have a group of guys in one place who do similar things, but as soon as you go outside of that group, you might find a perfectly good man who doesn't do the same thing. So that cannot be what masculinity is. The error is to think about manliness in isolation. Gender is made for relationship. Take it out of relationship—you lose what it is.

But still, you say, when I play (or watch) football, it makes me feel like a man. It is undeniable and has nothing to do with women.

I answer that it has everything to do with women, not their presence but their absence. Picture this. Imagine that you scored a ticket to an epic final contest between the Giants and the Patriots, or the Cowboys and the Redskins. It promised to be the mother of all Super Bowls and your seat was on the 50 yard line, section A. Perfect. You barely contain your excitement as you enter the stadium through one of the special lower doors, reserved for people with the best seats. You fist pump as you see the empty seat waiting for you. After you plop down, dizzy with the view, you turn to your right. You are sitting next to a smiling woman. You turn to your left. Another woman, swigging a beer. You then look around and notice that all of your section A are women, laughing and joking around. As you scan the crowd, it seems that the entire stadium is filled with women, with a few guys hanging around, looking like they wished they were somewhere else. How would you feel, then? You might enjoy the game, and maybe get a date, but would just being there make you feel like a man? Let me suggest that what you are enjoying in football watching is camaraderie with other men, which is important to one stage of manhood. A large group of us have responded to and share this physical activity and that is a good thing. But if you were the only guy in America who showed up for the Super Bowl, it wouldn't make you feel that this is a manly activity at all. Similarly, if you are a woman who likes to go shopping, do not mistake that feeling for what it is that makes you a woman. Shopping may feel womanly to you because you've met so many other women doing it and you happen to love it too. Feels great, doesn't it? It is the fellowship with other women that is making you feel womanly about shopping.

A man doesn't find out what it is to be a man by going out in the woods and cutting himself with stones. If he is doing it with other men, the affirmation he may feel in doing it is real. But it is exercising courage in knowing and loving women that makes us men. And vice versa. Women need men, too, to know who they are. As Christians, we want to be careful not to mistake cultural stereotypes for something more, lest we contribute to the exclusion of the exceptional people that do not fit in. We err by judging a man a failure as a man if he cannot work a barbecue or does not own a truck. Likewise, we blunder in deeming a woman unseemly when she eschews romantic comedies. Churches must guard against making gender-specific ministries that alienate those who do not fit the mold. Take me, for example. I'm a real man. And I have never drunk a can of beer in my life. My whole life. Do you wanna step outside and make something of it?

We cannot get away from gender in cultural forms though. How come? Because although culture does not give us gender, gender is always expressed through culture. You might want to repeat that last sentence to let it sink in. There is no expression of gender that is not culturally mediated. Gender and culture are like candied apples. The candy part is your culture. There is always an apple in there but, depending on what culture it gets swirled around in, it comes out having a different taste. You may say, "Who needs the candy? That stuff just gets caught in your teeth, anyway. Why not just have the apple, *au natural*?" Here the candied apple analogy breaks down, because gender never comes *au natural*. It is always covered in culture. It is like trying to find a plain apple on the boardwalk of a beach town. You cannot. And you cannot get gender except expressed through cultural norms. It is actualized through your culture.

To give rest, you need to build with cultural practices, whether it is making a bed or procuring watered land. To make someone secure, you need to address fears arising from cultural norms, like mortgage payments or nearby hostile tribes. To submit or find God's mission or divinely assist, you need to address changing cultural lies like slavery or greed, or current weaknesses in the church like a lack of discipling. Even being in charge may mean different things at different times, from handling the horses to showing up for a court of law. So, in this way, your culture is like your clothing when you go outside—you cannot take it off or step out of it any more than you can just go out naked. You have to wear it.

This makes for the variety through time and place that God loves, but it also makes for some exegetical confusion for us. Gender operates beneath a culture. But, at all times, it has got to pop its head out through that specific culture. And cultures always present us with an admixture of good and bad. The apostle Paul understood this, so long ago . . .

> [2]Now I commend you because you remember me in everything and maintain the traditions even as I delivered them to you. [3]But I want you to understand that the head of every man is Christ, the head of a wife is her husband, and the

head of Christ is God. [4]Every man who prays or prophesies with his head covered dishonors his head, [5]but every wife who prays or prophesies with her head uncovered dishonors her head, since it is the same as if her head were shaven. [6]For if a wife will not cover her head, then she should cut her hair short. But since it is disgraceful for a wife to cut off her hair or shave her head, let her cover her head. [7]For a man ought not to cover his head, since he is the image and glory of God, but woman is the glory of man. [8]For man was not made from woman, but woman from man. [9]Neither was man created for woman, but woman for man. [10]That is why a wife ought to have a symbol of authority on her head, because of the angels.

[11]Nevertheless, in the Lord woman is not independent of man nor man of woman; [12]for as woman was made from man, so man is now born of woman. And all things are from God. [13]Judge for yourselves: is it proper for a wife to pray to God with her head uncovered? [14]Does not nature itself teach you that if a man wears long hair it is a disgrace for him, [15]but if a woman has long hair, it is her glory? For her hair is given to her for a covering. [16]If anyone is inclined to be contentious, we have no such practice, nor do the churches of God. (1 Cor. 11:2–16)

This passage explains the relationship of gender and culture.[1] As we already saw in chapter 4, women are to be active in the church. Paul praises the Corinthians at the beginning of the passage for precisely this reason: "I commend you because you . . . maintain the traditions. . . ." (v. 2). The Corinthian church was involving women. A big part of Paul's oral tradition about worship must have included women's participation. They held on to it despite opposition on all sides.

In the customs of first-century Judaism, it seems, a woman was not a participant in the synagogue service.[2] She could approach the temple before it was destroyed, but only as far as the Court of the Women. She could be present at a synagogue service or be a donor to the synagogue but, based on early Jewish religious instruction texts, it is doubtful that she could normally speak in the service.[3] In later centuries, in places around the Mediterranean Sea, inscriptions indicate that wealthy or upper-class women could become synagogue heads or elders.[4] But this was long after the time of 1 Corinthians. A woman's presence back then would not suffice to make up the requisite quorum of ten.[5] So this passage exhibits first-century Christian church gatherings that broke the rules of what women should be doing in synagogue worship. This meant a cultural clash with the significant Jewish population in Corinth.[6]

In addition to their Jewish culture, Corinthian Christians were immersed in Hellenistic culture. Corinth, though now a Roman city, had deep roots in its Greek past. *Ekklēsia* is the Greek word for church. Before New Testament writers co-opted the term, the word meant an assembly in a Greek city. Women were also not allowed in the Greek *ekklēsia*. But in the new *ekklēsia*, that of Jesus Christ, there they were, praying, prophesying, participating. So Paul is really praising them for standing against Greco-Roman cultural norms as well. He is saying, "I know it has been hard, because you come from a Jewish or Greco-Roman background and you feel like it is not natural for a woman to be publicly praying and prophesying, yet you have held fast to how I have taught you. You are recalling the very scriptural roots of the gospel, that woman also is an image-bearer of God."

We, likewise, can make choices about our culture's gender falsehoods, rejecting today's degradation of women via pornography and the injustice of unequal pay. We can contradict sexual harassment, still a reality in many workplaces.

Nonetheless, other cultural conventions Paul did not want them to break, conventions that proclaimed gender reality but which a minority in the Corinthian church wanted to challenge. Paul wanted them to think through how they were engaging culture, which requires resisting but also embracing at the same time. What he wanted them to embrace was the cultural expression of head coverings.

What does the apostle think about long hair on women? That is, what does he mean in saying that long hair "is her glory . . . given to her for a covering" (v. 15)? If you think Paul would walk into the Woodabe tribe of Africa, where the women shave their heads and the men wear long hair and makeup, and say, "It is disgraceful that you, a woman, have short hair," you are mistaking his point. Or if you think that Paul would stride up to Hudson Taylor, first missionary to nineteenth-century China, who grew his hair into a long braid down his back and wore a scholar's dress to his worship services, and would pull him aside to whisper, "Hud, knock it off! You are acting like a woman!" you are again missing Paul's point.

Paul argues about what embarrasses them in what they are doing— not what is moral in what they are doing. He uses the terms "disgrace" in verses 6 and 14 and "proper" in verse 13, each of which are uncommon terms in Paul used just a handful of times. Here they are best translated as "failing or succeeding in what feels right culturally." These words are about meeting, or failing to meet, expected norms. Terms of decorum, terms of cultural conformity. Verses 5–6 are a prolonged clarification about what is disgraceful to them, what makes them feel ashamed, as a woman or man, where they live. Doesn't it say something about gender, he asks, that a woman feels ashamed in violating a hair custom, regardless of what the custom is? So, today in Cincinnati, Paul might say, "Doesn't a man who wears a skirt to a formal ceremony feel ashamed?" Yes, no matter how good his legs are. Paul would not say that in Scotland, but he would say it in Ohio. Head coverings were not moral but cultural, a matter of seemliness, fitness, propriety. So he calls head coverings a "practice" (v. 16), a habit. Head-covering practice, he says, is a habit in all our churches of the Roman Empire.

Again, in verse 13, Paul calls upon *their* judgment: "Judge for yourselves" on this matter. Paul is assigning them homework in understanding their culture: is it "proper," according to Roman gender standards, for a woman to publicly pray with her hair uncovered? He asks, "Does not nature [*hē phusis*[7]] . . . teach you . . . ?" (v. 14). In this question, Paul does not mean "nature" like what is biologically natural. For one, what is natural is for men to have long hair too, unless they get a haircut. For another, Paul is not going to contradict Numbers 6:5: in order to make himself holy to the Lord, a Nazirite would grow his hair long.[8] In fact, Paul let his hair grow while he was at Corinth in connection with a religious vow he had taken (Acts 18:18). He had actually worn his hair long while planting their church! He is not trying to utter a timeless truth about men's and women's hair. Rather, he means, as the NIV translates well, "the very nature of things,"[9] that is, "the natural feelings in your contemporary culture." In short, he is restating his question from verse 13 to them about what they consider "proper."[10] In a gender-minimizing downtown New York City culture, for example, Paul's question might be, "Doesn't a man still feel ashamed wearing a woman's cut of jeans?"

What Paul says fits with what we can tell about the culture in first-century Corinth. First, long hair was considered disgraceful on a man.[11] Epictetus, first-century Roman teacher, chided a student who showed up with an elaborate "do," which he called a dreadful spectacle and asked the student, "Are you a man or a woman?"[12] Second, short hair on a woman was not popular.[13] Achilles Tatius, father of the modern novel who lived in second-century Alexandria, has one story in which a woman character was shaved. He writes, "She has been robbed of the crowning glory of her hair."[14] Sounds just like Paul. So, short hair for men, long hair for women. That was considered "natural."[15] At the same time, long, flowing, uncovered hair on a married woman, in public functions, was disgraceful[16] while men in these cultures (Greek, Roman, Jewish) did not cover their heads.[17] In the nature of things, her hair was given to her as her glory, given not by God but by first-century Corinthian culture. And covering it was a sign of her married status.

So what did it mean to buck this custom? It seems that, at that time in Roman society, wealthy, licentious socialites replaced their matronly robes with ostentatious and provocative clothing, thus dishonoring their husbands. Some women in the church were following these socialites' example of independence. By refusing to pull their hooded robes up over their heads in a public setting, Christian wives were signaling that they were willing to act independently, as if they were not married.[18] Don't do this, says Paul. Buck this craze.

So Paul does not want us to follow all custom or cultural conventions blindly. You can tell that by his disregard of synagogue convention in insisting on women's participation, as well as his previous discussion of not eating at idol feasts in the passage just before this (10:23–11:1). But Paul is saying that clothes are an important matter of gender. The cultural convention was getting at something real in the relationship between the wife and her husband. Embedded in the public custom was a display of what was happening in the home. Authority or not, mission collaboration or not. That is why Paul thinks of the Genesis 2 passage (11:8–9).

The universal cultural mediator of gender is clothing. Clothing stands for your culture, a veritable synecdoche of your culture. You cannot but wear your culture when you put on your clothes. And clothes are always saying something genderly. The expression "Clothes make the man" may or may not be true in a fashion sense, but it is certainly true that clothes tell us someone *is* a man. People use clothes to distinguish one from the other. It is why unisex clothing stores never catch on. There remains a women's department in all clothing stores. This is the real teaching of Paul's head-covering passage: we should wear our gender-distinguishing culture into worship. To obey Paul's teaching today would mean using culturally appropriate ways to proclaim gender distinction in our worship.

The Old Testament counterpart to the head-coverings teaching of 1 Corinthians 11 is Deuteronomy's prohibition against cross-dressing

(Deut. 22:5). Wisely, the Bible never says dresses are for women, pants are for men. That would not work in Shanghai. And what might signify masculinity today in Paris might not in the next decade. So, rather, Deuteronomy says, whatever is man dress and woman dress in that moving target called your own culture, respect it and use it to say that you are woman, or a man. Hudson Taylor was actually obeying Paul's passage in adopting Chinese custom.

This is God's call to us. Wear your culture, deftly discerning the difference between it and the gender being expressed. Respectfully consider cultural expression when it comes to gender distinction. Make it part of your worship service. In some cases Christ's people will defy the culture (e.g., having women fully participate in church worship). In other cases they will embrace the culture (e.g., wearing head coverings). Going to the hardware store or starting a campfire may be masculine, if it does something for your wife or a woman in your life. If it doesn't, it has nothing to do with being a man. In the household teaching of Titus 2, the gender-distinction behavior is advised "that the word of God may not be discredited"[19] (v. 5 RSV). In this case the Cretan culture expected the right thing. This was an opportunity for the women of the new covenant community to show to Crete the wisdom of God's Word. God's heart is for His church to show a watching world the powerful truth of the Triune equality and asymmetry in ways that they can understand. He would have all gaze upon the arresting goodness of our death for each other and the stunning beauty of people enjoying who they are and who they together mirror.

PART 3
The Inner Wood
The Dynamics of Getting Close

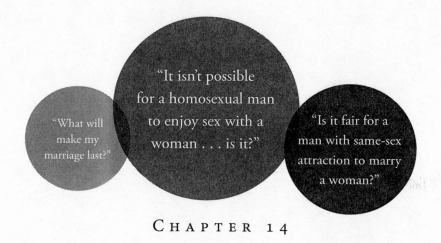

"What will make my marriage last?"

"It isn't possible for a homosexual man to enjoy sex with a woman . . . is it?"

"Is it fair for a man with same-sex attraction to marry a woman?"

CHAPTER 14

The Purpose of the Genders: A Gift to Foster Intimacy

S ilva's eyes glistened as he remembered how "the tenderness, the patience of my wife toward me on our wedding night awakened me to exploring . . . we began to explore one another . . ." My heart was touched in this "Does She Matter?" (DSM) interview as I listened to how Silva and Alexa, who also had a history of same-sex attraction (SSA), came to be one flesh. As I expected, SSA did indeed present an obstacle to physical intimacy in these marriages. As Edwin put it, "It is difficult because they [women] are different. And, in our case, where we had to work through that, initially without the sexual dynamic, it was really hard. Because there wasn't even . . . you couldn't kind of patch things up with sex." What I did not expect was the repeated confession from these men that emotional intimacy overcame this seemingly insurmountable obstacle of SSA. Even though I did not ask a question specifically about this, most participants made some kind of statement, in passing, regarding how sexual intimacy with their wives grew from emotional intimacy with them:

Edwin: "Real sexual intimacy grew out of that emotional
intimacy."

Fibeo: "[Titillation from] the female body . . . always . . . was
kind of a reach to me. . . . [Yet the] times I got . . . excited . . .
was all emotional and psychological."

Ted: "I was very worried when I knew . . . that we were gonna be
together, I was worried about that, you know, like how do I be
with a woman and all that. . . . And all that's been so minor."

Theo: "When I'm sharing . . . with [my wife], I'm aware that
it's building . . . it's doing something for us at an intimate
level . . . like physically in the bedroom."

These men are not "faking it" when they have sex with their wives.
They do not need to fantasize about men in order to reach release with
their women. Overcoming such an impediment as this confirmed the
power of emotional intimacy to make marriages successful, lending
credence to Emotionally Focused Therapy's contention that "the most
appropriate paradigm for adult sexual intimacy is that of an emotional
bond."[1] It is not the experience of all men, but the testimonies of the
DSM study men, as well as the witness of the Higher Ground guys from
our Greenwich Village ministry[2] who have gone on to intergendered
marriage, comport with quantitative findings that some in mixed-
orientation marriages experience a lessening of SSA over time.[3]

Marriage in America is in trouble. Economists and public policy
scholars Stevenson and Wolfers charted U.S. marriage and divorce
rates from 1860 to 2005.[4] Their data, including recent U.S. Census
Bureau findings, show an unmistakable long-term trend of increasing
divorce. Marriage historian Stephanie Coontz tells how a Cornell
professor made the prediction in 1891, preposterous at the time, that if
trends continued, by 1980 more marriages would end by divorce than
by death. Coontz notes that as it turned out, he was off by only ten
years.[5] Marriages have been lasting less and less long.

Even marriages that last suffer greater distress. According to Wilcox,
"in the early 1970s, seventy percent of married men and sixty-seven
percent of married women reported being very happy in their marriages;
by the early '80s, these figures had fallen to sixty-three percent for men
and sixty-two percent for women. Thus marital quality dropped even as

divorce rates were reaching record highs."[6] And marriage rates themselves have declined by almost half since 1970.[7] Coontz summarizes her historical survey of matrimony bleakly: "everywhere [around the world] marriage is becoming more optional and more fragile."[8] As this fact has become undeniable, many more scholars, therapists, policymakers, and journalists openly wonder about the future of marriage in America.[9]

There are bright spots for marriage, however. Vaughn R. A. Call and Tim B. Heaton, Brigham Young University sociologists, find that when both spouses attend church regularly, the couple has the lowest risk of divorce.[10] Less divorce does not necessarily mean more happiness in marriage. But it isn't just fewer divorces. "Most studies indicate that religious practice is associated with higher levels of marital quality."[11] Church attendance or having faith commitments correlate with greater romance,[12] sexual satisfaction,[13] and overall marriage satisfaction.[14] Greeley states it as "indisputable: the family that tends to pray together . . . tends to stay together."[15]

Recall from our discussion on pages 28–29, that as sociologists, psychologists, policymakers, and marriage counselors focused attention on what makes marriages flourish, their answers converged upon emotional intimacy. A variety of disciplines now understand achieving emotional closeness to be the prime determiner of a happy marriage. It makes marriages last longer, grow stronger, and endure the more formidable shocks of life. It is the stuff of solid unions.

This raises a question. What is distinctive in the specific practices of strongly identifying Christians that may increase emotional intimacy, that key to marriage longevity? According to Wilcox, wives of conservative Christians report higher levels of appreciation, affection, understanding, and time spent together in their marriages.[16] Arizona State University researcher Margaret R. Wilson and University of Alabama sociologist Erik E. Filsinger found very similar intimacy results for husbands.[17] What is giving Christian marriages their edge in intimacy?

One feature of Christian marriage is increasingly peculiar among the general population. It is couples making gender differences of the kind described in part 2 of this book. A longstanding body of survey research establishes that "traditionalist gender ideologies are alive and well among . . . evangelicals."[18] "Traditionalist gender ideology" is not necessarily biblical ideology,[19] but it may be getting at it at times. Wilcox, who studies the place of gender distinction in marriage among Christians, finds them doing husbandly authority and gender-inspired division of labor in the home.[20] A 1996 survey revealed that about 85 percent of conservative Protestants endorse husband headship,[21] a surprising percentage, given the cultural changes of the last half century.[22] In spite of cultural changes, economic tightenings, and marriage books de-emphasizing difference, Christian marriages remain distinctive in making gender matter in belief and practice.[23] Could these habits be the secret ingredient to their pie of marital satisfaction?

In the Bible, gender distinction produces dramatic outcomes. The struggle over it in a single marriage brought the great Esther of the Old Testament to power in the Persian Empire (Esther 1). The New Testament also ascribes great potency to gendered behavior, emphasizing it as God's direct command (1 Cor. 14:37), making it the focal point of teaching about marriage (Col. 3:18–19; Eph. 5:22–33; 1 Peter 3:1–7), and even investing it with the capability to convert (1 Peter 3:1) and sanctify souls (Eph. 5:25–27). This last citation, from Ephesians, is part of the apostle Paul's defining explanation of intergendered marriage. There he quotes Genesis 2:24, just as Jesus did in His defining passage on marriage: "Therefore a man shall leave his father and mother and hold fast to his wife, and the two shall become one flesh" (Eph. 5:31). Recall that we used Jesus' quotation of this verse in chapter 5, "Gender Matters in Relationship," to talk about how gender is the cause of marriage. This time, in Paul, what precedes the quotation's "therefore" is a discussion of intimacy in the midst of gender distinction practices.

As we reviewed in our introduction, verse 28 of the Ephesians passage encourages husbands to think of their wives as their own bodies, a profound image of intimacy. The passage goes on (v. 29) to elaborate on that intimacy. A husband is called to nourish and cherish his wife in the same way that he cares for his own body, defining a kind of intimacy that promulgates growth. The passage implies a development through intergendered relationships that differs from the benefits of relationships with others of the same gender.

The text then says, "Therefore . . . the two shall become one flesh" (v. 31). In other words, therefore people get married. Paul's quotation of Genesis 2:24 in Ephesians 5 differs from the same quotation in the book of Mark, using a different Greek prepositional phrase, *anti toutou* rather than *heneken toutou*, to translate the Hebrew "therefore."[24] Paul's preposition, usually meaning, "in the place of," or "in behalf of," more easily lends itself to an interpretation of purpose than cause. Thus, in behalf of intimacy, or for the benefit of intimacy, people marry. Paul is saying that these kinds of growing experiences of intimacy are the purpose of marriage.

Reading Ephesians 5 with Mark 10 gives us the New Testament summary of the "therefore" of the Genesis two-becoming-one-flesh. Jesus says that marriage's cause is gender. Paul says that marriage's purpose is intimacy. If the two are to agree, it must be because gender specialties advance the experience of intimacy. Asymmetry is used to make love.

This is the final and most enlightening point about gender to which the Bible leads us. Gender was given to us to foster intimacy. On the firm ground of equally sharing God's image, differences deliver us into the inner woods of close relationships, where the intoxicating fragrance of love convinces us that things really are all right and that our lives are possible.

The power of this gender-wrought intimacy is undeniable. The SSA men who now know physical intimacy with their wives testify to it. The DSM interviews, themselves, an unexpected joy to conduct, also confirm it. Nick used the word "amazing" ten times to describe Laura and what she did for him. By the end of Steven's interview, he had remarked seven times how much he loves spending time with Madeline. In light of the many problems that plague marriages today, it was refreshing to hear long-married men merely delighting in their wives.

Canadian psychologists at the University of New Brunswick, in their study of emotional intimacy in homosexual relationships, indicate some potentially large differences in experiences of intimacy between hetero- and homosexual couples.[25] They attribute these differences, in large part, to attitudes present in the culture in which sexual minority relationships occur, but the discussion suggests that there may be other causes. Unfortunately, as homosexuality researcher Tyrel J. Starks concedes, "currently, the literature related to sexual orientation is ambiguous with regard to the relationship of sexual orientation . . . and intimacy."[26] The DSM study husbands found that, for them, their monogendered relationships were "reasonable facsimiles" which could achieve some level of intimacy and love, but which ultimately was limited. These husbands felt that they could not achieve with a man the intimacy enjoyed with their wives. Probing as to exactly why brought forth a variety of reasons . . .

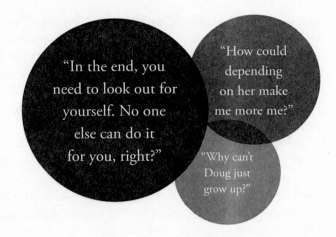

CHAPTER 15

Deeper Still: Dynamics of Intergendered Intimacy

To explain exactly how gender distinction cultivates emotional intimacy like Paul says, we need a way to talk about that intimacy. How do we measure it? How do we help people talk about their experience of it? We need a vocabulary of how it works. But when we try to get in there and actually define it, we come up against the difficulty of all intimacy entails.

Social science researchers know this difficulty. Cornell psychologist Cindy Hazan, an expert on human mating and pair-bonding, whose research has been featured in documentary films and news articles around the world, partnered with Phillip Shaver, former executive officer of the Society of Experimental Social Psychology and former president of the International Association for Relationship Research, who also studies social relationships and emotions at the University of California, Davis. Twenty years ago, Hazan and Shaver openly complained of the lack of a comprehensive theory of close relationships in their field.[1] A review of earlier sociology, psychology, and marriage studies reveals the cause of their complaint. Some too narrowly equated intimacy with, for example, self-disclosure.[2] Other definitions were too broad, such as "a mutual need satisfaction."[3] But a review of relationship literature today still discloses no universal standard definition. In the following few paragraphs, I ask the reader to bear with just a sampling to get an idea of the variety.

Hazan and Shaver sought a unifying definition in attachment theory. Proponents of attachment theory[4] hold that styles of adult romantic love translate from affectional bonds in infancy and childhood[5] because bonding patterns remain largely stable into adulthood.[6] That is, you form certain ways of loving (or not loving) as an infant or a child that stay with you when you grow up. Consequently, the theory focuses on the feeling of security as fundamental.[7] Marriage therapies derived from this theory speak of "the safety of intimacy" and define emotional connection as the presence of a "safe haven," a place of trust and security.[8] A popular book on such Emotionally Focused Therapy was written by Archibald D. Hart and his daughter Sharon Hart Morris. As the former dean of the School of Psychology at Fuller Theological Seminary and the director of the Haven of Safety Relationships in Pasadena, California, respectively, Hart and Hart Morris write, "[T]he greatest predictor of marital . . . longevity is the presence of trust."[9] This formulation is helpful. Trust is undoubtedly a crucial element of intimacy. But are there others?

Wilson and Filsinger follow the jargon-heavy but frequently used marriage quality scale of Graham Spanier called "dyadic marital adjustment"[10] ("dyadic" means involving two people). Spanier's scale uses thirty-two variables categorized in four dimensions. The first of these is "consensus," or degree of couple agreement about important issues and tasks. The second is "satisfaction," involving frequency of quarreling, kissing, and confiding, as well as commitment to the relationship. The third is "cohesion," pertaining to frequency of sharing ideas, common interests, and working together. The final dimension is "affectional expression," which looks at the couple's agreement about affection and sex.[11] This dyadic adjustment scale captures a lot and proved to be a resilient way of speaking of a quality of marriage among sociologists.[12] But the framework does not isolate intimacy. Emotional closeness is instead spread across the variables.

Sex therapist Philip Colgan, attempting a broader definition in his study of same-sex relationships, defines "intimacy functioning" as having affective components of trusting in and caring for, behavioral components of listening to and responding to, and cognitive components of affirming the relationship's value and faith in its dependability.[13] Other definers speak of companionship, feeling accepted, understood, safe and supported, sharing, and complementariness.[14]

Alternatively, many marriage therapists use the Personal Assessment of Intimacy in Relationships (PAIR), which conceives of five types of intimacy, including emotional intimacy.[15] The measure, developed through contributions from family professionals, marriage enrichment group participants, graduate students, and therapists asks subjects questions such as, "Does your partner listen to you?" "Can you state your feelings and have your partner understand them?" "Do you sometimes feel neglected or sometimes lonely when together with your partner?" Worthington, following the PAIR assessment, defines intimacy as "a sense of unity or bonding."[16]

There is something else to intimacy, though, implicit in some of these scales: the way it makes you find yourself. As University of Ottawa professor of psychology and founding director of the International Centre for Excellence in Emotionally Focused Therapy Susan M. Johnson and University of Quebec psychologist Paul S. Greenman explain, "Patterns of interaction with loved ones are the arenas in which individuals . . . define themselves."[17] Some researchers go further than others in seeing emotional bonding as shaping a person's identity, but it is obviously germane. Greeley agrees that the most important direct influence on the happiness of a marriage is making the spouse feel important,[18] another way of speaking of this identity-forming constituent.

Bewildered? The plethora of intimacy measures and definitions tends to confuse rather than clarify, doesn't it? Another complication: Which are impacts of intimacy and which are activities of intimacy? Or even prerequisites to intimacy? These questions compound the challenge of arriving at a wording that best captures the experience.

Why is it so hard to say what closeness is? Again, I suggest that it is because emotional intimacy is central to the meaning of image-bearers, their display of God. God is many faceted, a fact of which the early theologians who tried to enumerate His attributes became increasingly aware. What we can recognize of His character makes for many connections between the Members of His Trinity—sharing and trust, dependence and companionship, unity and support.

It seems best, then, to define intimacy with a collective approach, regarding the different ways researchers and therapists talk about intimacy as probably capturing a part of the experience. Let us suppose that the surfeit of definitions uncovers intimacy as a jewel of many facets, reflecting the wealth of human experience and identity in bearing God's image. To help get a handle on the discussion, the following list groups the various descriptions encountered in the literatures under seven headings that help demarcate the different facets (see "Seven Facets of the Jewel of Intimacy" on the next page).

Thinking of intimacy in these seven terms—unity, sharing, trust, dependence, support, companionship, and identity formation—allows a conversation about how relationships are doing.

Now, these are abstract categories. No one goes around saying, "I have a high level of unity with my husband." But people can talk about the quality of their fights and how they get resolved. In the DSM interviews, I discerned the degree of sharing by listening to what items the husbands uniquely shared with their wives. Intimacy means sharing the bad: fears such as job insecurities; weaknesses such as points of temptations or unworthiness; troubles such as HIV status or struggles with the kids; and things gone wrong such as deaths and dysfunctions in one's extended family. The vulnerability showed how intimately people were sharing. Similarly, dependence comes out in a question such as, "What would it be like if she were suddenly gone from your life?" First responses to that question tell a great deal. Ones I heard ranged from "I'd get over it" to "functional loneliness forever—I would never remarry."[19] What about trust? It ranges from the practical: that the spouse has the checkbook and the other's passwords, to the relationship oriented: that they would work out difficulties, that her motives were good even when he is hurt, that he won't use her weaknesses against her, and that the spouse would never leave. All these kinds of things are what we speak of when we speak of intimacy.

One reason intimacy measurements proliferate is because the different diamond facets mean more or less to different people. When I asked husbands what comprised intimacy with their wives, they varied in valuing dependence or trust, feeling supported or companionship. Sharing dominated in the DSM men's values, but not in every case. In another study of mixed-orientation couples, those with good marriages most often cited friendship and companionship as the best aspects of their marriage.[20] Intimacy among husbands and wives, or close friends or siblings, is rich and sundry. Paying attention to all elements of it

Seven Facets of the Jewel of Intimacy

I. Overall Definition of Intimacy:
>   A sense of bonding
>   Intense emotional relationship
>   Love

II. Facets of Intimacy:
>   1. Unity
>>   Ability to resolve conflict
>>   Forgiveness
>>   Lack of quarreling
>>   Agreement or solidarity regarding issues and tasks
>   2. Sharing
>>   Ability to share feelings and express one's self
>>   Confiding
>>   Self-disclosure
>>   Sharing ideas
>>   Responding to one another
>>   Listening to one another
>>   Working together
>   3. Trust
>>   Belief in the relationship's dependability
>>   Feeling safe
>   4. Dependence
>>   Relief at not having to do it all myself
>>   Confidence in one another
>   5. Feeling Supported
>>   Not feeling neglected
>   6. Companionship
>>   Best friend, friendship
>>   Expressions of affection
>>   Don't feel lonely when together
>   7. Identity formation
>>   Understand who I am
>>   Made to feel important
>>   Made to feel accepted
>>   Complementariness
>>   Hurts and joys are felt to be understood

allows us to cast a wide net when hunting for intimacy. The facets are also interrelated. For example, deeper sharing happens because of greater trust, and dependence is one way of talking about a partner's support. As Nick suggested, "it is kind of like the domino effect." So asking about all seven allows people to speak in their own terms about the intimacy they enjoy.

The DSM study, in which I did exactly that, was great in allowing time to listen to guys talk. I got to hear many reasons why the men treasured their wives. As I pressed them about why they felt that they could not share the same intimacy with a man, a host of explanations issued forth. I eventually distinguished twenty-eight distinct reasons for intergendered intimacy! These responses left no question that these happy husbands have found an intense intimacy through intergendered union, and that the womanhood of their partners played a critical part in the depth of that intimacy—they would say an indispensable part. All of this declares what the apostle long ago taught, that gender is a gift given to build intimacy in relationships. Some of these reasons focused more on the inherent qualities of their wives, differences in nature as these men experienced them. Others involved their wives' gendered practices. It was not just what they did, but who they were, doing what they did, that made these husbands feel, as one confessed, "to depend on her makes me more me."

Some DSM explanations for intergendered intimacy were straight-forward, such as making a baby together. In one particularly moving account, procreating another person forged powerful bonds within the couple. Other reasons were not so obvious. Men frequently mentioned less competition in life with a woman, a "face-to-face posture," which was unique, they felt, to an intergendered relationship. The lack of testosterone-fueled rivalry would encourage unity, of course, but also sharing and vulnerability. The man, to a woman, would confess his inner workings. Explaining how noncompetitiveness also fostered trust by removing limits to disclosure, Fibeo appreciated how Cathy, being a woman, did not try to "one upmanship me in everything, compete, have the upper hand, so I could trust. . . ." Furthermore, the husband's own uniqueness in the relationship cultivated his identity: "I don't feel like she's trying to take that away from me or put herself on an equal footing with [manhood]. . . . I don't think that she tries to steal my identity."

These comments should not go unappreciated. All relationships, intergendered or monogendered, can be hindered by feelings of antagonistic competition. As soon as we enter into an attitude of competition, we lose the truth about gender. As soon as our hearts dip to think about who's better, who is more deserving of privilege, whose place before God is more important, we enter into the realm of the fall, where gender deteriorates. All of us need help in forming redeemed patterns of being with one another. If difference is a platform or gift that works against unhealthy competition, it would make sense as a tectonic force for intimacy in a relationship.

The most frequently identified way that gender distinction lit up every facet of intimacy was, simply, differentness itself. "Richness comes from differentness," the DSM husbands contended. Each bringing distinction to the relationship fosters unity; relying on each other's varied responsibilities builds trust; her gendered acts of service, distinct from his, support him; his complementing her secures his identity; his not doing what she does—or not being able to—creates greater healthy dependence. Averred Nick,

> There's no one I depend on, on planet Earth, more than I depend on Laura. And I think it has everything to do with the fact that we complement each other . . . because she's a woman and I'm a man. I couldn't depend upon a man in the way that I depend on Laura, no. I don't think that that's possible. I could depend on a man. I don't think it would reach the depths that it does with Laura.

Or as Theo put it: "It's . . . [a] greater place, . . . being dependent . . . upon the other, not of the same."

Men often find sharing internal things tiresome, but these men talk up a storm about themselves when with their wives, just to find out how womanhood responds. The men also talked about how their wives, in contrast to their past male partners, bring an emotional awareness that cultivates companionship: "A woman brings a lot of life." The exceptional emotional richness of women encourages even deeper sharing and trust: "Most women have the ability to understand and feel things at a different level from men, so I get a deeper connection from her perspective." "Her sensitivities . . . give me room to risk things that with a man I would never risk." Fred creatively pictured the emotional complementarity thus: "Men are like strings, women like balloons. Women rise in lofty splendor, but need the string to be tied down. But men, without them, are just strings dropped in the mud." (I am guessing that this revelation came to Fred while he was taking their children to a fair.)

The wife's virtues, often dissimilar to the husband's, constituted another cluster of reasons that gender matters: "Her femininity allows me to let my guard down." "A different makeup, her womanhood . . . increases my understanding and has helped to unravel lies about me." "Her . . . gentle spirit, it invites me in [to a place of] security [that] unites us." One husband eulogized, "She is very much an undergirding support of everything I do, and very strong. . . . It's all very feminine. There is nothing masculine about her strength, which I love. I find . . . security and support in that."

A little reflection elucidates. Deepening complement is only possible where diversity is present and appreciated. The more two people are interchangeable, the less they truly need each other. They do not come to know themselves in ways that change them. Thus, losing distinction consigns relationships to shallow water. If, on the other hand, one brings to the union a unique specialty, or an intent to develop something that the other does not, each will be prized more deeply. They learn that they do not need to look out for themselves.

The table on the next page summarizes all the different reasons intergendered relationships foster the facets of intimacy.

I phrased the interview questions, "How does her womanhood affect X?" to allow the participant to choose to answer along the lines of essence (her being a woman in contrast to being a man) or practice (what she does to be feminine). The discussion of inherent female traits and conscious womanly practices intertwined. As we have seen, we err if we make womanhood about just one or the other (equating the female with the feminine or, on the other hand, not respecting gender's platform). Both seemed important to what gender distinction meant to these husbands. The table labels the different reasons as to whether its dynamic is one of primarily essence, primarily practice, or both. The scatter of these letters shows the intertwining significance of both in the ingredients of their intergendered intimacy.

Perhaps the most profound collection of reasons that the DSM men associated with their intergendered unions concerned personal growth (#3 in the table): "Her femininity has very much enhanced my masculinity." "It's not like my wife is particularly more mature than the [men] that I was with. . . . It's just the two of us together . . . having to. . . . It's just deeper. It is." "A different makeup, her womanhood . . . increases my understanding and has helped to unravel lies about me."

The challenge of the "other" arose in response to questioning about why, if intergendered relationships were preferable, some of them remained, for a time, in monogendered ones. Besides the answers of "I didn't know what I didn't know" or "I didn't think it was possible," there were other deeper answers such as "To not be challenged," "Cowardice," "So I didn't have to learn anything new," and "It is easier to be dependent on a guy." Edwin shared, "It was a huge risk for my wife and me to step into who we really were as men and women."

The Dynamics of Gender Distinction Fostering Intimacy for Husbands

E: Primarily a matter of essence; P: Primarily a matter of practice; B: Both practice and essence
Listed by frequency of response

E	P	B	#1 Differentness Itself (Essence or Practice) Fosters:	
		B	Unity	from complementation
E			Sharing	from motivation to find out how womanhood responds
	P		Trust	from having to rely on other's different responsibilities
E			Dependence	from the "other" creating greater place of being dependent
	P		Dependence	from her taking on unique responsibilities, e.g., in home
	P		Being Supported	from her gendered acts of service specifically to support me
E			Companionship	from her womanhood supplying what is missing
E			Identity	from a security in how I complement her
			#2 Absence of Competition Fosters:	
		B	Unity	from allowing face-to-face posture
		B	Sharing	from vulnerability to confess, to speak of my workings
		B	Trust	from removing suspicion, sharing limits, bringing walls down
		B	Identity	from giving me a secure uniqueness
			#3 Resulting Growth Fosters:	
E			Unity	from her nature calling me toward pleasing, doing more
E			Unity	from her need calling me toward covering
		B	Sharing	from her service helping me regarding SSA
	P		Trust	from her trust in me encouraging my trust in God (for her)
E			Being Supported	from her womanhood informing that I haven't failed as a man
		B	Identity	from her desire helping me become a man
E			Identity	from her need calling me forth to secure her
			#4 Difference in Emotion Fosters:	
E			Sharing	from women feeling at different level, making deeper connect
E			Trust	from sensitivities giving me room to risk
E			Dependence	from making us interdependent
E			Companionship	from encouraging open silliness in me
			#5 Difference in Virtue Fosters:	
		B	Unity	from gentle welcome
E			Sharing	from her womanhood increasing my understanding of me
E			Being Supported	from her strong femininity
		B	Identity	from her femininity enhancing my masculinity
			#6 Ability to Bear Children Fosters:	
E			Unity	from the bond of making new life together

In fact, one reason these husbands first sought an intergendered union was a lack of spiritual growth in their monogendered ones: "It left me self-focused." "To be perfectly honest with you, when I was in a relationship with a man, I wanted a man to take care of me." Now, instead, her nature, need, service, and desires called him forth to be proactive for her: "Her femininity makes me want to do more . . . pulls me to where I would want to please her." "The mystery of male and female union . . . is about 'other'. . . . [I]t called out of me fruit. . . . I'm more awakened to being me. I'm a different man."

Theo explained the dynamic at length,

> I need to dig down . . . more to be able, as a man, to meet her needs as a woman, in a way that is very different than meeting the needs of a guy. . . . One man knows typically what another man desires or needs in many different ways. And women tend to know the same for other women. It's that harder thing of . . . more of that mystery coming together and the unknown. . . . Yeah. I couldn't say that enough . . . having to dig down deeper. . . . It's impossible for two men to be challenged to the depth that opposite-sex relationships are going to challenge us. . . . I can actually become more than I ever thought I would be . . . to be more than I've ever been before, in relationship to her, to meet her needs, to be for her what she needs.

But the "other" also surprised the men with comfort: "[H]er . . . choosing to receive from me and to need from me . . . yes, that is definitely calling me to be far more than I am." "[B]ecause she rested into me, it gave me a desire . . . that's what's building me."

This is how it works: an intergendered relationship requires engagement with the otherness of woman, the demands and rewards of which engagement develop him into a more mature man, and so, paradoxically, more himself. This operation emotionally bonds him to the woman who brought it out. This may be why none of the husbands I interviewed would trade what they have now for what they had. Her comfort and confrontation called him to grow as a man. He grew up through his engagement with a woman. Of all the reasons cited for intergendered unions, being "called out by other" may be the deepest.

One interviewee likened this engagement with the other to physical training in a gym or sport (with God as the trainer):

In some fashion, it's like working with a trainer who knows that I can get to a certain point, but I'm going to be puking and dying, you know, through this rigorous training of getting there. But yet I can achieve. I can actually become more than I ever thought I would be. And I think that in some fashion is what gender difference is like. . . .

We could put it another way. The woman brought the man to learn how to lay down his life.

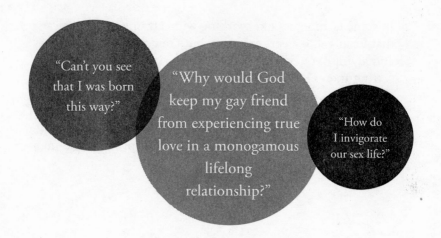

"Can't you see that I was born this way?"

"Why would God keep my gay friend from experiencing true love in a monogamous lifelong relationship?"

"How do I invigorate our sex life?"

CHAPTER 16

Sex: Respecting the Platform of Distinction

This was complicated. I asked my new friend Rod to repeat what he had just said, because I was sure that he couldn't have said what I thought he just said. He did repeat it. Then I asked him to repeat it again because I didn't believe what I was now sure he said. It just didn't fit the profile. I wanted to be certain I understood.

"Are you saying that you feel completely oriented toward men?"

"Yes."

"And you did not experience these desires until you came to New York . . . ?

"Yes."

". . . when you were in your late twenties?"

"That's right."

"Before that you had usual physical desires for girls but not SSA, Rod?"

"Yes."

In the course of supporting those with unwanted same-sex attractions, Higher Ground found that it was not a one-size-fits-all. I expected to always hear the same opening line, "Ever since I remember . . . ," but it wasn't that way. I met guys like Rod whose SSA started later in life. I met women whose SSA had nothing whatsoever to do with emotions, just straight physical desire for other women. These were unusual, but they go to show that there is not just one story. Our sexuality is complex.

And it is almost always messed up. There are a multitude of perversions and obstacles to this most precious joining, this gift God gave us for our journey to the inner wood of intimacy. It is a wonder, considering all the things that go wrong, that any of us are able to have a halfway healthy and wholesome climax. Obstructions abound because all that is wrong with our identities is expressed in sex. Our failure to commit. Our selfishness. Our ingratitude. All the ways we err in our gender come out in sex. All the ways we have been hurt also lie in bed with us. We are all so far from holy sex that it is a miracle that God tolerates it at all. But He is like that. The Lord loves to give us delights. Behold His mercy in the vitality of His creation to afford us the damaged pleasure that we yet enjoy. And He can make us better.

To get better, we all need to first challenge what feels natural to do, whether it is ogling women who are not our wives, pursuing same-sex relationships, or committing adultery. For those of you with them, I know that your same-sex desires feel natural. You may feel like they have always been there. And they bring such pleasure. But the Bible asks us to entertain the possibility that, while they are doing some good things for us, they are, in other ways, harming us. Some actions that benefit us in some ways will kill us inside.

Consider the thief who steals a loaf of bread. He gets it home and cuts a great slice, warms it in the oven and melts butter on it. He then brings it to his lips. Does it not taste delicious? Furthermore, when he swallows it, will it not nourish his body? Will his body's cells not profit from that buttered slice of stolen bread? Could there actually be benefits there for the thief? But is the bread not stolen?

The answer to all these questions is yes. The fact of the matter of God's world is that we can do many things that continue to nourish us in some ways, because of the energy of His original good work, while they harm us in others, because of our misuse. In fact, if they go against what God directly tells us to do, they are slowly destroying us, even as they sweeten our days.

"But it feels so right!" said the adulterer in my office. Bill and I were having a frank discussion about his recent affair. I was awfully glad that Bill was talking to me—it is always a great sign of hope when sinning people actually make it into the pastor's office. And he was being straight with me. So I was not going to pull any punches either. When Bill talked about how things were just so easy with this other woman, I didn't contradict him. When he, visibly brightening, eulogized the affirmation he got from her and how it built him up, I didn't disagree. But then I asked him to hold those benefits in a scale with the destruction this experience was bringing to his wife and young daughter, as well as to himself. Then there was no real comparison. Of course he knew it was wrong, even though it felt so right. Even though he was oriented toward adultery.

Many things can feel right and good when seen from the perspective of some benefits we accrue. But we are much deeper than that. A sexual act can feel good on one level but, more deeply, be alienating us from ourselves and from God. Even the fruit of the tree of knowledge of good and evil was "good for food" (Gen. 2:9). Eve found that fruit pleasant and good to eat (Gen. 3:6). That is, as she was chewing, she found the fruit pleasurable. Pleasure is a good thing. But not this time. The fruit was still death to eat (2:17). Similarly, same-sex attraction may feel so very natural. The very real comfort from acting on it can be overwhelming, especially if you have been isolated by your desires. It is a small step from there to concluding, "I was born this way."

In point of fact, however, you weren't. There are now well over a half dozen studies that have looked at the sexual orientations of identical (monozygotic) twins found in population registries.[1] The most recent one looked at the Swedish Twin Registry, the largest population register of twin births in the world.[2] They show that there is not a likelihood, if one turns out to have a same-sex orientation, that the other will. These twins have the exact same genes and equivalent prenatal conditions. It is only after birth that they start to have differences, because their experiences, their environment, and their wills won't be the same.

Specifically, the largest study based on 7,652 twins finds that if one has a same-sex orientation, the probability that the other has also is only, at most, 39 percent for men and 19 percent for women.[3] If people were born gay, those numbers would be around 100 percent. This is pretty conclusive evidence that if genes play a role in sexual orientation, it must be a minor role.

So, no. No one is born gay. But you could have known that even without twin studies. Our sexuality is way too complex for that. This does not mean that you have simply chosen your homosexuality either.

Numerous genetic, environmental, experiential, and volitional factors upon factors have brought us to where we are as sexual adults. In *Higher Ground*, we helped men who understood their SSA as a desire for manhood that did not get met. This was because the majority of the guys did have that experience. They did not feel that they fit in earlier in life. They felt an intense desire for manhood but there was a disconnect with masculinity, something that went wrong. And here the histories can vary quite a bit: a horror of abuse, a failed or nonexistent father relationship, or just an absence of affirmation as a man. Then that unmet desire to be a man became a desire for a man.

These days it is common to deny that any change is possible for SSA guys, but to say that is not fair to them. As I write this today, I received an email from Alfred, a man I counseled with Ada, his girlfriend, a few years ago, when they felt trepidation about getting engaged. Alfred had explained his SSA to Ada, and they came in to ask me whether they should break off their romance. They worried that marriage could not really work for them. I walked with them through that early part of their relationship, encouraging them about the different possibilities the future of an SSA-affected couple could hold. The email from Europe, where Alfred and Ada now live happily married, includes a photograph of the two of them in their bliss, which I wish you, dear reader, could see. The way they hang upon one another. The look in their eyes. It says it all. I found myself wondering what they would have missed if I had handed them the line that change was impossible.

In fact, in their extensive literature review, former Wheaton College professor of psychology Stanton L. Jones, along with Mark Yarhouse, find that "nearly every study ever conducted on change of [sexual] orientation [by SSA people] found some evidence of change,"[4] especially if the attempts were religiously motivated. Their own rigorous longitudinal study found that 45 percent of those with unwanted SSA were able to experience positive change, and 38 percent reached a state of contentment (conversion or contented abstinence),[5] a success rate higher than, for instance, pharmaceutical treatment of depression.[6] Professor of sociology and past president of the Society for the Scientific Study of Sex Pepper Schwartz explains that "most people have a wider repertoire (of sexual arousal) that changes according to personal association. We change our appetites as we grow older."[7] This does not mean that change is easy or the experience of a majority. But, in my interviews of now contented husbands with a history of SSA, I had to conclude that over time, under the right circumstances, people do learn different ways to be aroused.

What might those circumstances be? The argument of this book is that, if distinction makes for intimacy, it is unwise for us to build on the platform of similarity, including sexual similarity. Genesis 2:24 (Adam and Eve "becoming one flesh") and verse 25 (their being naked and unashamed) should be understood to be, first of all, about sex. Paul reads it so in 1 Corinthians 6:16, in his case to the urban Christians of Corinth to eschew prostitution. Recall that that first union was specifically because of gender difference (as explained in chapter 5, "Gender Matters in Relationship"). So God is thereby telling us to reserve our closest physical relationships to be intergendered, to respect the platform of difference upon which gender has its play.[8] He does this because relationships are really about His own internal community of love. Following His directive here promises the circumstances of life transformation. He wants to get us there.

The image of God is fulfilled in relationship. Conversely, the disintegration of that image is seen in the loss of love. Genesis goes on, in the story of Sodom and Gomorrah (chapter 19), to show the image disintegration brought about by the fall in chapter 3. The blindness inflicted on the Sodomites (19:11) and the breakdown of Lot's wife to salt (v. 26) both graphically expose what Sodom culture was doing to those who embraced it, which unfortunately included Lot and his family.[9] His marriage, which should have displayed the divine image, was instead disintegrating.

What was the sin of Sodom and Gomorrah? Later Scriptures' commentary shows that their problems were multiple. Periodically the prophets, when God is especially angry, compare Israel to the two depraved cities (e.g., Lam. 4:6; Amos 4:11). In fact, each of the major prophets comments on that story and all the details they cite must have contributed to what was the cities' total dissolution. Isaiah brings up Sodom and Gomorrah (Isa. 1:9, 10, 21; 3:9) to condemn Israel's oppression of the poor, lack of justice (Isa. 1:10, 17; 3:12–15), and not respecting gender (3:12).[10] Jeremiah speaks of adultery, lying, and abetting criminals (Jer. 23:14). Ezekiel, likewise, accuses Israel of the guilt of "your sister" Sodom, calling them out for not helping the needy, arrogance, complacency, prostitution, promiscuity, and forbidden sexual practices, using the word for same-sex relations found in levitical law (Ezek. 16:48–50). The New Testament letter of Jude explains the sin of Sodom as sexual immorality and, again, giving themselves to the pursuit of forbidden desires (Jude 7). So Sodom showed how the image of God disintegrates as we depart from the righteousness of God, including leaving the platform of intergendered love.

Note that God went to great lengths to preserve Sodom. Abraham went in God's power to rescue the people of Sodom when they earlier were carried off (Gen. 14:1–24), and he then intercedes with God for them to be spared (Gen. 18:22–33), a request God seems eminently agreeable to if evidence can be found that things are not so bad, that there remains some righteous preservation of His image in the city. God longs to lead us out of our sexual disintegration, just as he led out Lot and his daughters.

The differences He has given us, first in the platform of male and female, then in gender distinction, have the power to pull us out of the familiar and, as we saw in the previous chapter, make us more than we could be. The rest of us have just as great a need to repent about our sex life. Even married folks. Sometimes especially married folks. There are numerous ways we can wrong each other in sharing this gift. One way is to withhold it from one another. Another is to celebrate it alone, even with our partners there. Contrary to the representation in movies, the quality of physical experience grows with time in a healthy marriage, because it takes time for trust to build.

Sometimes couples find that sex starts to fall off in a marriage. They might even seek help to invigorate their sex life. When they do, there are charlatans aplenty, peddling exotica to try to liven things up. But it is foolishness. Because, as English actor Peter Ustinov once observed, "Sex is a conversation carried out by other means. If you get on well out of bed, half the problems of bed are solved." Indeed. And there is one big secret that is often missed in the search for novel appliances.

The secret is this: certain differences create the healthy sparks of physical intimacy. Sex is a gender-intensive activity. Sabino Kornrich, of the Center for Advanced Studies in the Social Sciences at Juan March Institute of Madrid, and Julie Brines and Katrina Leupp of the University of Washington show that American couples with more gender distinct housework arrangements have more (and more vigorous) sex.[11] (As we argued in chapter 8, it is not the breadwinning/housework that is important but the securing/giving rest that may be beneath it.) These researchers also explain how popular perception on this point came to be opposite, with people today erroneously thinking that equal housework fosters more sex.[12] They explain their results: "Introducing more distance or difference, rather than connection and similarity, helps to resurrect passion in long-term, stable relationships."[13] Other studies show that wives in intergendered relationships have more sex than those in monogendered ones.[14] Over time, sex in lesbian relationships tends to dwindle, a finding which Schwartz has termed "lesbian bed death." Schwartz herself is a proponent of "peer marriage," which attempts to remove all hierarchy and stress only equality. Nonetheless, in her extensive interviews of all kinds of married people, Schwartz found that "peer couples struggled with their sex lives more than did traditional couples."[15] She holds out hope that things could be different, but concedes that "the raw dynamics of hierarchy have sexual power."[16]

Even usual fantasies teach us that asymmetry is better for sex. When the lovers described in chapter 2 of the Song of Solomon coo to each other in their reciprocal way, they use specifically different imagery to picture each other:

> As a lily among brambles,
>> so is my love among the young women.
> As an apple tree among the trees of the forest,
>> so is my beloved among the young men. (2:2–3)

They do not exult in each other as both flowers or both apple trees. Rather, what excites the woman in the poem is the man as a stag (2:9, 17) and the woman as a dove arouses the man (v. 14). It is their differences, and the different things they do, that excite them. When most people start talking about their sexual fantasies, though often twisting the beneficial asymmetries into dark regions, they can still be seen to contain the goodness of asymmetry within them. No one gets excited about dreaming of being the same. No one is sheepish about admitting how they are aroused by equality. Equality is an essential component of the relationship, but it is not the focus in the bedroom. Rather, gender asymmetries arouse.

If the Scriptures are right, then erasing gender lines make us less human, not more. Following the lines of gender should make us feel alive and create the sparks that need to be there. And it does. It gives us more energy for being who we were meant to be. And it leads to lovemaking that is intensely intimate, the kind where partners can look into each other's eyes or say each other's names during the act. Difference: the strawberries bring out the taste of the champagne. The garlic brings out the richness of the olive oil. The chocolate brings out the sweetness of the peanut butter.

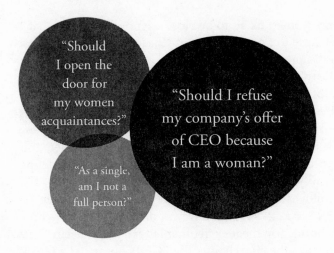

"Should I open the door for my women acquaintances?"

"Should I refuse my company's offer of CEO because I am a woman?"

"As a single, am I not a full person?"

CHAPTER 17

Continuum of Closeness: When Gender Does and Doesn't Matter

We began this book noting that relationships run along a continuum. The mailman from chapter 2 with whom you should not have an affair, the colleague who needs encouragement, or the parent who deserves your transparency all attest to varyingly appropriate degrees of closeness.

When I worked for Chase Manhattan Bank, I didn't understand this continuum of varying appropriate relationship distance. So I was often trying to bring my wife to work functions where spouses weren't really welcome. Some bank event would come up and I would make the request, "Well, can Mary K. come?" And my boss would always get this puzzled expression, as if this was a new question. I was not being sensitive to the appropriate level of work relationships. I wanted Chase to be one big family. I wanted my spouse to know my co-workers and they to know her. I wanted us all to be close friends. I now see that I basically wanted Chase to be a church. But Chase isn't a church. It's a bank. I was often disappointed.

We have made the point that gender matters when things are close. This is why the biblical teachers distinguish gender in some contexts but not others. Besides marriage and family, the Bible distinguishes gender in the Old Testament covenant community and in the New Testament church relationships, which according to Jesus, Peter, and Paul, are meant to be family-tight. Jesus spoke of His first traveling community as a family (Mark 3:31–35, Matt. 12:46–50; Luke 8:19–21), and the apostles follow suit. They both call the church "the household of God" (1 Tim. 3:15; 1 Peter 4:17) as a way of directing believers how to behave. Paul elaborates on the idea in other letters. In Ephesians 2:19 (and Gal. 6:10), he calls the church, literally, "God's home." The Greek word, *oikeios*, means people who are related by kinship and form a closely knit group.[1] This is why, when Paul instructs Timothy how to qualify nominees for church eldership, he tells his ward to examine how the man manages his family, for "if someone does not know how to manage his own household, how will he care for God's church?" (1 Tim. 3:5 cf. v. 10). The parallel seems obvious to Paul. The elder-to-be is simply taking on a larger family, the family of God.

There are many examples of how God calls brothers and sisters to look to their spiritual community's needs in a gendered way, securing and resting, pursuing mission together, and promoting and paying close attention to those in close relationship. First, the Old Testament distinguishes gender in the covenant community relationships, outside of marriage. The laws and practices from these previous covenants do not directly apply to today, tailored as they were for a theocracy. But they do show how God has always made gender distinctions. So God commands men to be priests (Exod. 29:9, 29–30; 40:13–15), women to steward the land back to the sons (Num. 36:1–13), and both to distinguish dress in front of each other (Deut. 22:5). So Deborah seeks to promote Barak (Judg. 4:6–9), Abigail, to be the strong helper of David (1 Sam. 25:2–35), and Jael and the woman of Thebez, to give rest to the people of God, preserving their homeland (Judg. 4:17–21; 5:24–27; 9:52–55). In turn, Solomon stands up for and secures the mother of a stolen child (1 Kings 3:16–27). The prophet Moses rather than the prophetess Miriam must lead in the mission of God for the people (Num. 12:1–9), and pray for them and her (Num. 12:10–16). After Hannah, the mother of Samuel, fails to get comfort from her husband (1 Sam. 1:2, 6–8), she is secured by Eli, a priest in the temple at Shiloh. In the affirmation of this brother in the Lord, who will become her son's mentor, she finds contentment (1 Sam. 1:10–18). King Asa takes charge for the women by putting an end to prostitution. He must also take authority to remove his mother from the office of queen, on account of her idolatry, for the sake of all the people (1 Kings 15:9–13). In turn, a Shunammite woman makes a home for Elisha in the perfect place for his ministry (2 Kings 4:8–11). She gives him the rest he needs on the edge of the Jezreel Valley, a home base with easy access to the major highways in all directions.

Likewise, in the New Testament, gender comes into play in the relationships of the church as the family of God. So worship of God offered by the family's brothers and sisters must reflect the creation equality and asymmetries of the first worshipers (1 Cor. 14:33–36; 1 Tim. 2:8–15). So Stephen and Philip and five other men, specifically men, must act to secure the neglected widows of the community (Acts 6:1–7). And so Jesus chooses the leaders of the new kingdom mission to be men (Matt. 10:1–4; 19:28; Mark 3:13–19; Luke 6:12–16; 9:1–2; 22:30). This pattern of Jesus is imitated by the church when choosing a replacement for Judas Iscariot, one of the twelve. Needing a "witness to his [Christ's] resurrection," they choose from among two men, in spite of the fact that several mature women of standing, who were the first such witnesses, were obvious choices (Acts 1:13–26; cf. 6:2).

Tabitha (also called Dorcas) stands out as a mighty woman of God. In Acts 9:36, she is called *mathētria*, the feminine form of the word for "disciple." This feminine form is used only once in the New Testament, here of Tabitha, marking her eminence in the early church. The apostle Peter visits the church in Joppa after her death to find them weeping and grieving. As they cry, they show Peter the "tunics and other garments" she made for them (v. 39). As far as homemaking tasks of that time, supplying clothing was central, and clothes took a really long time to make. The verb "show" here is in the middle voice, meaning that the clothes the Christians were showing Peter they were probably wearing![2] That is, they were not just holding up some raiment, declaring, "Isn't this nice handiwork?" but rather, pointing to themselves, pleading, "Do you see how she has sustained us?"

It is this loss to the church that probably figured into Peter's decision to raise her from death. Other Christians were dying at this time and they go unraised. Not everybody gets called back. But Tabitha's industry was too valuable for this church to lose. Joppa was an important stopping point on the northern end of Palestine's coastal plain, where the gospel was spreading out from Jerusalem. Tabitha was essentially establishing a home for the entire congregation, those who lived as a light on the stepping stone to the land's main port of Caesarea. Peter's action after the miracle is telling. When he at last raises her to her feet, he gives the disciple back to the church (v. 41).

Before Tabitha, Mary Magdalene, Joanna and Susanna make places of rest for the new traveling Israel under Jesus (Luke 8:1–3). Following this pattern, Luke highlights how Lydia makes a home for Paul's ministry (Acts 16:12–40), just as did John Mark's mother (Acts 12:12–17) and the mother of Rufus (Rom. 16:13). Priscilla, the New Testament counterpart to Deborah, seeks to promote Apollos (Acts 18:24–28; with better results in Apollos than in Barak), and women like Euodia and Syntyche heroically empowered Paul's ministry (Phil. 4:2–3).[3]

I have seen many examples of brothers and sisters in Christ acting genderly to great effect with one another. One man, Theodore, answered our call to lead a ministry of worship in our church. He stepped forward to do this out of a newly felt responsibility for his sisters in the pews. The decision propelled him forward in his own life as his relationships with his sisters in Christ deepened. On another occasion, Mary K. came to me with a difficulty the solution for which I seemed unable to provide. I finally advised her to go consult a trusted elder in the church. His unique perspective as her brother reassured her. I was hugely grateful for his time securing his spiritual sister.

The larger the community, the more formalization is needed to enact right relationships. Our church experimented with different structures to ensure that we heard from women. We wanted to formally preserve their prophetic voice. The congregation found these extremely beneficial. Much more can be done in most churches to build these gender principles into the structure of collective behavior, like recognizing appropriate titles and establishing appropriate offices for women as well as men.

In church and home, your relationships are meant to be closer, fuller, and involve more of your identity, so there the Bible directs divine image-bearers to embrace your difference and explore what the complement means. Together you collectively identify the image of Christ. Further along the continuum, in marriage, the most intense relationship of all, as we have already seen, gender really matters.

Conversely, the more distant the relationship, the less gender matters. Acts like opening the door for a woman acquaintance, though maybe courteous, have little to do with being or growing to be a man. A mother declining to speak in a high school PTA meeting, because some man is dominating the microphone, does little in the way of expressing femininity. In the body politic or the workplace, for example, relationships do not usually attain to the level where gender distinction has a bearing. Along the continuum of connections, these are not personally intense enough; they do not reach the level of defining our identity. Gender specialties don't come into play. Women and men may bring their own sex-differentiated gifting to such jobs, but in such capacities, gender is not prominent and does not deserve special consideration. For example, male and female have distinctive sets of traits on average, but both can usually be good leaders. This is why the Bible does not charge women to not lead or teach outside the close family of the church. On the contrary, there is praise for women business executives, such as Lydia (Acts 16:14), or women leaders such as the Thessalonian elite (Acts 17:11–12). The Bible even gives us a story of an (eventually) brave secular queen (the book of Esther). The Scriptures' silence about anything wrong with these women in secular authority, and on the contrary clear approval of them in such positions, make the point that gender asymmetries do not come into play.

Recognizing this end of the spectrum means that Christians should welcome talented women political heads or corporation leaders and evaluate them on their merits of leadership just as any man. Gender need not be considered. And men should feel just as comfortable working under women, if they are good. A man need not feel his masculinity threatened by serving in the cabinet of Margaret Thatcher or as an intern to Hillary Clinton. I should feel no twinge of conscience when, at the gym, Jill Lovoti, one the country's top female bodybuilders, teaches me about weight training—and I don't, because she is so good at what she does. I want to learn from her.

Jake is a high school student (high school students are strange beings best described as quasi adults) who submits to Mary K. in writing papers and learns from her as she teaches her history class. Jake and my wife are both believers and both are comfortable with her being in charge because they both want Jake to learn how to write. They also both know, in a matter of a few years, he could become an elder over her if they are in the same church. Neither feels uncomfortable with either arrangement. I have watched Natasha, a mature woman in my church, don her lab coat in the morning and go take charge of the clinic where she works, governing mostly men all day. At night, she goes home to Alex, and it is clear that with him she is no longer the one in charge. She feels no conflict about the way her life is. She has told me how she loves submitting to her husband, and I know how good she is leading at her job. She and Alex get the continuum. Are you uncomfortable with her position?

Sometimes there are unique circumstances or exceptions to the demarcations I have made on the continuum. My academic congregant Ellie, who worked in a university lab, told me that my teaching did not apply to her working relationships because her boss was like a father to her. That kind of makes the point—in seeking for an image of closeness, her mind went up the scale to family. If a mentoring relationship gets that close, then I would say that gender starts to come into play. Sometimes, when work relationships get too close, though, it causes problems. But, whether it does or not, those relationships will never persist as the family of birth or of second birth ones are made to do. They are not meant to last as long. Ellie's mentoring experience, it turned out sadly, did not prevent her boss from firing her a year later. Even the best company is not really a family or a church.

So the answer to the opening quotation, asked by a studious Christian sister trying to live out what the Bible says about women, should be evident. Should my woman friend take the job as CEO of the company? The correct answer is: only if the compensation package includes stock options.

With all my talk about intimacy in marriage, my single reader may feel left out. Are you barred from this journey to the inner wood of intimacy? Does *not* getting married mean missing out on life? For the one asking this question there is ample consolation in the way of Christ. For marriage is not the only place for intimacy. There are three ways that God welcomes the single man or woman into the experience of intimacy.

The first is through family. Within a family, gender matters, not only in the marriage but in the whole household. So, in the New Testament, for example, ultimate responsibility for a minor's discipline is laid upon the father—Ephesians 6:4; Colossians 3:21; Hebrews 12:7–10, a sobering reminder to dads to stay engaged as the commissioned ones. Or Paul asks if the elder nominee is caring for his first family in a way that inspires their submission (1 Tim. 3:4–5). Sister-brother, father-son, mother-daughter, daughter-father, son-mother, and extended ties all provide different avenues of gendered closeness.

Because of the closeness of the ties in the families into which we are first born, relatives have an immense influence on what we become. I still remember the time my sleepy sister lay her head on my shoulder to doze, only to pop upright a few seconds later and say, "You have a bony shoulder!" Those words have shaped my image of myself to this day. Why have I never forgotten them? Because of family closeness, and its power for good or ill, in our lives.

People have searched hard for early causes of homosexuality. But of all the possible links and tenable ideas about the womb or early childhood, there is one overwhelming correlation. There is one variable that can be positively identified with greatly increased probability that someone will develop same-sex desires as they grow up. Scientists call it the strongest known biodemographic predictor of sexual orientation. It is birth order.[4] The more older brothers a guy has, the more likely he is to develop same-sex attraction. This correlation points again to the power of our family relationships. That power presents potential problems when relations go amiss. But it also promises great possibility for intimacy.

Even if your earthly family is in tatters, you are never single in the church. As cited above, Jesus, Peter, and Paul speak of the church as the household or family of God, and the New Testament is replete with familial imagery.[5] As author Wesley Hill astutely notes, Jesus promised that those who are left without their own families for His sake will receive "a hundredfold now in this time, . . . brothers and sisters and mothers and children. . . ." (Mark 10:30). And as Hill rightly points out, for single people being faithful to Christ, this means the church.[6] However short our churches may fall of this proclamation, it remains the case. In fact, the way back to health for many congregations would be to begin viewing and treating the church as a family, rather than modeling it on some other entity.

Because of the overall breakdown in intimacy in relationships, we think more and more that romantic bonds are the only ones that can fulfill us. As ethics professor Christopher C. Roberts provocatively suggests,

We cannot imagine existing in our culture without the haven of an erotic partnership, because our capacity to belong together in more chaste ways is so limited. In this light, it seems cruel and laughable to suggest that someone would be more fulfilled opting out of the quest for romance and cultivating chastity. A mixed community of virgins as well as married men and women simply does not feature in our imaginations. We cannot see its point.[7]

But, according to the Song of Solomon, brides are just a subset of sisters (Song 4:12; 5:1–2) and bridegrooms are a subset of friends (5:16). The larger category is the connection of Christ's body. Intimacy is yours to pursue, and something you and your sisters and brothers, should be pursuing with you.[8]

One time, Aretha, a young woman in my New York City church, began to get friendly with John, a guy who was not following Christ. This happens a lot. There are always plenty of non-Christians around. But the Scriptures tell Christians to limit those relationships to friendship, as romantic attachments call for sharing of the deepest part of ourselves, which is our faith in Christ (1 Cor. 7:39). Regrettably, Aretha's thing with John was swiftly becoming more than friendship. Some of the guys in the church took it upon themselves to approach John and talk to him about his spiritual life, asking what he believed and whether he had ever opened himself up to the gospel of Jesus. They did this out of concern for Aretha and let him know that.

You might think that Aretha was infuriated. She could have been, but she wasn't. Instead, she was deeply touched. She later told me how stirred she was that they were looking out for her, how safe she was made to feel in her city life. What they did made her secure. We are never single in the church of Christ.

There is yet another way of intimacy open to single individuals, and this path is unique to them. We find it spoken of in 1 Corinthians 7, where Paul counsels about divorce and remarriage. The passage is worth quoting extensively, noting especially verses 32, 35, 38, and 40:

> [7]I wish that all were as I myself am. But each has his own gift from God, one of one kind and one of another.
>
> [8]To the unmarried and the widows I say that it is good for them to remain single as I am. [9]But if they cannot exercise self-control, they should marry. For it is better to marry than to burn with passion. . . .

[25]Now concerning the betrothed, I have no command from the Lord, but I give my judgment as one who by the Lord's mercy is trustworthy. [26]I think that in view of the present distress it is good for a person to remain as he is. [27]Are you bound to a wife? Do not seek to be free. Are you free from a wife? Do not seek a wife. [28]But if you do marry, you have not sinned, and if a betrothed woman marries, she has not sinned. Yet those who marry will have worldly troubles, and I would spare you that. . . .

[32]I want you to be free from anxieties. *The unmarried man is anxious about the things of the Lord, how to please the Lord.* [33]But the married man is anxious about worldly things, how to please his wife, [34]and his interests are divided. And the unmarried or betrothed woman is *anxious about the things of the Lord, how to be holy in body and spirit.* But the married woman is anxious about worldly things, how to please her husband. [35]I say this for your own benefit, not to lay any restraint upon you, but to promote good order and *to secure your undivided devotion to the Lord.* . . .

. . . [38]So then he who marries his betrothed does well, and *he who refrains from marriage will do even better.*

[39]A wife is bound to her husband as long as he lives. But if her husband dies, she is free to be married to whom she wishes, only in the Lord. [40]Yet in my judgment *she is happier if she remains as she is.* And I think that I too have the Spirit of God. (1 Cor. 7:7–9, 25–28, 32–35, 38–40)

Paul discusses that perennial question, "To marry or not to marry?" He recognizes that each of us have different gifting that bear on this question. But it is hard to avoid Paul's meaning in verse 38, especially since it recalls Jesus' similar teaching (Matt. 19:12): being married is good; being single is even better. Given the other places of his exaltation regarding marriage (e.g., Ephesians 5), how could he say that?

When I set out to really write this book and get it done, I went off by myself. At my age and stage of life I am not used to doing that. I departed from all the people who depend on me, and took many weeks alone. While I was writing, I began to feel intense loneliness. I had taken trips before away from wife and family and church, for a week or maybe a few at most, and had started to have this feeling, this holistic longing that usually caused me to book a sooner flight home.

But this longer length of time brought on a new level of isolation. The longer I was away, the more it intensified. I had not been this alone since, well, since I was single. But then something else started to happen at the same time.

I started to enter into the presence of the Lord in a deep way. I got out a guitar again—fortunately there was one there where I was staying—which I hadn't played since, oh, I cannot remember. I sang songs to my God. I spent a long time praying. I renewed a part of our relationship that had not been so active since, well, since I was single. I remembered the point of my life. There it was, the joy of knowing Him. Was there anything greater than this?

Paul was wise. He recognized this phenomenon when he wrote about singleness. He says, in that passage, that the single person— and no gender distinction here—is all about pleasing the Lord (1 Cor. 7:32, 35). In contrast to the married person, who gets caught up in the matters of life with one's spouse, the single person gets caught up in God. Many single people know just what I am talking about. That is why I always look at single people with a sort of reverence. They are special. Do you want to talk about intimacy? Is there a greater intimacy to experience while on this earth?

Wesley Hill, a single man with SSA who has remained celibate in his walk with Christ, puts it this way: "If there is a remedy for loneliness, surely this must be it. In the solitude of our celibacy, God's desiring us, God's wanting us, is enough."[9] I have noticed this certain something with long-time single Christians, at least those who have not become bitter toward God in their singleness. They are those among us with a glow, lonely at times, intensely lonely, but also caught up in the Lord's pleasure. They are great ones in the Lord, sustained by Christ's purposes. It was good that I was afflicted on this trip, that I might relearn this precept.

All of us cannot experience all of life all the time. By getting married, we miss out on some things. By not getting married, we miss out on others. But no one—*no one*—need miss out on the love of God. This is His immense invitation.

"How close can we get?"

CHAPTER 18

The Immense Invitation

Behind our able guides, the Scriptures and real overcoming relationships, we have found our way to the inner wood of close connections. To my patient reader I offer apology for my no doubt faulty and lesser exegesis of these sacred texts, along with my no doubt inferior description of the people about whom I have written. This effort, though feeble, promises a way, I hope, through the confusing woods in which we are liable to wander in our unions. I cannot help but conclude that gender, as the Bible defines it, is our passage. He made us gendered to engender devotion to one another. The gift induces attachment.

One might anticipate that, upon reaching the troves of great intimacy, one would be free to discard the masculine and feminine, as one might let drop one's compass upon reaching the long sought after thirst-quenching stream. One might suppose that these gender principles, useful in the beginning, could be profitably laid aside as people really get to know each other. Everything leads me to believe, however, that the opposite is the case. The more intimate the relationship, the more pronounced the gender distinction. If we want more intimacy, we must lean into the specialties, not minimize or avoid them. Rather than beginner's principles, they are the pathway to press into greater and greater closeness.

One of my congregants, Susan, once complained to me that she often hears of Christ and the church as the metaphor for marriage. She pointed out that Paul also compares the First and Second member of the Trinity to men and women in relationship. She was right. That Paul certainly does in 1 Corinthians 11:3: "The head of a wife is her husband, and the head of Christ is God." Susan protested, "I want to hear about how I am like Christ as a woman!" I looked at her, thinking to myself, "Is she sure she wants to hear about that, Christ's relationship to the First? Does she really want to hear what goes into their confidence? Is she ready to consider exactly how Christ leaned into the asymmetry between God the First and Himself, as He expressed in rather extreme sayings like "I have come down from heaven, not to do my own will but the will of him who sent me" (John 6:38) or "I do nothing on my own authority, but speak just as the Father taught me" (8:28) or "I can do nothing on my own. As I hear, I judge, and my judgment is just, because I seek not my own will but the will of him who sent me" (5:30)? Does she wish to contemplate how Their intimate company is based on, as Jesus puts it, His doing only "things that are pleasing to" the First (8:29)?

Interpreting these statements as expressions of intimacy for a human relationship may offend us. It affronts our sense of healthy independence. But can we question whether independence is the right measuring stick for health?

In response to a long history of male abuse, modern women have been counseled to become more independent, to remove themselves from the vulnerable state pictured in 1 Peter 3:7's weaker vessels, to stand on their own two feet. It makes tragic sense. If women are in the weaker vessel of vulnerability and discern no protection, why should they not smash that vessel to make sure that they are never vulnerable? This smashing in turn encourages men to eschew the giving up of their lives for close women, and in the end we all become more independent of one another. The modern mind is considerably influenced by this way of thinking. Indeed, in a world of manly sinfulness, this may be the only recourse. But it cannot be so in the lives of Christians. The fact is, the more independent we become, women or men, the more intimacy eludes us. To try to solve the problems of men and women independently is to ensure failure, as well as to throw away opportunities for trust to grow and bloom between them. God rather wants trust to grow to such an extent that her joyful surrender of prerogative and his sober death to self become possible.

Still, some of the things I have said may seem unhealthy. What is the difference between great intimacy and codependence, the stunting persistence of abusive situations, the pathology of immaturity? The difference is that leaning into the specialties takes great strength, as the DSM guys insisted. As Theo declared of Melanie, "She sees the feminine as strong—that it's not weak. . . . My wife is by no means a milquetoast . . . by any stretch. She's from New Jersey, so, you know . . ."

For men to die to themselves is not pandering to their wives. It takes great character. When a man passes on a promotion because his wife is melting down with the kids and needs more of his input and presence, and he is derided by the guys for being a momma's boy, it takes fiber not to sway. When a woman chooses to forego the right to decide when her husband points to a map and says, "Our work lies here," and her relatives call her a doormat, it is an epic effort to persist. The great strength of character flexed to lay down one's life and to surrender prerogative bespeaks the health.

What did Jesus mean in saying that we must lose our life for His sake to gain it (Matt. 10:39)? He meant many things, no doubt. This is one: intimacy destroys some of our individuality. But this is necessary to become more than you were. Christ's way may not make sense to our way of thinking. But you lose life to gain God's internal experience of love. I am not the individual I was before my relationship with my wife. But that is a great thing. I am what I could not have been without her.

When all is said and done, great intimacy, seen from the outside, may look weird, like something is wrong with that much connection. Silva often revels unabashedly about his marriage, and how wonderful his wife is. He goes on and on. One time a Christian brother interrupted his exultation to say, quite frankly, that he had heard enough about Silva's @!#?@! marriage.

The Scriptures point us in this direction. Returning to the quintessential marriage passage, Ephesians 5:22–33, we find more disturbing statements: Verse 23 reads:

> For the husband is the head of the wife even as Christ is the
> head of the church, his body, and is himself its Savior.

Read carefully, the verse seems to encourage husbands to become "saviors" of their wives. This is likely to raise the hackles of Protestant Christians. We insist that there is only one Savior, Christ Jesus. It is true. No man can be a savior for another and many of our problems come from thinking someone can. Christ alone is the matchless one, our Rescuer. And yet, why would Paul bring in the role of savior to his discussion of a husband's headship just here? I can think of no other reason than the apostle wants husbands to aspire to, in some sense, save their wives.

Our discomfort only grows as the passage goes on. Verse 33 reads, literally, "Let the wife *fear* her husband." The Greek word for "fear," *phobeō*, is a very strong word.[1] Though most translations understandably try to soften it with the gloss "respect," this verb is used to describe people's reverence for God, as in "to fear God," the profound respect that we show God. The only other place in the Bible where someone shows this profound respect to another person with this verb is in Leviticus 19:3, concerning what people should do for parents.[2]

A husband cannot really be the savior of his wife like Jesus is, any more than a wife could actually fear her husband like she fears God. But Paul directs the husband to see his mission, more and more, as rescuing his wife like a savior, and the wife to be seeking, more and more, to give deeper and deeper reverence to her husband. The principles are to wax, not wan. So the apostle gives us ways to lean into gender distinction. The words pull us to give our all for one another, to go through death for one another.

Paul anticipates that we will not be able to fully get it or do it. Verse 32 of Ephesians 5, the verse right before, predicts that this may be beyond us. "This mystery is profound," says the apostle. Great intimacy is not simple or easy. In fact, our inability to follow these towering commands might crush us. Is entering this wood a pathway to our doom? Or is the grueling hike worth it? Our guide, the Scriptures, assures us that it is indeed worth it. A resurrection awaits on the other side of the dense foliage, a taste of something sacred, a dividend of the Divine.

Gender shows us God's love for us. Real love comes when we see that marriage is a metaphor for Christ and the church, not the other way around. The latter is the reality. Marriage was invented to mirror it. Paul is not thinking about marriage and saying, "Hmm, what is marriage like? Let me see . . . I know, I can use Christ and the church— that is a neat metaphor for talking about marriage." No. Christ and the church are not like marriage. Marriage is like Christ and the church. God invented marriage to explain His love for His own. He said,

"Hmm, what is one way I can make them feel every day what I want between them and Me? I know, marriage."

That means what goes on in marriage is a shadow play. The reason a husband and wife can think of themselves as becoming one flesh is because the church has become Christ's body. There's a union. The relationship was made to show how closely Christ holds you, as His very flesh. It is because you are playing out, in Christian marriage, the work of Christ and His church, that you must do it. You must play these parts to your currently unworthy costars, because in the process of doing it over time you each become more worthy. Over time you will find yourself gazing into the beauty of Christ in each other's faces.

Susan was right to want to hear about how she is like Christ. The two parallels of husband/wife that the New Testament gives us are: Christ/church and God the First/God the Christ:

	Husband	Wife
Ephesians 5:23	like Christ	like church
1 Corinthians 11:3	like God, the First Person	like Christ, the Second Person

Christ demonstrates both positions for us—both husband and wife. Christ, in relationship to God the First, models the wife for us. He submitted to the will of the First, surrendering to a lower and vulnerable place when He had every right not to. There is no way around His feminine act. The inner wood of our analogous intimacy is full of thorns that lacerate and tear at us in our union with Christ. Thorns that become our head covering. But the First then exalted Christ for making Himself the weaker vessel.

You also cannot get to the meaning of masculinity, as a single or married person, without grasping that Jesus Christ came for us as our Head. He initiated a sovereign dance of redemption in which He died for us, to reconcile us to God, while we were running, some of us still running, in the opposite direction. The husband is called to this kind of giving without getting back, accepting that his reward will eventually come from the Lord. Recall that our Head rose from the dead. The story will always end in glory.

Biblical commentator Warren Austin Gage elucidates how the operation on the first man, Adam, spoke of what Christ would endure to make us His.[3] Adam's side was wounded to make the first marriage (Gen. 2:21). So also, the last Adam, Jesus Christ (1 Cor. 15:45), was wounded in His side, on the cross, to secure and sanctify His bride, that is, us (John 19:34). Blood and water poured forth. The blood that gushed forth from the wound purchased us, and the water sanctified us. The Father put the first Adam into a deep sleep to produce his bride. The Father put the Son of Man into an even deeper sleep, the sleep of death, to yield His bride, that is, us. The love that that death broadcast still rings out across the ages for all who trust in Him. The first Adam awakened to behold his resulting bride in all her perfection. Jesus also rose from the dead and, in the final resurrection that will now follow, He will meet His bride in all her perfection. Behold the glade that we stumble into through the thorns of gender callings. We come to know nothing less than the unrelenting love of God for us.

There we were, Mary K. and I, having a fight on our vacation. Dwarfed beside the gorgeous browns of towering canyon walls, our now mostly grown children sat by the river patiently, long familiar with this perennial safety argument between their father and mother. That the argument was familiar did not make it easier. She did not feel that she could submit to me when her children's safety was at risk. I felt, just as strongly, that her misjudgment of the situation was costing us an opportunity we would never have again, and some important things in the relationship with one of my sons. I was certain that we would never be visiting Dinosaur National Monument all together again, and that I would never again get to swim with my son down Green River, gliding past landscape that was pure geological history. The more we talked, the less we could agree on whether braving the river was safe enough. Finally, as I could not think of a Scriptural principle to insist upon in the situation, inside I allowed my headship to be limited. I let my vision for the afternoon die. We returned to camp.

Later my oldest son, who was himself engaged to be married, approached me, standing beside the tent. He could see that I was still very bothered by the loss. He asked me, "But she is worth it, isn't she?" I paused, brought back to reality by his question. "Yes," I agreed. Under the desert sunset, all reservations about the incident left me: "Yes, she is!" Suddenly, through my gendered pursuit, I knew how God felt about me. Despite how irritating I can be, despite how I mess up His plans—wonder of wonders, He still keeps me near. As I felt that Mary K. was worth it, I must be worth it to Him too. Why does

God press gender upon us? So that we can come to know, really know, how He cherishes us.

One more great truth of Scripture motivates us in the gender journey. Something like the key to the universe hangs in the clearing ahead of us. For gender does not just bring us into God's love for us, it ushers us into God's love for God. In one of the more puzzling verses of the New Testament, Paul tells the Corinthian women to wear head coverings in their worship service "because of the angels" (1 Cor. 11:10). Theologian Sinclair Ferguson gives a sound reading of this verse when he points out that, in the apostolic understanding, when Christians gather together, "the veil between heaven and earth grows thin."[4] Jesus said that when we gather together, even in small numbers, He is present in our midst (Matt. 18:20). Just so, the church service lifts us up to a sacred place (Heb. 10:25; 12:22; Eph. 2:6). The Christian assembly for worship forms an extra-dimensional connection to that other realm, in which joyful worshiping angels are looking on. When we are preaching the Word, administering the sacrament, praying together, praising, functioning in fellowship, it makes a place close to heaven. Christians often feel this, which is why such passions rage about worship styles, and otherwise godly people come to blows. Churchgoers insisting on their liturgical style are recalling when they felt that thinning effect in the past. And they crave it.

When we enter a space where the veil grows thin, expressing our gender relations in culturally appropriate means (as discussed in chapter 13, "Culture: The Clothes of Gender") becomes critical. The angels present in the heavenly assembly are eagerly looking to see the image of God in us, created in us through Christ and displayed in our union together (1 Peter 1:12). That is why Paul tells the Corinthians to do head coverings "because of the angels." They need to see the divine image in our gathering, and you need gender expression to do that. Fundamental to His image are our genders in relationship. So we need to be visibly women and men in proper alliance, to worship well. Being women with men, and men with women, especially in worship, finds the relationship of Christ to God. This is how important gender is.

When there stops being masculine and feminine, there stops being the harmony that expresses God well in the world. This, unfortunately, is where we are today in Western culture. People are increasingly making choices to limit close relationships. Eric Klinenberg, director of the Institute for Public Knowledge at New York University, in his recent book, *Going Solo*, exposes the historically novel phenomenon of Americans living alone. In 1950, 4 million Americans lived alone. Today, more than 32 million do, accounting for 28 percent of American households, or one out of every seven adults. The rates are even higher in urban areas. More than 40 percent of all households consist of just one person in Atlanta, Denver, Seattle, San Francisco, and Minneapolis. In Manhattan, the figure is nearly 50 percent.[5] Klinenberg and American writer Dominique Browning[6] extol the virtues of this new "cult of the individual,"[7] but the trend of aversion to living with others dovetails with the similar decline of marriage: people are opting for lives involving less commitment, and thereby, less intimacy.

In contrast, the Scriptures direct and empower us to live close. The DSM interviewees, in addition to reasons we explored in chapter 15, "Deeper Still: Dynamics of Intergendered Intimacy," spoke of a deeper reason that they chose an intergendered marriage over a monogendered one: The monogendered relationship, Silva felt, "brings me to bow before another Head besides Christ." Edwin came to believe that "it does not create something reflective of God." Nick simply arrived at a point of realization, that in this union "I cannot find out who God is." Instead, they found that they came to understand God through living with a woman: "Gender distinction builds unity because we find out who God is together through doing marriage this way."

Perhaps the clearest way to see how the asymmetry cultivates intimacy is to view it in this most exalted relationship of all, the relationship of the Godhead. In what is held out as the most intense relationship of the universe, a functional adoption of headship and submission rests atop a fundamental equality. The Second Member of the Trinity, equal in power and glory, voluntarily submits (e.g., John 5:30; 8:28) in promotion of the First Member, and the First voluntarily assumes authority (e.g., Matt. 24:36; John 12:28) for the honoring of the Second's concerns. They thereby abide in one another (John 14:10; 15:10). In fact, in what may be the most profound asymmetry, the Second is represented as seeking only to do the will of the First (Ps. 40:8; John 4:34; 6:38; 8:29; Heb. 1:3; 10:7). Consequently, the Second now sits at the right hand of the First, that side-by-side seated scene conveying the greatest intimacy it is possible to enjoy. In 1 Corinthians 11:3, as Susan pointed out, Paul draws a comparison between this Trinitarian dynamic and men and women in relationship. His main point seems to be that married partners, also leaning into these specialties, reflect the image of God and develop His intimacy between themselves (1 Cor. 11:11–12).

One time, our church session met to fast and pray for our church. The vision of the church came from John 17, in which the Second is speaking to the First in prayer, so we were going through that chapter together trying to understand Jesus' extravagant words. When Jesus said, "This is eternal life, that they know you . . . and . . . whom you have sent" (v. 3), we could see that eternal life was about intimacy with God. But at certain points His words were just baffling:

> Yours they were, and you gave them to me. . . . All mine are yours, and yours are mine, and I am glorified in them. . . .
> . . . that they may all be one, just as you, Father, are in me, and I in you, that they also may be in us. . . . I in them and you in me, that they may become perfectly one. . . . Father, I desire that they also, whom you have given me, may be with me where I am, to see my glory that you have given me because you loved me before the foundation of the world . . . that the love with which you have loved me may be in them, and I in them. (17:6, 10, 21, 23–24, 26)

What? "I am in You," and "they are in Us," and "You in Me" and "I in them" . . . ? What is Jesus talking about? As we considered the love and the glory that was between these two, and, somehow us, what Jesus was saying dawned on us: They wanted us drawn up into Their relationship. Jesus wanted us with Him, sharing in Their intimacy.

The vast depths of God are brought out through the Trinity's boundless relationship. As Paul puts it, the Third searches out the depths of God the First (1 Cor. 2:10). And He wants us caught up in it. Through the thorns there is an enchanted moonlit meadow, deep in the inner wood, where delights await. God's invitation to us regarding intimacy is this: as far as you want to go, I will take you.

A Theology of Gender

Herewith are the principles elaborated in this book: six primary assertions, and nine derived secondary assertions, about gender, and the major Scriptures whence they arise. Key passages are in bold. Page numbers where the Scriptures are discussed or cited in the text can be found in the Scripture index.

1. God's Internal Being Experiences Intimacy

- **Matthew 28:19**; **2 Corinthians 13:13–14**—The Three in One
- Scenes of intimacy between the First and the Second:
  - **Psalm 110:1** with **Mark 12:35–37**; **Proverbs 8:30** with Matthew 11:19; Luke 7:35; 11:49; 1 Corinthians 1:24; 1:30 (The Wisdom of God rejoices before Him); Matthew 3:17; **11:27**; 12:18; 17:5; 26:39, 42, 44; Mark 1:11; 9:7; 12:6; Luke 3:22; 9:35; 10:22; 22:29; 22:42–44; John 1:1; 2:16; 5:17, 21, 26, 27; **10:30**; 12:28, 49–50; 14:10, **28**, 31; 15:10; **16:15**; 16:32; **17:10**; Ephesians 1:6; 2 Thessalonians 2:16–17
- Isaiah 11:2; 42:1; 61:1; Mark 1:12; John 14:26; **2 Corinthians 3:17–18**; Revelation 22:17—the Third upon the Second
- John 16:12–14; Romans 8:27; 1 Corinthians 2:10–11—the Third with the First
- 1 Corinthians 12:4–6; **Galatians 4:6**—the closeness of all Three

1a. God Desires to Share His Intimacy with Us
- 1 Corinthians 11:3 with 12; **Matthew 11:27**; **John 14:23**; 16:27; 17:26
- 1 Corinthians 11:3; Ephesians 5:23—Marriage a model for Christ's love in both wife and husband
- John 17:3, 6, 10, 21, 23, 24, 26—God wants us drawn up into Their relationship

1b. There Exists a Special Dispensation of Intimacy for Singles
- 1 Corinthians 7:7–40, after Matthew 19:10–12

2. The Gift of the Genders: Constituent of the Image of God

- **Genesis 1:26–27**; Colossians 3:10
- Genesis 5:1–2—Repetition of gender as important constituent of the image
- **1 Corinthians 11:11–12**; Ephesians 3:14-15—Both man and woman are out of God
- Deuteronomy 32:18; Psalm 90:2; Proverbs 1:20–33; Proverbs 8–9; Isaiah 66:13; Luke 15:8–10; possibly Psalm 131:2–3—Imagery suggesting the feminine contained in God (the representation of the masculine in God is too ubiquitous to cite)

  2a. Biological Sex Differences Are the Prior Platform for Gender
  - Genesis 1:24; 2:7, 18–22; 6:19—Creation of human gender after animal male and female
  - 1 Corinthians 12:4–6; Hebrews 2:4—God loves variety
  - Genesis 2:24–25 read by 1 Corinthians 6:16; Genesis 19:1–13 with Judges 19:22–25, Isaiah 3:12, Ezekiel 16:48–50, and Jude 6–8; Leviticus 18:22 and 20:13 with Exodus 20:14; Romans 1:26–27; 1 Corinthians 6:9–10; 1 Timothy 1:10–11—Physical intimacy (sex) meant to support intergendered intimacy

  2b. Culture is the Clothes of Gender
  - Deuteronomy 22:5—Respect gender through cultural forms of clothing
  - 1 Corinthians 11:2–16—Wear your culture into worship

3. The Parity of the Genders: The Same in Spirit

- **Genesis 1:27**; 5:1–2; Colossians 3:10—God's image proclaimed as both genders
- **John 5:21, 23**; Philippians 2:5-6—First and Second of the Trinity are equal
- **List** (in chapter 4)—"Women's Equal Spirituality Conveyed in the Bible"
- Genesis 1:28; Exodus 20:8–11; Deuteronomy 5:12–15—Commissioning and Sabbath command to both
- Leviticus 19:29; 21:9; Deuteronomy 23:17–18—Laws against prostitution to preserve image
- Numbers 27:1–11; Job 1:4; 42:15; Mark 10:12—Equal inheritance and access of women demonstrated
- 1 Corinthians 12:4–6—The same Spirit inspires all of God's gifts, services, and acts

3a. There Is Great Importance to Giving Women Voice
- Genesis 25:22–23; Exodus 15:20; Judges 4:4–7; 2 Kings 22:13–20; Luke 2:36–38; Acts 2:1–4 with verses 17–18, after Joel 2:28–29; Acts 21:9, 1 Corinthians 11:5, 13—Women have always prophesied to the people of God
- Luke 8:2–3; 23:55; 24:1–10; 24:6—Luke uses women as sources
- 1 Corinthians 11:1–2; 1 Corinthians 12:4–6; 1 Thessalonians 2:7—Paul's sensibilities show importance of women's experience

4. The Relevance of the Genders: Gender Matters in Relationship

- **Mark 10:6–8**, joining Genesis 1:27 and 2:24—Jesus gives gender as the necessary cause of marriage
- **List** (in chapter 5)—"The Distinguishing of Gender in Scriptures about Marriage" shows how gender matters in close relationship
- Job 38:28–29; 1 Corinthians 7:2–28—Examples of the back and forth of gendered instruction
- Ephesians 5:22–33; 1 Timothy 2:8–15—Each for the other
- **1 Corinthians 11:11–12**—Each defined by the other

5. The Asymmetry of the Genders: Different Specialties for the Other

- **Genesis 2**—The creation narrative details three distinctions of Origin, Order, and Intent
- Genesis 3:16; Colossians 3:19; 1 Corinthians 11:16; 14:36; 1 Timothy 2:8—The fall distorts the distinctions
- Colossians 3:18–19; 1 Timothy 2:8–15—Christ restores the distinctions
- 1 Corinthians 11:10—The gender distinctions of God's image are necessary to worship well

5a. The Asymmetry of Order: The Firstborn and the Promoter
- **1 Timothy 2:12–13** on Genesis 2:7, 21–23
  - **John 5:30**; 6:38; 8:28, 29—The Trinitarian Second fully submits to the First
  - Psalm 40:8; Hebrews 10:7; **John 4:34**; 6:38; 8:29; Hebrews 1:3—The Second seeks only to do the will of the First
  - **Matthew 24:36**; John 12:28; Romans 8:34; Hebrews 1:13; 1 Peter 3:22—The First assumes authority to honor the Second's concerns

- ○ Genesis 27:19, 29; 49:3–4; Deuteronomy 21:15–17; Colossians 1:15–18—Principle of the Firstborn
- ○ Genesis 1:26–27 and 5:1–2 with usage of (ʾadam) in between, Genesis 3:6 with verse 9; Genesis 5:3; Leviticus 12:3; Job 38:3; 40:7; Romans 5:12–21; 1 Corinthians 15:22, 45–49—Principle of the man's representation
- ○ Genesis 2:23; 3:20 (with Gen. 1:28 with 2:19; 17:5, 15)— Man naming the woman as authority
- ○ Leviticus 4:22–26, 27–31—The symbolism of masculine sacrifice for leaders' sin offering
- ○ Numbers 30:3–4, 6, 9, 11 with verses 5, 7–8, 11–16— Husbandly, fatherly daily engagement with women's concerns with override of vows
- ○ Numbers 36:1–12 (with 27:1–11)—Women's stewardship of inherited land back to the men
- ○ Exodus 28–29; 30:30; 40:14–15; Deuteronomy 17:15, 20; Matthew 10:1–4; Mark 3:13–19; Luke 6:12–16; Acts 1:13–26—Men called to offices of priest, king, and apostle
- ○ 1 Corinthians 14:29–35—Men called to judge prophecies
- ○ **1 Corinthians 11:3, 10**—Husbands called to be head of wives
- ○ 1 Timothy 3:4–5, 12—Men called to manage their households
- ○ **Ephesians 5:22–33; 1 Peter 3:1–7**; Colossians 3:18–19— Wives called to promote husbands to authority, as to the Lord, and husbands to take it
- ○ 1 Timothy 2:12; 1 Corinthians 14:34–35—Women called to promote men's communal leading in speech
- ○ Judges 4:18–24; 5:23–27; Proverbs 31; Luke 1:41–42, 49, 51, 52—The strength of women's asymmetry seen in military terms
- ○ Deuteronomy 24:1–4; Numbers 5:11–31; **Acts 5:1–10**; **Ephesians 5:22**; 1 Corinthians 11:1—Limitations set on gendered authority

5b. The Asymmetry of Origin: Man of the Solid Earth and Woman of the Resting Rib
- • **1 Corinthians 11:7–8** on Genesis 2:7, 21–23
  - ○ Genesis 2:23; 3:20—Man naming the woman as securer
  - ○ **Deuteronomy 24:5**—Law of newlyweds codifies the husband's securing function

- ○ Leviticus 19:29; Deuteronomy 23:17–18—Law against prostitution to secure women
- ○ Judges 1:11–13 with Judges 19–21—Contrast showing the gauging of society by women's security
- ○ Judges 3:7–11 with 1:11–15 and Judges 16—Achsah vs. Delilah in giving rest by making a home
- ○ Proverbs 14:1; **Proverbs 31:10–31**; **Titus 2:5**; (by contrast: Prov. 7:11; 1 Tim. 5:13)—Wifely focus on homemaking as a means of giving rest
- ○ **1 Peter 3:1–4**—Wifely giving rest
- ○ Genesis 29:10; Exodus 2:16–17; Ruth 3:9, 12–13, 14; 4:13; 1 Samuel 1:19; 2 Samuel 12:24; Proverbs 31:23, 28–29, 31; Ephesians 5:29; **6:4**; Colossians 3:21; **1 Peter 3:7**—Husbandly focus on making secure
- ○ Judges 4:17–21; 9:52–55; Luke 8:2–3; Acts 9:36–41; 12:12–17; 16:12–15; Romans 16:13—Sisterly focus on rest-giving
- ○ Ruth 2:9, 15–16, 22; 1 Samuel 1:10–18; Acts 6:1–7— Brotherly focus on making secure

5c. The Asymmetry of Intent: The Commissioned and the Divine Help
- • **1 Corinthians 11:9–10** on Genesis 2:15, 18, 20
  - ○ Ephesians 1:2–11—The First and Second distinguished (v. 2 and v. 3), the First determining the plan by the counsel of His will, the Second accomplishing it
  - ○ **Proverbs 8:22**, 30; John 1:3, 10; Colossians 1:16; **Hebrews 1:2**; 3:3—The Second acts as a workman creating from the plans of the First
  - ○ Exodus 18:4; Deuteronomy 33:7, 29; Psalm 115:9–11; 121:2; 124:8; 146:5—Examples of the divine help
  - ○ Exodus 28–29; Deuteronomy 17:15, 20; Matthew 10:1–4; Mark 3:13–19; Luke 6:12–16; Acts 1:13–26—Men called to offices of priest, king, and apostle, compared to Genesis 25:22–23; Exodus 15:20; Judges 4:4–7; 2 Kings 22:13–20; Luke 2:36–38; Acts 2:1–4 with verses 17–18, after Joel 2:28–29; Acts 21:9—Women included among the prophets
  - ○ Judges 1:11–15—Achsah helps Othniel to God's purposes for them and the kingdom by motivating and urging

- **Judges 4:6–10**—Deborah helps Barak to God's purposes for the covenant people by promotion, prophetic promise, and prophetic judgment
- **1 Samuel 25:2–35**—Abigail helps David by calling him back from error
- **1 Kings 2:1–4**—David makes manhood the apprehending of God's charge
- Exodus 2:1-10; Judges 5:28–30; 1 Kings 11:26; 14:21; 15:2; 15:10; 1 Chronicles 12:13; Esther 5:10–14; Nehemiah 2:6–9; Matthew 27:14–26—Women empowering mission in close men
- Proverbs 24:27; 1 Corinthians 9:5—Hints of the man's call to apprehend God's work
- **Acts 18:24–28**—Priscilla aids Apollos to do God's work for him
- Philippians 4:2–3—Euodia and Syntyche empower Paul's ministry
- 1 Timothy 2:10—The women of Ephesus called to adornment of good works for the community

6. The Purpose of the Genders: A Gift to Foster Intimacy

- **Ephesians 5:22–33**—Paul gives intimacy as the purpose of intergendered marriage
- Song of Solomon 2:2–3, 9, 14, 17—Varying imagery shows difference is given to heighten joy in one another

6a. The Continuum of Relationships Determines When Gender Matters . . .
- In marriage (**list** in chapter 5)
- And in the natural family:
  - Genesis 18:18–19; Ephesians 6:4; Colossians 3:21; Hebrews 12:7–10—Ultimate responsibility for the child's discipline rests with the father
  - 1 Timothy 3:4–5; Titus 1:5–7—Elders are screened by how they manage their family
  - Song of Solomon 4:12; 5:1, 2, 16—Brides are a subset of sisters, grooms are a subset of brothers
- And in covenant community, outside of marriage:
  - Deuteronomy 22:5—In the distinguishing of dress in community
  - Exodus 2:16–17; Ruth 2:9, 15–16, 22; 1 Samuel 1:10–18—In making secure

- ○ Judges 4:17–21; 9:52–55; 2 Kings 4:8–11—In the giving of rest, sometimes making a home
- ○ Exodus 29:9, 29–30; 40:13–15—In the appointment of priests
- ○ Numbers 36:1–13—In the stewardship of land
- ○ Numbers 12:1–9, 10–16—In discerning the mission of God
- ○ Judges 4:6–9, 17–21; 5:24–27—In the progress of the kingdom of God
- ○ 1 Samuel 25:2–35—In helping regard for covenant promises
- ○ 1 Kings 3:16–27; 15:9–13—In the attendance to community justice
- And in the church, which is the family of God (Matt. 12:46–50; Mark 3:31–35; Luke 8:19–21; Gal. 6:10; Eph. 1:5; 2:19; 5:1; 6:23; 1 Tim. 3:15; 1 Peter 4:17):
  - ○ 1 Corinthians 14:33–36; 1 Timothy 2:8–15—In authority/promotion in corporate worship
  - ○ 1 Corinthians 11:2-16—In the distinguishing of dress in worship
  - ○ Acts 6:1–7—In brotherly focus on making secure
  - ○ 1 Timothy 3:5, 10—In the evaluation of men to office
  - ○ Luke 8:2–3; Acts 9:36–41; 12:12–17; 16:12–15; Romans 16:13—In sisterly focus on rest-giving
  - ○ Matthew 10:1–4; 19:28; Mark 3:13–19; Luke 6:12–16; 9:1–2; 22:30; Acts 1:13–26; 6:2—In brothers leading the kingdom mission
  - ○ Luke 8:1–3; Acts 9:36, 39; 12:12–17; 16:12–40—In sisters furnishing the kingdom mission
  - ○ Acts 18:24–28; Philippians 4:2–3—In sisters empowering the kingdom mission
- But not outside these close relationships: Esther 2:17–18; Acts 16:14; 17:11–12

The Structure of Judges

We Need a King

The structure of the book of Judges teaches the spiritual and political deterioration in Israel after the exodus and before the monarchy. The people had a land and a law. But the rule by judges progressively defines the need of a covenantally faithful lord (like the Judahite David, as opposed to the Benjaminite Saul) to save the people from disintegration. Cycles of apostasy, oppression, crying out, raising up a judge, deliverance, and temporary rest break down by the end of the book. The latter judges, after Gideon, are worse than their earlier matching counterpart judges. By Samson, the land is not having any rest and they are not even crying out any more. External enemies are replaced by internal enemies.

The author gives the book's important messages through a brilliant selection and chiastic arrangement[1] of some of the historical events of the period. In a chiasm, the first thing matches the last thing (A and A'), the second thing matches the second to last thing (B and B'), etc., until the messages meet in a center pivot. Through these pairings the book explores themes of leadership, including the importance of women to the kingdom enterprise, corruption through idolatry and syncretism, tribalism vs. unity, and the need for faith in Yahweh as their real hero.

The Structure of Judges: We Need a King

A. **Introduction 1:** Unity for war on Canaan. Israel: "Who will go up . . . ?" LORD: "Judah" (1:1–36)

B. How Othniel got his wife (1:11–15)

C. Benjaminites fail to drive out Jebusites from Jerusalem (1:21), so Israel weeps before Yahweh over breaking His covenant (2:1–5)

D. **Introduction 2:** Israel forsakes LORD for Baalim (2:1–3:6) Will they obey commands given by the hand of Moses? (3:4)

E. **Othniel:** the secret of success of best judge: Israelite wife (3:7–11, along with 1:11–15)

F. **Ehud**, after eighteen years of subjugation (3:14), takes message to a foreign king (3:19) and slays Moabites at the fords of Jordan (3:26–30) and Israel saved from many Philistines by blunt instrument in hand of **Shamgar** (3:31)

G. **Deborah** calls **Barak** to hill country of Ephraim to save Israel (4:5–6), without Gilead (5:17)

H. The woman, Jael, cracks skull of Sisera with a domestic tool and ends the war (4:17–5:31)

X. **Gideon:** The flawed leader who wouldn't be king (three chapters: 6, 7, and 8)

H´. A woman cracks skull of Abimelech with a domestic tool and ends the war: (9:1–56)

G´. **Tola** arises from hill country of Ephraim to save Israel (10:1) and Gilead is troubled (10:3–17)

F´. **Jephthah**, after eighteen years of oppression (10:8b), sends messages to a foreign king (11:14, 28) and slays Ephraimites at the fords of the Jordan (12:6–7) and Israel still saved from many Philistines by blunt instrument in hand of **Samson** (15:14–17)

E´. **Samson**: the secret of downfall of worst judge: foreign "wife" (16)

D´. **Epilogue "2"**: Idolatry is rampant (17–18) They desecrate the priesthood by the hand of Moses' grandson (18:30)

C´. Levite avoids the Jebusites in Jerusalem and suffers from Benjaminites (19:1–30), so Israel weeps before Yahweh at the ark of His covenant (20:26–27)

B´. How Benjaminites got their wives (21:1–25)

A´. **Epilogue 1**: Dismemberment from war on Benjamin. Israel: "Who will go up . . . ?" LORD: "Judah" (19–21)

Notes

Introduction: Prohibitions Are Not Enough

1 Deuteronomy 5:18. All English Scripture quotations are from the English Standard Version unless otherwise indicated. Other translations used are the New International Version (NIV) and the Revised Standard Version (RSV). Greek quotations are taken from *Novum Testamentum Graece*, Nestle-Aland 27th edition (1993) and *Septuaginta* (Old Greek Jewish Scriptures), edited by Alfred Rahlfs (1935). Hebrew quotations are taken from *Biblia Hebraica Stuttgartensia* (1990; reproduced from the Leningrad Codex).

2 Others have found different ways to read 1 Timothy 2:12, questioning this meaning or its general application outside the situation of Ephesus. My reading and justification may be found in part 2, chapter 10 and especially chapter 12.

3 The question of "monogendered" relationships (aka same-sex unions) is discussed throughout the book, but especially in chapters 5 and 16.

4 Wesley Hill, *Washed and Waiting: Reflections on Christian Faithfulness and Homosexuality* (Grand Rapids: Zondervan, 2010), 60. Hill's book gives a sensitive account of faithfulness.

5 The term is coined in Mark A. Yarhouse, Jill L. Kays, Heather Poma, Audrey N. Atkinson, and Jennifer S. Ripley, "Characteristics of Mixed Orientation Couples: An Empirical Study," *Edification: The Transdisciplinary Journal of Christian Psychology* 4, no. 2 (2011): 41, 42.

6 Ibid., 41.

7 Amity Pierce Buxton, "Writing Our Own Script: How Bisexual Men and Their Heterosexual Wives Maintain Their Marriages after Disclosure," *Journal of Bisexuality* 1, nos. 2–3 (2001): 155.

8 Mark A. Yarhouse, Lisa M. Pawlowski, and Erica S. N. Tan, "Intact Marriages in Which One Partner Dis-Identifies with Experiences of Same-Sex Attraction," *American Journal of Family Therapy* 31, no. 5 (2003): 382–83. A follow-up study was done a year later: Mark A. Yarhouse and Robin L. Seymore, "Intact Marriages in Which One Partner Dis-Identifies with Experiences of Same-Sex Attraction: A Follow-Up Study," *American Journal of Family Therapy* 34, no. 2 (2006). A second follow-up study was done five years after that: Mark A. Yarhouse, Christine H. Gow, and Edward B. Davis, "Intact

Marriages in Which One Partner Experiences Same-Sex Attraction: A 5-Year Follow-Up Study," *Family Journal* 17, no. 4 (2009): 329–34.

9 Yarhouse, "Characteristics of Mixed Orientation Couples," 41.

10 Ibid., 48–49.

11 Qualitative research explores the meaning of people's experience through in-depth interviews. I spent time with ten husbands matching the study criteria (turning down more who kindly offered to be subjects). I did not have the resources to do a companion study with the wives, which is a lack in the original research, hearing only one side of the story. But I did feel I came to know these women, at least, through their husband's appreciative eyes. A published dissertation describes the full study: Samuel A. Andreades, "Does She Matter? Emotional Intimacy in Marriage in Light of Gender Distinction" (D.Min. thesis., Qualitative Research Report, Covenant Theological Seminary, 2013).

Scenic Overlook from the Bible: The Big Frolicking Circle on the Deep

1 This scene derives from Proverbs 8:1, 22–31, as chapter 1 below explains. I am indebted for some of the astronomical facts in this piece to Hugh Ross, *The Creator and the Cosmos: How the Greatest Scientific Discoveries of the Century Reveal God*, 3rd expanded ed. (Colorado Springs: NavPress, 2001), 145–99.

Chapter 1: We Have Lost the Trail of Relational Love

1 According to University of Virginia professor of politics Steven Rhoads, although feminism has many hues, eight out of nine types of feminism include the tenet that gender is socially constructed, Steven E. Rhoads, *Taking Sex Differences Seriously* (San Francisco: Encounter Books, 2004), 14. As one can imagine, this view leads to little agreement as to what makes a woman or a man.

2 So confess University of California professors of sociology Candace West and Don H. Zimmerman, in their seminal work on gender as a social construct, "Doing Gender," in *The Social Construction of Gender*, ed. Judith Lorber and Susan A. Farrell (Newbury Park, CA: Sage Publications, in cooperation with Sociologists for Women in Society, 1991), 13–15.

3 An example of this confusion is seen in the otherwise insightful book by Paul King Jewett, *Man as Male and Female: A Study in Sexual Relationships from a Theological Point of View* (Grand Rapids: Eerdmans, 1975). After pages and pages extolling the importance of gender for understanding ourselves, Jewett confesses, "Some . . . contemporary theologians are not so sure that they know what it means to be a man in distinction to a woman [or vice versa]. . . . [T]he writer shares this uncertainty. . . ." (p. 178). John Piper points out this example in "A Vision of Biblical Complementarity: Manhood and Womanhood Defined According

to the Bible," in John Piper and Wayne A. Grudem, *Recovering Biblical Manhood and Womanhood: A Response to Evangelical Feminism* (Wheaton: Crossway Books, 1991), 33–34.

4 Amy Allen, "'Mommy Wars' Redux: A False Conflict," The Stone, *New York Times*, May 27, 2012. http://opinionator.blogs.nytimes.com/ 2012/05/27/the-mommy-wars-redux-a-false-conflict/?_php=true&_ type=blogs&_r=0. (All newspaper article sources were read online and so contain no page numbers.)

5 For example, Thomas Walter Laqueur, *Making Sex: Body and Gender from the Greeks to Freud* (Cambridge: Harvard University Press, 1990), argues for remaking gender as we like, "as free as mind's play" (p. 243).

6 Jerram Barrs, *Through His Eyes: God's Perspective on Women in the Bible* (Wheaton: Crossway Books, 2009), 10.

7 John Piper, "Vision of Biblical Complementarity," 54.

Chapter 2: The God of Closeness Has Shown Himself

1 Everett L. Worthington Jr., *Hope-Focused Marriage Counseling: A Guide to Brief Therapy*, Expanded pbk. ed. (Downers Grove, IL: InterVarsity Press, 2005), xxv–xxvi, xxviii.

2 John M. Gottman and Nan Silver, *The Seven Principles for Making Marriage Work* (New York: Crown Publishers, 1999), 2.

3 Ibid., 19–20.

4 W. Bradford Wilcox, *Soft Patriarchs, New Men: How Christianity Shapes Fathers and Husbands* (Chicago: University of Chicago Press, 2004), 6. This finding came from careful examination of three different data sets: the General Social Survey (GSS), which is conducted by the National Opinion Research Center (NORC) and is one of the most widely used surveys of national attitudes and behaviors in the United States; the National Survey of Families and Households (NSFH); and the Survey of Adults and Youth (SAY).

5 W. Bradford Wilcox and Steven L. Nock, "What's Love Got to Do with It? Equality, Equity, Commitment and Women's Marital Quality," *Social Forces* 84, no. 3 (2006): 1322. A similar assessment is found in Mark T. Schaefer and David H. Olson, "Assessing Intimacy: The Pair Inventory," *Journal of Marital and Family Therapy* 7, no. 1 (1981): 47. Likewise, it makes sense if "emotions are the principal organizers of behavior," as stated by Susan M. Johnson and Paul S. Greenman, "The Path to a Secure Bond: Emotionally Focused Couple Therapy," *Journal of Clinical Psychology* 62, no. 5 (2006): 599.

6 Worthington, *Hope-Focused Marriage Counseling*, 69.

7 W. Bradford Wilcox, "The Evolution of Divorce," *National Affairs*, no. 1 (Fall 2009): 83.

8 Andrew M. Greeley, *Faithful Attraction: Discovering Intimacy, Love, and Fidelity in American Marriage* (New York: Tor, distributed by St. Martin's Press, 1991), 140.

9 Ibid., 141.

10 Susan M. Johnson, "The Contribution of Emotionally Focused Couples Therapy," *Journal of Contemporary Psychotherapy* 37, no. 1 (2007): 47.

11 Susan M. Johnson and Andrea K. Wittenborn, "New Research Findings on Emotionally Focused Therapy: Introduction to Special Section," *Journal of Marital and Family Therapy* 38, no. supp. 1 (2012): 18.

12 Ibid., 19.

13 Ibid.

14 Some scholars might object that wisdom in Proverbs represents Solomon's teaching on the practical skill in righteous living, whereas Paul, in 1 Corinthians 1, was addressing the Greek idea of wisdom, thus contending that the two cannot be read together as I do. But the language of Proverbs 8:22, "The LORD brought me forth" (NIV, קָנָה, *qnh*), and of verse 24, "I was brought forth" (חִיל, *khyl*), suggest more is in view than Solomon's teaching, at least a foreshadowing of Christ, who also personifies Wisdom in referring to Himself.

15 The Hebrew verb in verse 24 and verse 25, חִיל, (*khyl*) in the polal as it is here, properly means to bring into labor or bring to birth, as the NIV translates it. Consider, for example, its use in Psalm 51:5 (v. 7 in Hebrew text) and Job 15:7.

16 Mark 12:35–37 (Matt. 22:43–45; Luke 20:41–44); Mark 14:62 (Matt. 26:64; Luke 22:69); and so Peter (Acts 2:33–34) and the writer of Hebrews (Heb. 1:13, 10:13) follow suit.

17 Certainly the language of "sitting at the right hand of" connotes giving unparalleled authority. But that fact should not obscure the purposeful imagery used of thrones side by side. The Son gains prestige because He is indeed seated next to the Father.

18 The Second and the Third (John 14:26; Rev. 22:17) and the First and the Third (John 16:12–14) are also said to say the same things.

19 Luke 10:22, a parallel passage, similarly expresses the intimacy in Jesus' words.

20 Compare this to other similar statements in John 16:26–27 and 17:26.

Chapter 3: Gender Is Hard to Talk About for Good Reason

1 Shaunti Christine Feldhahn, *For Women Only: What You Need to Know About the Inner Lives of Men* (Sisters, OR: Multnomah, 2004), 15, 21–51.

2 Maureen Dowd, "We Offer More Than Ankles, Gentlemen," *New York Times*, January 12, 2013. http://www.nytimes.com/2013/01/13/opinion/ sunday/dowd-we-offer-more-than-ankles-gentlemen.html.

3 Charles M. Blow, "Real Men and Pink Suits," *New York Times*, February 10, 2012. http://www.nytimes.com/2012/02/11/opinion/blow-real-men-and -pink-suits.html.

4 John P. Bartkowski, *Remaking the Godly Marriage: Gender Negotiation in Evangelical Families* (New Brunswick, NJ: Rutgers University Press, 2001), 44.

5 The overwhelming majority of biblical descriptions of God use masculine imagery (presumably to convey authority), but feminine images are used five or six times: God as mother (Isa. 66:13; possibly Ps. 131:2–3); God "giving birth to" the mountains and the world (Ps. 90:2), and to Israel (Deut. 32:18); God represented as a woman in a parable (Luke 15:8–10); and, if God the Second Member is to be identified with the feminine character of Proverbs, Lady Wisdom (Prov. 1:20–33; Proverbs 8–9).

6 Lisa Abend, "In Sweden, Boys Won't Be Boys," *Time*, December 16, 2013, 40–44. http://content.time.com/time/magazine/article/0,917 1,2159265,00.html.

7 The ten New Testament gender distinction passages are Mark 10:2–12; Matthew 19:3–12; 1 Corinthians 11:1–16; 1 Corinthians 14:33–38; Ephesians 5:22–33; Colossians 3:18–19; 1 Timothy 2:8–15; 1 Timothy 3:1–15; Titus 2:1–8; and 1 Peter 3:1–7. Many other passages concern gender, but these explicitly teach gender distinction.

8 John Milton, *Paradise Lost*, ed. Merritt Y. Hughes (New York: Odyssey Press, 1935), book 9, lines 896–97.

Chapter 4: They Are Equal in Power and Glory

1 Anita Diamant, *The Red Tent* (New York: A Wyatt Book for St. Martin's Press, 1997).

2 References to this sociology of the ancient Near East are given in J. Richard Middleton, "The Liberating Image? Interpreting the Imago Dei in Context," *Christian Scholar's Review* 24, no. 1 (1994): 16, 18, esp. 21. This hierarchy, with women at the bottom, would be the current cultural view whether one takes the Genesis author to be a Jerusalem elite priest in sixth-century exile à la J. Richard Middleton, *The Liberating Image: The Imago Dei in Genesis 1* (Grand Rapids: Brazos Press, 2005), 201, 204, 211; or Moses himself as considered in Richard L. Pratt Jr., *Designed for Dignity: What God Has Made It Possible for You to Be* (Phillipsburg, NJ: P&R Publishing, 1993), 5, 9. A literary example showing slaves and women at the bottom during the classical period may be found in Aristotle's *Poetics*, 15, cited below (see n. 4). A contrary view is given in James B. Hurley, *Man and Woman in Biblical Perspective* (Grand Rapids: Zondervan, 1981), 53.

3 *Timaeus*, 90e–91a, in Plato, *Complete Works*, ed. John M. Cooper, and D. S. Hutchinson (Indianapolis: Hackett Publishing, 1997), 1289. Note that most scholars date *Timaeus* among Plato's last works, which if so means that this view of women represents his mature thought.

4 *Poetics*, 15, in Aristotle, *The Complete Works of Aristotle: The Revised Oxford Translation*, ed. Jonathan Barnes, 2 vols., Bollingen Series 71:2 (Princeton, NJ: Princeton University Press, 1984–95), 2:2327.

5 Hurley, *Man and Woman in Biblical Perspective*, 39.

6 In the Old Testament canon's last book, the prophet Malachi reports God's final complaints against His people, why He no longer regards their offerings. Malachi 2:14 bemoans unfaithfulness to wives. The NIV (1984 version), sensitive to the thrust of God's complaint that the husbands in their unfaithfulness are belittling the wives, follows the Septuagint in translating God's term for the wife as "partner." In other words, she should not be so demeaned because of her equality with the husband. These are among the last words of God in the Old Testament.

7 The term ἀδελφοῖς (*adelphois*), "to the brethren," in Colossians 1:2 includes both women and men, as shown by the previous parallel phrase in the verse, ἁγίοις (*hagiois*), "to the saints," obviously including women with men. That sisters are included is made explicit in the NIV translation.

8 Ross S. Kraemer, of the University of Pennsylvania, attempts to paint a better picture of the status of Jewish women in her essays "Jewish Women and Christian Origins: Some Caveats" and "Jewish Women and Women's Judaism(s) at the Beginning of Christianity," in *Women and Christian Origins*, ed. Ross Shepard Kraemer and Mary Rose D'Angelo (New York: Oxford University Press, 1999), 35–79. While she adds nuance to the picture, she does not show that "Jesus' behavior toward women . . . is actually generally consistent with . . . the rabbinic norms. . . ." (p. 7), as claimed. Specifically, she does not demonstrate that attitudes toward women were substantially better than what we can infer from the Mishnah and early Jewish writers cited. For the evidence of this, one may turn to Ben Witherington III's article "Women in the New Testament," in *The Anchor Bible Dictionary*, ed., David Noel Freedman, 6 vols. (New York: Doubleday, 1992), 6:957–61.

9 Philo, *On the Creation [of the World]* 59, in *The Works of Philo: Complete and Unabridged*, trans. C. D. Yonge, new updated ed. (Peabody, MA: Hendrickson, 1993), 165. Flavius Josephus, *Against Apion* 2.201, in *Josephus*, trans. H. St. J. Thackeray, 10 vols., Loeb Classical Library 186 (1926; repr., Cambridge: Harvard University Press, 1966), 1:373. Note that, again, this writing about women represents Josephus's mature thought. Talmud *b. Menahot* 43b.

10 Kraemer and D'Angelo, *Women and Christian Origins*, 38, 51, 69.

11 Judith P. Hallett in her essay, "Women's Lives in the Ancient Mediterranean," in Kraemer and D'Angelo, *Women and Christian Origins*, 18, 32. While Hallett provides subtlety in showing "sameness" of men and women sometimes expressed in literary evidence, she still understands this in a context in which women were clearly considered inferior to men (32).

12 Ovid, *The Love Books of Ovid Being the Amores, Ars Amatoria, Redmedia Amoris and Medicamina Faciei Femineae of Publius Ovidius Naso*, trans. J. Lewis May (Whitefish, MT: Kessinger Publishing, 2005), 117.

13 David Schaps, "The Woman Least Mentioned: Etiquette and Women's Names," *Classical Quarterly* 27, no. 2 (1977): 323–30.

14 Luke's Gospel and Acts (also Luke's composition) contain approximately 37,932 words, or 27.6 percent, and Paul's letters approximately 32,408 words, or 23.5 percent, of the approximately 137,660 words of the New Testament.

15 R. MacMullen, "Women in Public in the Roman Empire," *Historia* 29, no. 2 (1980): 208–18. The brief but extremely helpful discussion on these points, in Ben Witherington III, *The Acts of the Apostles: A Socio-Rhetorical Commentary* (Grand Rapids: Eerdmans, 1998), 334–39, also gives discerning references.

16 Consider simply the specific women in Luke's Gospel: Peter's mother-in-law (4:38–39), woman with a hemorrhage of blood (8:43–48), the widows about whose treatment Jesus gets upset with the Pharisees (20:47), the widow Jesus praises for her gift of a mite to the temple (21:1–4), the women at the crucifixion (23:49, 55–56), the women at the tomb (24:10–11); and, uniquely Lucan, Mary, mother of Jesus (1:26–56), Elizabeth, mother of John the Baptist (1:5–61), Anna the prophetess (2:36–38), widow of Nain, for whom Jesus raises a dead son (7:11–17), the sinful woman who, in gratitude for forgiveness, anoints feet of Jesus (7:36–50), certain events with Martha and Mary, sisters of Lazarus (10:38–42), the woman, crippled for eighteen years (13:10–17), the daughters of Jerusalem Jesus comforts while carrying His cross (23:27); likewise uniquely, the women at the empty tomb (24:22–24), women who minister (8:1–3), the woman with the lost coin in the parable (15:8–10), and the widow in the parable of the unrighteous judge (18:1–8). This list, compiled by C. H. Talbert, and cited in Darrell L. Bock, *Luke*, 2 vols., Baker Exegetical Commentary on the New Testament (Grand Rapids: Baker, 1994), 1:710, shows how integral women are to the life events of, and also to the very thought of, Jesus. Luke obviously wants to stress their importance to the coming of the kingdom of heaven.

17 Jesus designates those doing the will of God as being more in truth His mother and sisters. He directs this feminine designation to "his disciples," clarified in Mark's account as His followers in general (Mark 3:32, 34), which included women.

18 Some argue that the γυναῖκας (*gunaikas*) of verse 11 are the wives of deacons as the word for woman, γυνή (*gunē*), could mean either "woman" or "wife," whereas others contend that these women are deaconesses. Whether they be wives or an order of women, the women being addressed had some kind of recognized position, since they require qualifications, and those qualities of character are similar to what is required of men aspiring to serve as elders or deacons.

Romans 16:1–2 seems to indicate, and Pliny the Younger (106 CE), attests to, the early church having an order of women deacons.

19 Tal Ilan, "Gender Issues and Daily Life," in *The Oxford Handbook of Jewish Daily Life in Roman Palestine*, ed. Catherine Hezser (New York:

Oxford University Press, 2010), 59. Ilan is professor of Jewish Studies at the Institut für Judaistik of the Free University Berlin.

20 Talmud *y. Sotah* 3.4. Consider Hurley's fuller discussion in *Man and Woman in Biblical Perspective*, 62–63, 71–74, 83–84.

21 Some scholars have argued that Jewish women could divorce their husbands, but they argue on slim evidence. Josephus (*Jewish Antiquities* 15.7.10) and Rabbinic law clearly put divorce as the sole prerogative of the husband. Early Judaism specialist Michael Satlow is equally unimpressed by such arguments. See Michael L. Satlow "Marriage and Divorce," in Hezser, *Oxford Handbook of Jewish Daily Life in Roman Palestine*, 352–53. Satlow is professor of religious studies and Judaic studies at Brown University.

22 Marriage historian Stephanie Coontz, *Marriage, a History: From Obedience to Intimacy or How Love Conquered Marriage* (New York: Viking, 2005), 86.

23 A woman's right to divorce is espoused in Jesus' teaching: Mark 10:12. (Coontz notes that by the late republic of Jesus' time, the Roman Empire allowed wives to initiate a divorce [*Marriage, a History*, 79–80]. But this was because Romans became so casual about what made a legal marriage anyway.) By the next century, Christians were using this right. Justin Martyr, *Second Apology*, chapter 2, describes a persecution upon the Christians for performing such a divorce, and the Shepherd of Hermas, *Mandate* 4, which is on divorce, hints at a parity of the genders in 1[29]:8 and 1[29]:10. Later Christian law, when it allowed divorce for adultery, permitted the innocent wife to divorce her guilty husband, as well as the innocent husband to divorce his guilty wife.

24 Coontz, *Marriage, a History*, 80.

25 Ibid., 86.

26 Gary A. Rendsburg, "Unlikely Heroes: Women as Israel," *Bible Review* 19, no. 1 (2003): 16.

27 Question 9 of the Larger Catechism, *The Westminster Confession of Faith and Catechisms: With Proof Texts* (Lawrenceville, GA: The Orthodox Presbyterian Church, 2007), 160. The equality of the Trinity's Members is indirectly expressed in many places in the Bible, for example, in John 10:30 and Acts 5:3–4.

28 Although she overstates the case, Sarah Sumner, *Men and Women in the Church: Building Consensus on Christian Leadership* (Downers Grove, IL: InterVarsity Press, 2003), interacts helpfully with some of the fathers, e.g. 43, 59–62. Daniel Doriani soberly surveys the major theologians of church history in a helpful appendix, "A History of the Interpretation of 1 Timothy 2," in *Women in the Church: A Fresh Analysis of 1 Timothy 2:9–15*, ed. Andreas J. Köstenberger, Thomas R. Schreiner, and H. Scott Baldwin (Grand Rapids: Baker, 1995), 213–67 (app. 1). Christopher Chenault Roberts, *Creation and Covenant: The Significance of Sexual Difference in and*

for the Moral Theology of Marriage (New York: T&T Clark International, 2007), 13–70, provides depth as well. It seems that even Augustine did not understand what Augustine thought about women.

29 Richard Bauckham, *Jesus and the Eyewitnesses: The Gospels as Eyewitness Testimony* (Grand Rapids: Eerdmans, 2006), 48–51, 129–32.

Chapter 5: Gender Matters in Relationship

1 Covenant Theological Seminary professor of Old Testament C. John Collins provides a helpful summarizing classification of theologians' three major understandings through history of the *imago Dei*, calling them the Resemblance, Representative and Relational views. He discusses them, complete with bibliography, in C. John Collins, *Genesis 1–4: A Linguistic, Literary, and Theological Commentary* (Phillipsburg, NJ: P&R Publishing, 2006), 61–67; C. John Collins, *Did Adam and Eve Really Exist? Who They Were and Why You Should Care* (Wheaton: Crossway, 2011), 93–104. Bruce A. Ware also gives a three-view categorization (Structural, Functional, Relational) and helpful discussion in "Male and Female Complementarity and the Image of God," in *Biblical Foundations for Manhood and Womanhood*, ed. Wayne Grudem (Wheaton: Crossway Books, 2002), 71–92.

2 Karl Barth, *Church Dogmatics*, ed. G. W. Bromiley and T. F. Torrance, trans. G. W. Bromiley. 4 vols. 2nd ed. (Edinburgh: T&T Clark, 1955–75), 3:2. Another example is Emil Brunner, *Dogmatics*, trans. Olive Wyon, 3 vols. (Philadelphia: Westminster, 1950–79), vol. 2. Though Barth and Brunner differ on gender roles, they both find the meaning of *imago Dei* in relationship.

3 Hurley, *Man and Woman in Biblical Perspective*, 97.

4 For this prepositional phrase, ἕνεκεν τούτου (*heneken toutou*), Mark 10:7 and Matthew 19:5 follow the ancient Greek translation called the Septuagint (third to second century BCE) for their quotation of Genesis 2:24.

5 Like most similar conjunctions, ἕνεκεν (*heneken*) can be a marker of purpose (instead of cause), but that meaning is rare for this term, and the context of Jesus' argument here excludes it.

6 Robert W. Wall, "1 Timothy 2:9–15 Reconsidered (Again)," *Bulletin for Biblical Research* 14, no. 1 (2004): 82n2.

7 William Ickes and Marilyn Turner, "On the Social Advantages of Having an Older, Opposite-Sex Sibling: Birth Order Influences in Mixed-Sex Dyads," *Journal of Personality and Social Psychology* 45, no. 1 (1983).

8 Scriptures explicitly prohibiting homosexuality are Leviticus 18:22; 20:13, both derived from Exodus 20:14; Jude 6–8, derived from Judges 19:22–25, itself referring to Genesis 19:1–13; in addition to Romans 1:26–27; 1 Corinthians 6:9–10; and 1 Timothy 1:10–11.

Chapter 6: Sex Differences Form the Platform of God's Gift

1 Carol Ann Rinzler, *Why Eve Doesn't Have an Adam's Apple: A Dictionary of Sex Differences* (New York: Facts on File, 1996), 38–39.

2 Ibid., 86–87, 16.

3 Leslie Brody, *Gender, Emotion, and the Family* (Cambridge: Harvard University Press, 1999), 116.

4 An idea of the extent of the differences can be found in Rinzler's treatment of them from a medical perspective in *Why Eve Doesn't Have an Adam's Apple*. Her work is now eighteen years old but is still useful in bringing many areas together.

5 Ibid., 96, 126, 127–29.

6 Find Hyde and McKinley's essay "Gender Differences in Cognition: Results from Meta-Analyses," as well as John T. E. Richardson's evaluation "Conclusions from the Study of Gender Differences in Cognition," in *Gender Differences in Human Cognition*, ed. Paula J. Caplan, Mary Crawford, Janet Shibley Hyde, and John T. E. Richardson, Counterpoints (New York: Oxford University Press, 1997), 34, 35, 37, 48, 131. Consider Rinzler, published at about the same time: "Girls master language and speech faster than boys do" (*Why Eve Doesn't Have an Adam's Apple*, 84–85, 116–17).

7 Kathryn Dindia and Daniel J. Canary, *Sex Differences and Similarities in Communication*, 2nd ed., Lea's Communication Series (Mahwah, NJ: Lawrence Erlbaum Associates, 2006), 11.

8 Rinzler, *Why Eve Doesn't Have an Adam's Apple*, 9, 134, 48.

9 Leslie R. Brody and Judith A. Hall, "Gender and Emotion in Context," in *Handbook of Emotions*, ed. Michael Lewis, Jeannette M. Haviland-Jones, and Lisa Feldman Barrett, 3rd ed. (New York: Guilford Press, 2008), 399. A recent example is Uta-Susan Donges, Anette Kersting, and Thomas Suslow, "Women's Greater Ability to Perceive Happy Facial Emotion Automatically: Gender Differences in Affective Priming," *PLoS ONE* 7, no. 7 (2012): 1–5. Although Donges et al. find women better at recognizing when a face is happy, they do not find the same for sadness, but they do cite research that has. Rinzler, *Why Eve Doesn't Have an Adam's Apple*, 48, cites such also.

10 Brody and Hall, "Gender and Emotion in Context," 398–99.

11 Ibid., 402–03.

12 Brody, *Gender, Emotion, and the Family*, 101–27. Brody forcefully argues "that even if there are biological differences between males and females, these differences may be the result, not the cause, of variations in emotional expressiveness" (127).

13 Judith A. Hall and Marianne Schmid Mast, "Are Women Always More Interpersonally Sensitive Than Men? Impact of Goals and Content Domain," *Personality and Social Psychology Bulletin* 34, no. 1 (2008): 144.

14 Jennifer L. Peterson, "Gender Differences in Sexual Attitudes and Behaviors: A Review of Meta-Analytic Results and Large Datasets,"

Journal of Sex Research 48, nos. 2–3 (2011): 14–16; Jennifer L. Peterson and Janet Shibley Hyde, "A Meta-Analytic Review of Research on Gender Differences in Sexuality, 1993–2007," *Psychological Bulletin* 136, no. 1 (2010): 21. Elsewhere, Hyde summarizes moderate to large differences as those in smiling, emotional expressiveness, sensitivity to nonverbal cues, and attitudes toward sex ("Epilogue," in Dindia and Canary, *Sex Differences and Similarities in Communication*, 393).

15 I grabbed this graph from Michael Mills, "How Can There Still Be a Sex Difference, Even When There Is No Sex Difference?," *PsychologyToday.com*, The How and Why of Sex Differences (January 26, 2011). Used by permission. A similar graph can be found for many sex trait distributions.

16 Hyde et al., for example, contend "that girls and boys, men and women, are more alike than they are different" ("Epilogue," 393), or likewise Kathryn Dindia, who maintains "that sex differences exist but they are overwhelmed by similarities" ("Men are From North Dakota, Women are From South Dakota," in Dindia and Canary, *Sex Differences and Similarities in Communication*, 3). This formed the basis of the argument of the much earlier work by Carol Tavris, *The Mismeasure of Woman* (New York: Simon & Schuster, 1992), explicitly stated, e.g., on page 54.

17 This is by no means a new observation. A particularly thoughtful and accessible discussion of the difficulties of interpreting sex differences is given in Mary Stewart Van Leeuwen, *Gender and Grace: Love, Work and Parenting in a Changing World* (Downers Grove, IL: InterVarsity Press, 1990), 54–71. In discussing a graph of sexually dimorphic verbal ability (p. 58), she notes how, at the time of her writing, overlapping scores of sexual traits always account for at least a third of each group. A more academic criticism of essential differences is given in Brody, *Gender, Emotion, and the Family*, chapter 6. The overlapping distribution of math scores is discussed in Tavris, *Mismeasure of Woman*, 41–43, although the understanding of real difference in math scores has been sharpened since then.

18 Commonly scholars use "gender" to refer to the psycho-social-cultural characteristics that either exist or are constructed in light of "sex," the biological differences between male and female.

19 Sex difference researchers may also speak of "doing gender" as I do, but they do it as part of their approach casting gender as socially constructed (e.g., Dindia and Canary, *Sex Differences and Similarities in Communication*, 179–94, 415–16). There is value to their investigations, which show how the gender of one person stimulates that of the other, but they fail to see gender, as I do, as a God-given call to a reality for which we were made.

Chapter 7: The Grand Asymmetries of Gender Give Us Specialties

1 On the question of whether two individuals, Adam and Eve, lived in history, I read the biblical author as saying that they did, but the

arguments drawn from the text's teaching about women, men, and gender do not depend upon it. The challenges to the historicity of Adam today arise from some striking developments in three areas: the proliferation of ancient hominids in paleoanthropology, the eminently useful biological clock in genomics, and the growing sensitivity to issues of time and place in hermeneutics. In short, there are ways of putting these discoveries together with a historical Adam when the text is closely read. A recent defense of the first couple's historicity that is sensitive to modern challenges, especially the hermeneutical ones, may be found in C. John Collins, *Did Adam and Eve Really Exist? Who They Were and Why You Should Care.*

2 Calculated by books, Paul gives us almost 50 percent, or 13 out of the 27 books, of the New Testament. This is assuming we accept Paul's authorship in the books that claim it, which I do. But calculated by Greek words, Paul's letters contain some 32,408 words out of the 137,660 of the New Testament, or 23.5 percent.

3 Other writers have observed the three distinctions in the Genesis narrative, also sometimes noting how Paul finds them theologically significant. Recent ones include Ware, "Male and Female Complementarity and the Image of God," 81–85; and Hurley, *Man and Woman in Biblical Perspective*, 206–7. Elisabeth Elliot, *The Mark of a Man: Following Christ's Example of Masculinity*, new pbk. ed. (Grand Rapids: Revell, 2006), 48, finds four distinctions.

4 C. S. Lewis, *Perelandra: A Novel* (London: John Lane, 1943), 44.

5 The Hebrew word תַּרְדֵּמָה (*thardhemah*) occurs seven times in the Old Testament, usually signifying a portentous experience at God's hands, such as Abram's sleep before God cuts a covenant with him (Gen. 15:12), the sleep that Job claims precedes God's terrible utterances (Job 33:15), the sleep vision claimed by Job's friend, Eliphaz, giving him the knowledge to correct Job (Job 4:13), the sleep from God's hand upon Saul's men before David reveals his righteousness to them (1 Sam. 26:12), and the prophetic sleep to which God puts Israel in their blindness (Isa. 29:10).

6 James G. S. S. Thomson, "Sleep: An Aspect of Jewish Anthropology," *Vetus Testamentum* 5, no. 4 (1955): 422–23.

7 Ibid., 426.

8 The word תְּשׁוּקָה (*teshuqah*) is attested in Samaritan and Mishnaic Hebrew with the meaning "urge, crave, impulse." Some look to its only other biblical use in Song of Solomon 7:10, "I am my beloved's, and his desire is for me," for the meaning of this word, where it connotes sexual desire. But, besides the cultural distance between Genesis and Song of Solomon, sexual desire is not a likely meaning for this sentence of judgment since such desire, in the Genesis account, is a gift (Gen. 1:22, 28) and not the result of the fall.

9 Paul uses masculine inclusive terms in the sentences, because Corinthian men were also involved in the wrongful attempts to erase gender

distinction in worship, but I am inferring that he is primarily anticipating contradiction by the upper-class Corinthian women, who took offence at such restrictions.

10 So ends the last book of Milton, *Paradise Lost*, book 12, lines 648–49.

11 Some authors see a progression in the status of women from old to new covenant, or an elevation of status for women at Pentecost (as in Van Leeuwen, *Gender and Grace*, 35), but there is not much justification for seeing such a change. Whatever ministry women are seen doing after Pentecost they are seen doing before it in the Bible.

12 Another possible referent of "the law" in 1 Corinthians 14:34 is Genesis 3:16, the description of consequences pronounced because of the woman's sin. That is, Paul may be naming the book of Genesis, a member of the five "books of Moses," as part of the law, as in the common division of the Hebrew Scriptures into "the law and the prophets." But the Numbers passage about vows, cited in the text, is the more likely referent, as it concerns submission of women in the covenant community. A third possible referent is the worship instruction restricting the office of priest to men (Aaron's sons, e.g., Exod. 28:1, 4, 41; 29:9, 44; 30:30; 40:14–15).

Chapter 8: The Asymmetry of Origin: The Man of the Solid Ground and the Woman of the Resting Rib

1 The verb of Deuteronomy 24:5 is sometimes translated "rejoice with his wife," based on a textual variant that puts the verb וְשִׂמַּח (*vesimmach*) in qal form (וְשָׂמַח, *vesamach*). But the direct object marker on the word for "wife" makes the Masoretic piel reading more likely to be original, meaning the husband is making his wife merry or happy, i.e., securing her.

2 Daniel Isaac Block, *Judges, Ruth*, New American Commentary (Nashville: Broadman & Holman Publishers, 1999), 95–74. As Achsah traveled south, she realized that the area around Kiriath-sepher, if we are to identify it with Debir, was considerably drier than her home in Hebron. Caleb gave her the upper and lower water sources (Josh. 15:19; Judg. 1:15). These springs lie some distance from the hill of Debir and are the only water source for the site.

3 Sally K. Gallagher, *Evangelical Identity and Gendered Family Life* (New Brunswick, NJ: Rutgers University Press, 2003), 5.

4 Some may read Titus 2:5 as not gender specific, meaning that Paul could just as easily have instructed the young men to be "busy at home." I must disagree, as Paul specifically divides up the genders in writing this passage. The yin-yang singsong pattern of addressing one and then the other is prominent, the men being addressed in verse 2 and verse 6. Note also how the woman's home command is directly followed in verse 5 by the definitely gender specific "be . . . submissive to their own husbands."

5 There is a textual variant in our Greek manuscripts with this word in Titus 2:5, with later miniscules and church fathers reading οἰκουρούς (*oikourous*) or "staying at home," a much more common word. But the reading of the earlier manuscripts, along with Clement of Rome, οἰκουργούς (*oikourgous*) "working at the home," is to be preferred, not only because of the external textual evidence but also because it is far more likely that a scribe would change the uncommon word to the common one than vice versa. Bruce Metzger and the Editorial Committee of the United Bible Societies' Greek New Testament agrees: Bruce M. Metzger and United Bible Societies, *A Textual Commentary on the Greek New Testament; a Companion Volume to the United Bible Societies' Greek New Testament (2nd Ed.)* (London, New York: United Bible Societies, 1994), 585. (A contrary scholarly opinion is given in Frederick Field, *Notes on the Translation of the New Testament* [London: Cambridge University Press, 1899], 220–22.) Thus, Paul is not advising wives to stay at home so much as take on the emphasis of the home, to consider homemaking their duty.

6 The significance of the word used in Titus 2:5 lies in the related common words, associated with a sedentary life, words that Paul does not use. He avoids the common word that crops up as a variant in some texts, οἰκουρος (*oikouros*), which seems to be used by second-century physician Soranus (another textual variant in our text of his *Gynecology*), discussing the idea that menstruation is needed for women in their homebound and sedentary life, "VI. Whether Catharsis of the Menses Fulfills a Helpful Purpose," in *Gynecology* (Baltimore, MD: Johns Hopkins Press, 1956), 23. Paul also does not use οἰκουροκαθέδριος (*oikourokathedrios*), associated with a sedentary life as well. Nor does he use ἐνδημέω (*endēmeō*), "to stay at home." He wants the women of Crete to be *working* at making the home.

7 *The Epistles of Clement* (Complete Text), ed. Allan Menzies, in *The Ante-Nicene Fathers. Translations of the Writings of the Fathers Down to A.D. 325*, ed. Alexander Roberts, James Donaldson, and A. Cleveland Coxe, 10 vols. (Buffalo: Christian Literature Publishing Company, 1885–96), 9:229.

8 Alfred DeMaris and Monica A. Longmore, "Ideology, Power, and Equity: Testing Competing Explanations for the Perception of Fairness in Household Labor," *Social Forces* 74, no. 3 (1996): 1043, 1064–67.

9 Research comparing happiness in marriages that try to divide up chores equally with those where the wife focuses on the home is conflicted. Rhoads concurs that research is mixed (*Taking Sex Differences Seriously*, 260). Sabino Kornrich, Julie Brines, and Katrina Leupp, "Egalitarianism, Housework, and Sexual Frequency in Marriage," *American Sociological Review* 78, no. 1 (2013): 27, cite research showing that couples with more equal division of home labor are less likely to divorce, but also acknowledge that research is mixed (47n1). A number of studies find that more gender-traditional women have happier marriages: Wilcox and Nock, "What's Love

Got to Do with It?," 1323, 1339. In their particularly penetrating study of the social factors contributing to the decline of marriage, W. Bradford Wilcox and Jeffrey Dew find that community-supported, religious wives and husbands in Louisiana who embrace "gender role traditionalism," as they call it, are much more likely to have high marital quality and are much less likely to get divorced than those who don't: W. Bradford Wilcox and Jeffrey Dew, "Is Love a Flimsy Foundation? Soulmate versus Institutional Models of Marriage," *Social Science Research* 39, no. 5 (2010): 696–97. There are other variables involved in their data that could account for this result, and their definition creates strictures where the Bible does not, but it at least suggests that this gender distinction may not be the purveyor of misery for women. In fact, historian James A. Sweet and sociologist Larry L. Bumpass, the latter also being a former board member of the National Academy of Science's Board on Children and Families, using the several large National Surveys of Families and Households, show that couples embracing gender distinction in housework are less likely to divorce: Larry L. Bumpass and James A. Sweet, *Cohabitation, Marriage and Union Stability: Preliminary Findings from NSFH2* (Madison: University of Wisconsin, Center for Demography and Ecology, 1995), 18. According to Wilcox and Nock's review of research in this area, "it appears that women in marriages characterized by more traditional gender beliefs and practices are happier" (Wilcox and Nock, "What's Love Got to Do with It?," 1339). As we've seen, the Bible does not argue for "traditional gender practices," but giving a woman and a man distinction as rest-giver and securer.

10 For example, Coontz traces the origin of the man–sole breadwinner/woman-homemaker model of marriage to the spread of wage labor in the late eighteenth century (*Marriage, a History*, 105, 146, 154–55). We can also note, in agreement, that later twentieth-century conditions in America that allowed a single income to sustain a rich lifestyle for an entire family were aberrant. Nancy Pearcey, *Total Truth: Liberating Christianity from Its Cultural Captivity* (Wheaton: Crossway Books, 2004), 325–48, cited in the text, also provides thoughtful analysis.

11 Pearcey, *Total Truth*, 343.

12 Brian Schulz, (lecture on Bedouin practice, Jerusalem University College, Jerusalem, Israel, June 30, 2014).

13 Perhaps by contrast, the women of Proverbs 7:11 and 1 Timothy 5:13 are not focused on their home but flitting from it.

14 According to Coontz, division of home sustenance jobs by gender has been a consistent practice in the general population throughout history, whether it was the hunter-gatherer wife concentrating on digging and foraging, while the husband focused on hunting large game; or it was the feudal couple both helping with the harvest, but the husband focusing on the outdoor agricultural labor (a "plowman") and the wife on preparing flax, brewing beer, making cheese, and washing their clothes in the village stream;

or it was the later urban husband working a trade with his wife as a partner keeping the books or acting as his agent (*Marriage, a History*, 38, 66, 110, 114–15). Sometimes these supported gender equality and specialties and sometimes they contradicted them.

15 Similarly, the narrative of 1 Samuel 1–7 is chiefly about establishing Samuel, through his interactions with Eli, as the authority to provide the foundation of God's kingdom on earth. But the passage cannot help but explain Eli's securing effect on Hannah, so that "her countenance was no longer sad" (1 Sam. 1:18 RSV).

Chapter 9: The Asymmetry of Order (Part 1): The Firstborn

1 Gordon J. Wenham, *Numbers: An Introduction and Commentary*, Tyndale Old Testament Commentaries 4 (Downers Grove, IL: InterVarsity Press, 2008), 215.

2 Iris Marion Young, *Intersecting Voices: Dilemmas of Gender, Political Philosophy, and Policy* (Princeton, NJ: Princeton University Press, 1997), 102, 105–6, 122.

3 So also concludes Collins, *Genesis 1–4*, 138, and Bruce K. Waltke, *Genesis: A Commentary* (Grand Rapids: Zondervan, 2001), 89.

4 First Corinthians 14:34, concerning women's silence in the service, is explained more fully in chapter 10, "The Asymmetry of Order (Part 2): The Promoter," as restraining women from taking part in the judging of prophetic utterances.

5 These reasons come from Herman N. Ridderbos, *Paul: An Outline of His Theology* (Grand Rapids: Eerdmans, 1975), 380–81.

6 The debate about whether "head" means "source" or "authority" seems less than profitable to me. Those in favor of "source" point to 1 Corinthians 11:8; Ephesians 4:15; Colossians 2:19; and to the order of the statements in 1 Corinthians 11:3, as well as to how the "person of the highest rank" meaning is rare in Greek literature. Those who favor "authority" point to 1 Corinthians 11:10; Ephesians 1:22; Ephesians 5:22–24; Colossians 1:18; 2:10; and, again, to consistent use of the term "head" throughout the Septuagint: Judges 11:11; 2 Samuel 22:44; Psalm 18:43; Isaiah 7:8–9; Lamentations 1:5. One is liable to feel that the meanings are not completely separate in Paul's mind. But even if we adopt the meaning of "source," as biblical commentator Gordon D. Fee defines it, "a unique relationship predicated on one's being the source of the other's existence," what is to be gained? How is that to be applied in our lives? Paul still expects the wife to apply that by submitting to her source. Even so, the comprehensive review of the Greek word κεφαλή (*kephalē*) that roundly defeats the connotation of "source" may be found in Piper and Grudem, *Recovering Biblical Manhood and Womanhood*, 425–68, and Grudem, *Biblical Foundations for Manhood and Womanhood*, 145–202.

7 Less than 10 percent of American evangelicals hold a thoroughgoing egalitarian view of marriage, according to Gallagher, *Evangelical Identity and Gendered Family Life*, 77.

8 Ibid., 69.

9 A number of researchers of evangelical practice assert that, despite what they say, conservative Christians do not practice husbandly authority in their marriages, their supposed headship is largely symbolic, and the language of headship lingers over a pragmatic egalitarianism. Bartkowski, in his study of a large Texas church, finds such "heterogeneity" between beliefs and practice (*Remaking the Godly Marriage*, ix, 6, 16, 122–27). Melinda Lundquist Denton finds the connection between gender role ideology and decision-making practices among conservative Protestants to be "loose," Melinda Lundquist Denton, "Gender and Marital Decision Making: Negotiating Religious Ideology and Practice," *Social Forces* 82, no. 3 (2004): 1151. Christian Smith, in his sensitive study of evangelical practice, similarly finds "the final say of the husband [to be] more an ideological safety net than a routine reality," Christian Smith, *Christian America? What Evangelicals Really Want* (Berkeley: University of California Press, 2000), 185. And as Gallagher puts it, "their traditionalism is largely symbolic. In practice, most are pragmatically egalitarian" (Gallagher, *Evangelical Identity and Gendered Family Life*, 103, elaborating on Sally K. Gallagher and Christian Smith, "Symbolic Traditionalism and Pragmatic Egalitarianism: Contemporary Evangelicals, Families, and Gender," *Gender and Society* 13, no. 2 [1999]: 211, 217, 223, 226–28). But I found that such statements are not sensitive to the rhythm of these marriages. Because the couples are mutually cognizant of their arrangement, the submitting happens much earlier than when the decision is actually finalized. Christian complementarian couples operate with a very real but inherent leading and submission that may not be visible to outside observers, analogous to the leading and following that transpires during formal dancing. It is very real to the dancers, but when it is done well, it is rarely noticed by onlookers (Andreades, "Does She Matter?," 64–65, 87–88).

10 The Greek word translated "vessel" is σκεῦος (*skeuos*), which can mean object, instrument (human), or even just a thing. But we can be certain that Peter is thinking of a dish or vase because of his connecting it to the term τιμή (*timē*), "honor," in the verse. Other places speaking of "honorable vessels" clearly mean containers: 2 Maccabees 5:16; Romans 9:21; 2 Timothy 2:20, 21; and, metaphorically, 1 Thessalonians 4:4.

11 I am indebted to John Calvin for the suggestion he offers in *Commentaries on the Four Last Books of Moses, Arranged in the Form of a Harmony* (1563), trans. Charles William Bingham, 45 vols. in 22 vols., Calvin's Commentaries (1852; repr., Grand Rapids: Baker, 1981), 1:501–2.

12 Betsey Stevenson and Justin Wolfers, "The Paradox of Declining Female Happiness," *National Bureau of Economic Research*, Working Papers Series, no. #14969 (2009): 1, doi: 10.3386/w14969.

Chapter 10: The Asymmetry of Order (Part 2): The Promoter

1 "Women," in *The Koran*, trans. N. J. Dawood, 50th anniversary ed., Penguin Classics (London; New York: Penguin Books, 2006), 64. Compare also the instruction to the wives of the prophet in "Prohibition," ibid., 398.

2 First Timothy 2:12's conjunction of διδάσκω (*didaskō*) and αὐθεντέω (*authenteō*) easily forms a hendiadys, a figure of speech in which two words connected by a conjunction are used to express a single notion that would normally be expressed by an adjective and a substantive, such as using "grace and favor" to mean "gracious favor," or using "eat and run" to mean "eat quickly." The best way to understand Paul's use of these two terms is to read him barring not teaching *and* exercising authority, but "authoritative teaching." Some note that the semantic range of the uncommon word αὐθεντέω (*authenteō*) includes negative domineering, and try to read Paul's hendiadys as forbidding only domineering teaching, but the contrast of the second part of the sentence, "rather, she is to remain quiet," and the contrast of verse 12 with verse 11, "Let a woman learn [not teach]," argue against that reading.

3 Bruce K. Waltke, *The Book of Proverbs*, 2 vols., New International Commentary on the Old Testament (Grand Rapids: Eerdmans, 2004), 2.516–17.

4 Erika Moore, as cited in Waltke, *Book of Proverbs*, 517.

5 Tremper Longman III and Daniel G. Reid, *God Is a Warrior*, Studies in Old Testament Biblical Theology (Grand Rapids: Zondervan, 1995), 112.

6 The song of Hannah (1 Sam. 2:1–10), whose vocabulary and themes Mary draws upon in her song, also employs martial language: "The adversaries of the LORD shall be broken to pieces; against them he will thunder in heaven" (v. 10).

7 Wilcox gives a thorough sampling of authors theorizing this view in *Soft Patriarchs, New Men*, 159.

8 Ibid., 181. This is not to say that religion or teaching on biblical authority is never used for abuse. Diane Langberg gives illustrations of such, for example, in *On the Threshold of Hope: Opening the Door to Hope and Healing for Survivors of Sexual Abuse* (Wheaton: Tyndale House, 1999), 120. The fact remains that higher incidence of domestic violence does not occur among Christians. As Langberg puts it, "There is no exact profile of a family in which [abuse] occurs." But even beyond that, Wilcox found that, conversely, "churchgoing conservative Protestant men register the lowest rates of domestic violence of any group" in American households (*Soft Patriarchs, New Men*, 207, 213).

9 The conspicuous lack of oil in the sacrifice required by this law strongly symbolizes the lack of joy in the disintegrating marriage. Consider the way oil represents gladness in Psalm 45:7; 1 Samuel 10:1. Wenham gives further explanation of the symbolism of the sacrifice in this passage (*Numbers*, 94–95).

10 Regarding the transition to household instruction in Ephesians 5, some argue that verse 22 goes with verse 21, and should not be broken up from it. "Submit to one another . . . and wives submit to your husbands," but this is a mistake. Verse 21 goes with and ends the previous passage, as the fourth nominative masculine participial phrase of the sentence beginning in verse 18. As it is masculine, it can only be modifying "be filled with the Spirit" as the other participles do. The argument that verse 21 belongs with verse 22 because there is no main verb in verse 22 is not true. There is a verb: it is "to be," implied. Literally, the text is: "Wives, be to your own husbands, as to the Lord." This is clarified in verse 24 and verse 33 as being in terms of submitting. Note that, in the next three phrases of verse 23, the verb "to be" is implied twice as well, and explicitly stated only once. Finally, the inclusio of verse 33 ends the passage (as 6:1 changes the address from husbands and wives to children), referring back to verse 22 as its beginning.

11 Another example of a wife who should have disobeyed her husband is Naomi, who follows her husband, Elimelech, out of the covenant land into Moab (Ruth 1:1).

12 As Coontz casually claims in one description, "The doctrine of difference inhibited emotional intimacy" (*Marriage, a History*, 189). Other illustrating statements in her book may be found on pages 178, 181, 184, 188.

13 There are various degrees of egalitarianism, and some claiming an egalitarian view would still affirm some different responsibilities for men and women in marriage, but I adopt the text's more narrow definition, coming from Wilcox and Nock, "What's Love Got to Do with It?," for the sake of comparison.

14 Wilcox and Nock, "What's Love Got to Do with It?," 1322. Wilcox and Nock explain why this is supposed to happen. First, common tasks should result in mutual understanding from shared experiences and so a richer emotional life. Second, the elimination of patriarchal authority removes social distance and so promotes intimacy. Third, egalitarian-minded men are expected to be more open to a counterstereotypical masculinity conducive to emotional expression, and so closeness. For these three reasons, egalitarian marriages are predicted to be characterized by more "interpersonal closeness, trust, communication and mutuality" (ibid., 1323).

15 Three sources stating a positive egalitarian link with marital happiness are, first, Paul R. Amato, David R. Johnson, Alan Booth, and Stacy J. Rogers, "Continuity and Change in Marital Quality between 1980 and 2000," *Journal of Marriage and Family* 65, no. 1 (2003): 1–22. In the

two surveys they examined, they note greater decision-making equality between spouses appearing to have improved marriage quality (p. 21). Second, John Mordechai Gottman, *What Predicts Divorce? The Relationship between Marital Processes and Marital Outcomes* (Hillsdale, NJ: Lawrence Erlbaum Associates, 1994), 57, says his observational research indicates that asymmetric power is more common among dissatisfied couples than satisfied ones. Third and lastly, an Oregon study by Judith H. Hibbard and Clyde R. Pope, "The Quality of Social Roles as Predictors of Morbidity and Mortality," *Social Science and Medicine* 36, no. 3 (1993): 217, found unequal decision-making power in marriage predicted higher risk of death (and so, one assumes, marital unhappiness) in women. In more general population data, on the other hand, Greeley finds that the feeling of being valued by the spouse is a more powerful contributor to marital happiness than a sense of equality (*Faithful Attraction*, 113). He did not distinguish between husbands and wives in this measure, namely, it holds for both.

Chapter 11: The Asymmetry of Intent: The Commissioned and the Empowerer

1 A happy (and lavishly illustrated) corrective on vocation is Amy L. Sherman, *Kingdom Calling: Vocational Stewardship for the Common Good* (Downers Grove, IL: InterVarsity Press, 2011).

2 The 2009 Shriver Report finds that mothers are the primary breadwinners in 40 percent of American families. Maria Shriver, *A Woman's Nation Changes Everything: A Study by Maria Shriver and the Center for American Progress*, ed. Heather Boushey and Ann O'Leary (Washington, DC: Center for American Progress, 2009), 6.

3 Joanne Lipman, "The Mismeasure of Woman," *New York Times*, October 23, 2009. http://www.nytimes.com/2009/10/24/opinion/24lipman.html.

4 From Henry Miller's essay "The Universe of Death," in *The Cosmological Eye* (Norfolk, CT: New Directions, 1939), 120.

5 Cushan-Rishathaim, King of Aram Naharaim (NIV), named in Judges 3:8 and 10, could refer to a number of different historical characters, but if he was coming over from Mesopotamia (ESV/RSV), the reach of his empire indicates a powerful enemy, more powerful than the local neighbors the Israelite judges otherwise confronted. This comports with the book's pattern of things starting out good, with the best, most accomplished judge, and ending with the least effective, Samson, who never once leads the tribes into battle. So though it is rather simply stated, Othniel's "hand prevailing" against Cushan-Rishathaim is an extraordinary accomplishment.

6 We would be prudent to refrain from calling Deborah a judge. The text tells us that she was a prophetess (Judg. 4:4), a spokesperson for God to the people, but she is never actually called a judge. Instead, her description is enigmatic. In contrast to the other judges, no reference to

her inspiration or empowerment by Yahweh is given. God does not "raise her up." She is not said to "save Israel," even though she seems to be very involved in the salvation. She does not head the troops (v. 10), is absent from the actual battlefield (vv. 15–17), and the Lord delivers into Barak's hand, not hers (v. 14). So she is not, at least, a judge like the other judges. Some point to the sentences stating that she "was judging Israel" (v. 4) and the sons of Israel came to her "for judgment" (v. 5), and it is true that she acts as a stopgap in the vacuum of leadership that was Israel at that time. But her goal is to promote the would-be Barak to the role of deliverer. By her own confession, she is not a "savior of Israel," but a "mother in Israel" (5:7). A detailed argument may be found in Block, *Judges, Ruth*, 193–96, and Robert H. O'Connell, *The Rhetoric of the Book of Judges*, Supplements to Vetus Testamentum 63 (Leiden: E. J. Brill, 1996), 107–8.

7 Again, the Judges author uses a chiastic structure to narrate the story of Deborah and Barak and Jael and Heber in chapter 4. When Deborah's conversation with Barak is understood as the center, Deborah's placement in verse 5 is clearly contrasted with Heber's in verse 11.

8 E.g., 1 Kings 11:26; 14:21; 15:2; 15:10; 1 Chronicles 12:13; etc. The many references to the mother's origin when a king begins his reign can often be seen to predict the righteousness of the reign.

9 Ken Tada, "Caregiving: A Cause for Christ," *Tabletalk*, October 1, 2011, http://www.ligonier.org/learn/articles/caregiving-a-cause-for-christ/.

Chapter 12: Gender Specialties: Banishing Independence

1 Imagery of Apollos in Alexandria described in chapter-opening scenic overlook is drawn from Flavius Josephus, *The Jewish War*, rev. ed., trans. G. A. Williamson, rev. E. Mary Smallwood, Penguin Classics (New York: Penguin, 1981), 171–73, 282, 286.

2 William D. Mounce, *Pastoral Epistles*, Word Biblical Commentary 46 (Nashville: Thomas Nelson, 2000), 143.

3 Though some church fathers, such as Ignatius, Irenaeus, Justin, and Tertullian, suggest that "the woman" of verse 15 is Mary, the end of the chain of childbirth, recognizing her as Eve had its supporters in the nineteenth century, as cited in Charles J. Ellicott's commentary of 1864, *The Pastoral Epistles of St. Paul*, rev. 3rd ed. (London: Longman, 1864), 38–39. Stanley Porter also cites several commentators who argue, as I do, that Paul means that Eve will find her ultimate salvation through Christ, who will eventually come through her childbirth. Stanley E. Porter, "What Does It Mean to Be 'Saved by Childbirth'? (1 Timothy 2:15)," *Journal for the Study of the New Testament* 49 (1993): 90nn8–9.

4 In the Greek sentence of 1 Timothy 2:15, σωθήσεται δὲ διὰ τῆς τεκνογονίας (*sōthēsetai de dia tēs teknogonias*), the verb τεκνογονέω (*teknogoneō*), to bear children, is made a noun and given the definite article.

Chapter 13: Culture: The Clothes of Gender

1 First Corinthians 11:10, speaking of the observing angels, is more fully explained in chapter 18, "The Immense Invitation."

2 Ilan, in the *Oxford Handbook of Jewish Daily Life in Roman Palestine* simply says, "[T]o what extent women actively participated in the synagogue service in the Land of Israel in the Roman period remains unclear" ("Gender Issues and Daily Life," 61). There could have been more participation outside of Palestine, but Talmudic evidence argues against it.

3 From early Jewish literature, see Tosefta *Megillah* 3:11: "They do not bring a woman to read in public." Also, Mishnah *Sukkah* 3:10 forbids women (along with slaves and minors) from reading the Hallel liturgy.

4 Three inscriptions (out of over thirty citing Heads of Synagogues) mention women Synagogue Heads: Rufina, Sophia, and Theopempte. Rufina's may only be estimated as "probably second century," and the other two not earlier than fourth to fifth century. They possibly worked only with women, or on a team, but perhaps not. Jewish women "elders," probably religious, are named unambiguously in six inscriptions, three dating from the fourth to fifth century and three dating from third to sixth century. (One dubious one could come from anywhere from the first century BCE to third century CE), Bernadette J. Brooten, *Women Leaders in the Ancient Synagogue*, Brown Judaic Studies 36 (Chico, CA: Scholars Press, 1982), 5, 11, 13, 23, 32, 41–45, 54–55. These decidedly later exceptions to Jewish male leadership are fascinating puzzles in Jewish development, but they do not make first-century women likely participants in the synagogue service.

5 Witherington, "Women in the New Testament," 957; F. F. Bruce, *The Acts of the Apostles: The Greek Text with Introduction and Commentary*, 3rd rev. and enl. ed. (Grand Rapids: Eerdmans, 1990), 358.

6 See Act 18:1–4. In addition, the "Synagogue of Hebrews" inscription found in Corinth, though later than the apostolic age, suggests a significant Hebrew population.

7 "Nature" is a rare word in the New Testament, compared with Greek literature, because "natural theology," that is, making a theological argument from what we see in nature, has no place in their thinking, according to Gordon D. Fee, *The First Epistle to the Corinthians*, New International Commentary on the New Testament (Grand Rapids: Eerdmans, 1987), 526n11. Just so, I posit that we would err to read Paul making such an argument here.

8 Paul was also well aware of 2 Samuel 14:25–26, where we read that Absalom is praised for his handsome, long hair that weighed "two hundred shekels."

9 The term φύσις (*phusis*) can mean the natural state in this vicinity, the lay of the land, which is how, for example, Herodotus uses it: *Histories* 2.5, in *The Landmark Herodotus: The Histories*, ed. Robert B. Strassler, trans.

Andrea L. Purvis (New York: Pantheon Books, 2007), 118. This meaning naturally lends itself to "what is natural culturally."

10 The question of verses 14b–15a connects grammatically to verse 13, introduced as it is by οὐδὲ (*oude*). This question about "the nature of things" is likely a restatement of what is "proper," πρέπον (*prepon*), not what is right. Paul is elaborating on his question about what feels right culturally.

11 Jerome Murphy-O'Connor, *St. Paul's Corinth: Text and Archaeology*, 3rd rev. and expanded ed. (Collegeville, MN: Liturgical Press, 2002), 114. The art of that time shows men usually with short hair. At the museum of Corinth, one can see two statues from a relief called "Captive's Façade," depicting how the Roman conquerors triumphed over their disgraceful captives: barbarians with shoulder-length curly hair. Murphy-O'Connor also notes that long hair on a man was associated with homosexuality.

12 Ibid., 91–92.

13 Fee, *First Epistle to the Corinthians*, 511n81; Murphy-O'Connor, *St. Paul's Corinth*, 92. Bruce, *Acts of the Apostles*, 105, cites the shaving of Bernice's head, who had undertaken a Nazirite vow, as a voluntary humiliation.

14 Achilles Tatius, *Achilles Tatius*, trans. S. Gaselee, Loeb Classical Library 45 (New York: G. P. Putnam's Sons, 1917), 8.6, p. 399.

15 Consider also the writer Lucian, who sees "a woman with her hair closely clipped in the Spartan manner, boyish-looking and wholly masculine," *The Fugitives*, 27, in Lucian and others, *Lucian*, 8 vols., The Loeb Classical Library (London, New York: W. Heinemann; Macmillan, 1913), V, 85. And, again, Lucian: "[Megilla's head] shaved close, just like the manliest of athletes," *Dialogi meretrici* 5:3 in ibid., VII, 383.

16 Numbers 5:18 indicates that the suspected adulteress must wear loosed hair as part of her shame. Philo, a contemporary of Jesus living in the first half of the first century, was a Greek-speaking Jewish philosopher in Alexandria. In commenting on the Numbers passage, he uses Paul's exact language, talking about the priest "removing her kerchief," so she is "bareheaded" during the rite (spec.leg. 3.60). Two frescoes from Pompeii, show religious ceremonies, and women with their hair covered (Fee, *First Epistle to the Corinthians*, 509n71; Leon Morris, *The First Epistle of Paul to the Corinthians: An Introduction and Commentary*, Tyndale New Testament Commentaries [Grand Rapids: Eerdmans, 1983], 148). "Evidence from Paul's era shows that women did not appear in public with long, flowing hair" (Fee, *First Epistle to the Corinthians*, 509). Fee also notes how rites of Dionysus, Cybele, and Isis, in which disheveled hair and head thrown back were almost trademarks of the frenzied worship of women in these cults (509n75).

17 Fee, *First Epistle to the Corinthians*, 507.

18 Gregory R. Perry, "Phoebe, Paul and Other Διάκονοι [*Diakonoi*]: God's 'Go-Betweens' for a New Social Order" (unpublished article, Covenant Theological Seminary, Creve Coeur, MO, 2010), 12–15.

19 The final phrase of Titus 2:5, taken by itself, could mean that distinguishing gender is simply a cultural thing: "When in Rome, promote and provide rest to your husband. . . ," but the identity of Titus 2's teaching with other places where Paul ties it to creation clarify that the instruction is not just for Cretans.

Chapter 14: The Purpose of the Genders: A Gift to Foster Intimacy

1 Susan M. Johnson and Leslie S. Greenberg, "Emotionally Focused Marital Therapy: An Overview," *Psychotherapy* 24, no. 3S (1987): 553.

2 As stated earlier, the Higher Ground Ministry was originally called G.A.M.E., the Gender Affirming Ministry Endeavor. The name was changed in 2014.

3 The Yarhouse longitudinal follow-up study found a lowering in the mean reported level of SSA from prior to the marriage to later times as the marriage continued ("Intact Marriages . . . A 5-Year Follow-up Study," 330).

4 Betsey Stevenson and Justin Wolfers, "Marriage and Divorce: Changes and Their Driving Forces," *Journal of Economic Perspectives* 21, no. 2 (2007): 27–52.

5 Coontz, *Marriage, a History*, 181. Especially toward the end of the hundred years, divorces increased. From 1960 to 1980, the annual rate of new divorces per thousand people doubled (Stevenson and Wolfers, "Marriage and Divorce," 29).

6 Wilcox, "Evolution of Divorce," 86.

7 I give the fuller discussion behind this conclusion, including analysis of the graph on page 29 of Stevenson and Wolfers, "Marriage and Divorce," in Andreades, "Does She Matter?," 1–4.

8 Coontz, *Marriage, a History*, 4, 306.

9 Wilcox, "Evolution of Divorce," 89. This fact served as one of the pillars in William Bennett's influential argument for cultural decline in the United States: William J. Bennett, *The Index of Leading Cultural Indicators: Facts and Figures on the State of American Society* (New York: Simon & Schuster, 1994).

10 Vaughn R. A. Call and Tim B. Heaton, "Religious Influence on Marital Stability," *Journal for the Scientific Study of Religion* 36, no. 3 (1997): 382.

11 Nicholas H. Wolfinger and W. Bradford Wilcox, "Happily Ever After? Religion, Marital Status, Gender and Relationship Quality in Urban Families," *Social Forces* 86, no. 3 (2008): 1312, cite relevant studies. An additional list is found in Margaret R. Wilson and Erik E. Filsinger, "Religiosity and Marital Adjustment: Multidimensional Interrelationships," *Journal of Marriage and Family* 48, no. 1 (1986): 147. Increase in marital

quality from religious faith was also in the findings of Wilcox and Nock, "What's Love Got to Do with It?," 1325, 1339, 1342.

12 Greeley, *Faithful Attraction*, 126.

13 Ibid., 85.

14 Ibid., 190.

15 Ibid., 67. Greeley specifically details the powerful role of prayer on pages 118–19, 189–90. Prayer, he notes, is a much more powerful predictor of marital satisfaction than even frequency of sexual intercourse. Even Pennsylvania State University sociology researcher Alan Booth and his colleagues, whose particular marriage study produced the unusual result of no correlation between low divorce and religious identification, acknowledge that a perceived achievement in "covenant connection with the Divine," in what they called "fundamentalist religion," might indeed bring about higher marriage quality and account for the large number of studies that do find an impact: Alan Booth, David R. Johnson, Ann Branaman, and Alan Sica, "Belief and Behavior: Does Religion Matter in Today's Marriage?," *Journal of Marriage and Family* 57, no. 3 (1995): 661–71.

16 Wilcox, *Soft Patriarchs, New Men*, 206.

17 Wilson and Filsinger attempt to clarify the connection between religious faith and good marriage by examining four measures in 190 couples: (1) degree of couple agreement about important issues and tasks; (2) frequency of quarreling, kissing, and confiding; (3) frequency of sharing ideas and working together; and (4) expression of affection and sex. The first three of these measures articulate emotional intimacy. The researchers find that things like attending and supporting a Christian church, experiencing repentance and forgiveness, and believing strongly in God associate strongly with these first three dimensions in the husbands ("Religiosity and Marital Adjustment," 147–48, 149–50).

18 Bartkowski, *Remaking the Godly Marriage*, 5; Gallagher, *Evangelical Identity and Gendered Family Life*, 46. While Bartkowski (e.g., pp. 43, 57) and Gallagher (e.g., pp. 40–46) attempt to be sensitive to egalitarian evangelicals as a "burgeoning" competing force, the force remains, as Christian Smith says, a "fairly small minority" (*Christian America?*, 171). In Gallagher and Smith's joint study, only 5 percent of evangelical respondents espoused an ideal of solely mutual submission ("Symbolic Traditionalism and Pragmatic Egalitarianism," 227).

19 "Gender role traditionalism" in the Wilcox and Dew study means believing that "families suffer when a wife works full time, the husband's job is to provide and the wife's job is to look after the family, it's best if the man works and the wife stays at home, childcare is primarily the wife's responsibility, and women are better at childcare than men 'by nature'" ("Is Love a Flimsy Foundation?," 693). This does not line up with biblical teaching but overlaps it.

20 Wilcox, *Soft Patriarchs, New Men*, 57. Wilcox's landmark study proceeds to examine practices in three domains: (1) household labor; (2) parenting; and (3) "emotion work," that is, husbands attending to the needs of wives. He unfortunately does not investigate the practice of husbandly authority in detail because the data from which he worked, the General Social Survey (GSS) and the National Survey of Families and Households (NSFH), did not include questions of headship (95). Survey evidence from as recently as the 1990s shows that the former, labor-oriented views constitute the beliefs of a majority of conservative Christians (as well as a significant minority of mainline churchgoers) (83–84). Among those actively involved in their churches, the percentage holding to labor-distinction goes up even higher (194).

21 Ibid., 95.

22 The cultural shift is documented in Denton, "Gender and Marital Decision Making," 1154. For one example (among many), in 1977, 76 percent of Americans believed that it was better for the man to work outside the home and for the woman to focus on the care of the home and family. By 1993, only 37 percent did (Wilcox, *Soft Patriarchs, New Men*, 4).

23 Note 9 of chapter 9 above explains why some researchers' contrary impression is not accurate. Some hold that conservative Protestantism is more ambivalent over gender distinction than its biblically focused discourse would lead one to expect, but those researchers are missing the way these Christians are living out gender.

24 Paul's quotation does not follow the Septuagint, like the Gospel quotation of the Genesis verse does in Mark 10:7.

25 Jacqueline N. Cohen, E. Sandra Byers, and Lindsay P. Walsh, "Factors Influencing the Sexual Relationships of Lesbians and Gay Men," *International Journal of Sexual Health* 20, no. 3 (2008): 163–64, 172.

26 Tyrel J. Starks, Brenda O. Gilbert, Ann R. Fischer, Rebecca Weston, and David L. DiLalla, "Gendered Sexuality: A New Model and Measure of Attraction and Intimacy," *Journal of Homosexuality* 56, no. 1 (2009): 14. For example, Philip Colgan reports on problems that gay men have with achieving intimacy. He also attributes these to the people around them not accepting or affirming the gay men's sexuality. Philip Colgan, "Treatment of Identity and Intimacy Issues in Gay Males," *Journal of Homosexuality* 14, no. 3/4 (1987): 115. On the other hand, Cohen, Byers, and Walsh assert that committed same-sex relationships provide intimacy ("Factors Influencing the Sexual Relationships of Lesbians and Gay Men," 162). And some longitudinal studies purport *greater* intimacy in monogendered couples: see Kimberly F. Balsam, Theodore P. Beauchaine, Esther D. Rothblum, and Sondra E. Solomon, "Three-Year Follow-up of Same-Sex Couples Who Had Civil Unions in Vermont, Same-Sex Couples Not in Civil Unions, and Heterosexual Married Couples," *Developmental Psychology* 44, no. 1 (2008): 102, 113; Lawrence A.

Kurdek, "Are Gay and Lesbian Cohabiting Couples Really Different from Heterosexual Married Couples?," *Journal of Marriage and Family* 66, no. 4 (2004): 880; and Lawrence A. Kurdek, "Change in Relationship Quality for Partners from Lesbian, Gay Male, and Heterosexual Couples," *Journal of Family Psychology* 22, no. 5 (2008): 701. Yet these studies come with some significant caveats. Starks et al. are right to be cautious. As Balsam et al. put it, "In contrast to the enormous literature on heterosexual marriage, there has been far less research on same-sex relationships" ("Three-Year Follow-up of Same-Sex Couples," 103).

Chapter 15: Deeper Still: Dynamics of Intergendered Intimacy

1 Cindy Hazan and Phillip R. Shaver, "Deeper into Attachment Theory," *Psychological Inquiry* 5, no. 1 (1994): 76–77.

2 Valerian J. Derlega and Alan L. Chaikin, *Sharing Intimacy: What We Reveal to Others and Why* (Englewood Cliffs, NJ: Prentice-Hall, 1975).

3 Howard J. Clinebell Jr. and Charlotte H. Clinebell, *The Intimate Marriage* (New York: Harper & Row, 1970), 66, 68, 83.

4 First explored in John Bowlby and Institute of Psycho-Analysis (Great Britain), *Attachment and Loss*, 3 vols., International Psycho-Analytical Library, 79, 95, 109 (London: Hogarth P.; Institute of Psycho-Analysis, 1969–80), written in the wake of Bowlby's dissatisfaction with psychoanalysis in explaining the behavior of institutionalized children.

5 Cindy Hazan and Phillip R. Shaver, "Romantic Love Conceptualized as an Attachment Process," *Journal of Personality and Social Psychology* 52, no. 3 (1987): 511.

6 Cindy Hazan and Phillip R. Shaver, "Attachment as an Organizational Framework for Research on Close Relationships," *Psychological Inquiry* 5, no. 1 (1994): 7; Hazan and Shaver, "Deeper into Attachment Theory," 70–71.

7 Hazan and Shaver, "Attachment as an Organizational Framework for Research on Close Relationships," 9, 17. "Secure lovers described their most important love experience as . . . trusting" (Hazan and Shaver, "Romantic Love Conceptualized as an Attachment Process," 514–15).

8 For example, Archibald D. Hart and Sharon Hart Morris, *Safe Haven Marriage: Building a Relationship You Want to Come Home To* (Nashville: W Publishing Group, 2003), xi, 87. The goal of the couples' therapy itself is to create safety, says Susan Johnson in "Contribution of Emotionally Focused Couples Therapy," 48, 49. Johnson also uses the term "safe haven" on page 51.

9 Hart and Hart Morris, *Safe Haven Marriage*, 61. They also include emotional availability and sensitive responsiveness as predictors, but trust remains supreme.

10 Graham Spanier, "Measuring Dyadic Adjustment: New Scales for Assessing the Quality of Marriage and Similar Dyads," *Journal of Marriage*

and Family 38, no. 1 (1976): 15. Spanier was recently indicted for conspiracy and resigned as president of Pennsylvania State University, but long before this he worked as a family sociologist, founded the *Journal of Family Issues*, and published widely.

11 Wilson and Filsinger, "Religiosity and Marital Adjustment," 147–48.

12 Spanier speaks of hundreds of studies using the scale in Graham B. Spanier and Linda Thompson, "A Confirmatory Analysis of the Dyadic Adjustment Scale," *Journal of Marriage and Family* 44, no. 3 (1982): 731. He also gives a helpful overview of the scale there.

13 Colgan, "Treatment of Identity and Intimacy Issues in Gay Males," 101.

14 Cohen, Byers, and Walsh, "Factors Influencing the Sexual Relationships of Lesbians and Gay Men," 163.

15 Schaefer and Olson, "Assessing Intimacy," 50–51.

16 Worthington, *Hope-Focused Marriage Counseling*, 68.

17 Johnson and Greenman, "Path to a Secure Bond," 599.

18 Greeley, *Faithful Attraction*, 119.

19 Dependence is tricky. One must discriminate between unhealthy dependence, termed "codependence" in older literature, and the healthy interdependence of married life. But I do not see a harmful dependence in extreme expressions of grief at the thought of spousal loss. Interview answers did not necessarily reflect what one would actually do if a wife were suddenly gone, but how much the men thought it would hurt to be without their wives. That is a measure of intimacy.

20 Yarhouse et al., "Characteristics of Mixed Orientation Couples," 48–49.

Chapter 16: Sex: Respecting the Platform of Distinction

1 Earlier twin-SSA studies were biased in their sampling, but twin registries have allowed a much more uniform selection of data. Such studies began in Australia in 1991. A large U.S. study was then conducted in 1997: Scott L. Hershberger, "A Twin Registry Study of Male and Female Sexual Orientation," *Journal of Sex Research* 34, no. 2 (1997): 212–22. Then Australia and the United States conducted more twin studies in 2000: J. Michael Bailey, Michael P. Dunne, and Nicholas G. Martin, "Genetic and Environmental Influences on Sexual Orientation and Its Correlates in an Australian Twin Sample," *Journal of Personality and Social Psychology* 78, no. 3 (2000): 524–36; Kenneth S. Kendler, Laura M. Thornton, Stephen E. Gilman, and Ronald C. Kessler, "Sexual Orientation in a U.S. National Sample of Twin and Nontwin Sibling Pairs," *American Journal of Psychiatry* 157, no. 11 (2000): 1843–46. These were followed by several studies in Scandinavia, the largest being the Swedish study described in the text: Niklas Långström, Qazi Rahman, Eva Carlström, and Paul Lichtenstein, "Genetic and Environmental Effects on Same-sex Sexual Behavior: A Population Study of Twins in

Sweden," *Archives of Sexual Behavior* 39, no. 1 (2010): 75–80. Lichtenstein is a psychiatrist at the Karolinska Institutet in Stockholm. All 43,808 twins born in Sweden between 1959 and 1985 were invited to participate in a Web-based survey that comprised a wide range of questions about personal behaviors and experiences. A gigantic European twin register with a projected 600,000 members is being organized, so we can expect further studies along these lines.

2 Långström et al., "Genetic and Environmental Effects on Same-sex Sexual Behavior," 76.

3 Ibid., 77.

4 Stanton L. Jones and Mark A. Yarhouse, *Ex-Gays? A Longitudinal Study of Religiously Mediated Change in Sexual Orientation* (Downers Grove, IL: IVP Academic, 2007), 78, 94. Several dozen studies on change in orientation were published in the 1950s through 1970s, but serious research disappeared when the *DSM* (this time, I do mean: *Diagnostic and Statistical Manual*) removed homosexuality as a disorder from its pages in 1973. In the last ten years, there has been a resurgence of such studies, with more rigorous standards and similar results.

5 Ibid., 283. "Positive Change" meant a lessening of SSA. "Contented abstinence" meant SSA became either missing or present only incidentally and in a way that did not bring about stress. A heterosexual relationship was possible along with a lack of compulsion to act on SSA. "Conversion" meant substantial conversion to heterosexual attraction such that homosexual attraction was either missing or present only incidentally and in a way that did not bring about stress. The subject experienced either a successful heterosexual sex life or satisfactory heterosexual attraction in a dating relationship (not acted on due to moral constraints).

6 Ibid., 283–84, 403.

7 Pepper Schwartz, *Love between Equals: How Peer Marriage Really Works* (New York: Free Press, 1995), 78.

8 Again, as cited in chapter 5, Scriptures prohibiting homosexuality are Leviticus 18:22 and 20:13 flowing from Exodus 20:14; Jude 6–8 flowing from Judges 19:22–25, itself flowing from Genesis 19:1–13; Romans 1:26–27; 1 Corinthians 6:9–10 and 1 Timothy 1:10–11.

9 Genesis 19:1. Lot's presence "sitting in the gate," the place where elders and officials sat to adjudicate legal matters and govern the community, suggests that he had become more Sodom than the Sodomites. He had entered in to such an extent that he had become part of it. Hence Lot's willingness to see his daughters violated (v. 8) and his hesitation in leaving the city (vv. 15–16). He couldn't seem to believe there was life outside of his city. He could no longer remove himself from his culture.

10 Genesis 19:30–36. Later on, the behavior of Lot's two daughters demonstrate that they too adapted the depraved cultural norms.

11 Isaiah 3:12 levels the criticism that "women rule over" the people. It is either an expression of the men's failure to rule, or a feature of judgment on the community when, within His people, women rule them. Not that women cannot be in charge in a culture, but the family of God relationships have soured if the women need to lead the charge with God's people. Things are awry.

12 Kornrich, Brines, and Leupp, "Egalitarianism, Housework, and Sexual Frequency in Marriage," 30, 42–43.

13 Ibid., 27.

14 Ibid., 27, 28.

15 A recent example is this finding: "Lesbians reported less frequent sexual activity than married heterosexual women." E. Sondra Solomon, Esther D. Rothblum, and Kimberly Balsam, "Money, Housework, Sex, and Conflict: Same-Sex Couples in Civil Unions, Those Not in Civil Unions, and Heterosexual Married Siblings," *Sex Roles* 52, no. 9/10 (2005): 561, 568. Solomon and her colleagues studied siblings, some involved in intergendered relationships and some involved in monogendered ones, to control for sociological factors in their comparison.

16 Schwartz, *Love between Equals*, 71.

17 Ibid., 85.

Chapter 17: Continuum of Closeness: When Gender Does and Doesn't Matter

1 Consider the use of the word οἰκεῖος (*oikeios*) in 1 Timothy 5:8, about providing for relatives, *especially* for members of one's own "family."

2 Bruce, *Acts of the Apostles*, 249.

3 The "leading women" of Thessalonica (Act 17:4) were probably so named because they were recognized as benefactors. With fewer activities open to women in the ancient world, many of the upper class would take up the role of financial donor to worthy causes (consider the appellation again for the Berean women in Acts 17:12). One imagines that these women, upon their conversion under Paul's preaching, became his benefactors as well.

4 Anthony F. Bogaert, "Biological versus Nonbiological Older Brothers and Men's Sexual Orientation," *Proceedings of the National Academy of Sciences* 103, no. 28 (2006): 10771.

5 E.g., in the foremost epistle of church unity, consider the "sons" of Ephesians 1:5, the "beloved children" of Ephesians 5:1 and the "brothers" of the "Father" of Ephesians 6:23.

6 Hill, *Washed and Waiting*, 111.

7 Roberts, *Creation and Covenant*, 227.

8 Consider the purity, strange to us, of Paul's brotherly relationship to the church as the bridegroom's friend, getting her ready for Christ, the Bridegroom, in 2 Corinthians 11:2.

9 Hill, *Washed and Waiting*, 108.

Chapter 18: The Immense Invitation

1 There really are only two choices of meaning. When people in the Bible, or in Greek literature for that matter, get frightened or terrified or have to run away, φοβέω (*phobeō*) is the word used. Since Paul's sentence is a command, we can rule out this meaning: Paul does not want wives to be terrified of their husbands. The other meaning is a deep reverence.

2 The Greek verb φοβέω (*phobeō*) is used in the Septuagint to translate the Hebrew verb יָרֵא (*yare'*), as it does in Leviticus 19:3. The noun form φόβος (*phobos*) is used a couple times of the respect due masters by servants (1 Peter 2:18; Eph. 6:5), but this is unusual. The noun form, as well as the verb, when being used for reverence rather than being afraid, is otherwise only applied to God (e.g., 1 Peter 2:17: "Honor everyone. Love the brotherhood. Fear God. Honor the emperor."). Peter applies the noun form once to a wife's behavior toward her husband as well (1 Peter 3:2).

3 Warren Austin Gage, *The Gospel of Genesis: Studies in Protology and Eschatology* (Winona Lake, IN: Carpenter Books, 1984), 90.

4 Sinclair Ferguson, "The Church and the Sacraments" (class lecture, Reformed Theological Seminary, Orlando, FL, January 1999).

5 Eric Klinenberg, *Going Solo: The Extraordinary Rise and Surprising Appeal of Living Alone* (New York: Penguin Press, 2012), 1–3.

6 In addition to Klinenberg's book, a typical article is Dominique Browning, "Alone Again, Naturally," *New York Times*, January 5, 2012, http://www.nytimes.com/2012/01/08/fashion/why-men-cant-stand-to -be-alone-after-a-breakup-or-a-divorce.html. Another is Eric Klinenberg, "One's a Crowd," *New York Times*, February 4, 2012, http://www.nytimes.com/ 2012/02/05/opinion/sunday/living-alone-means-being-social.html.

7 Klinenberg, *Going Solo*, 14.

Appendix 2: The Structure of Judges: We Need a King

1 To identify this chiasm, I have drawn on and added to the work of several rhetorical critics, most notably, D. W. Gooding, "The Composition of the Book of Judges," in *Eretz-Israel, Archeological Historical and Geographical Studies, vol. 16: Harry M. Orlinsky Memorial Volume*, ed. B. A. Levine and A. Malamat (Jerusalem: Israel Exploration Society, 1982): 70–79; Bruce K. Waltke and Charles Yu, *An Old Testament Theology: An Exegetical, Canonical, and Thematic Approach* (Grand Rapids: Zondervan, 2007), 592–93; Barry G. Webb, *The Book of Judges: An Integrated Reading*, Journal for the Study of the Old Testament: Supplement Series 46 (Sheffield: Sheffield Academic Press, 1987). For the Introduction/Epilogue pairs, K. Lawson Younger, *Judges and Ruth*, NIV Application Commentary (Grand Rapids: Zondervan, 2002), 30–33, was also helpful.

Works Cited

Abend, Lisa. "In Sweden, Boys Won't Be Boys." *Time*, December 16, 2013. http://content.time.com/time/magazine/article/0,9171,2159265,00.html.

Achilles Tatius. *Achilles Tatius*. Translated by S. Gaselee. Loeb Classical Library 45. New York: G. P. Putnam's Sons, 1917.

Allen, Amy. "'Mommy Wars' Redux: A False Conflict." The Stone, *New York Times*, May 27, 2012. http://opinionator.blogs.nytimes.com/2012/05/27/the-mommy-wars-redux-a-false-conflict/?_php=true&_type=blogs&_r=0.

Amato, Paul R., David R. Johnson, Alan Booth, and Stacy J. Rogers. "Continuity and Change in Marital Quality between 1980 and 2000." *Journal of Marriage and Family* 65, no. 1 (2003): 1–22.

Andreades, Samuel A. "Does She Matter? Emotional Intimacy in Marriage in Light of Gender Distinction." D.Min. thesis, Qualitative Research Report, Covenant Theological Seminary, 2013.

Aristotle. *The Complete Works of Aristotle: The Revised Oxford Translation*. Edited by Jonathan Barnes. 2 vols. Bollingen Series 72:2. Princeton, NJ: Princeton University Press, 1984–95.

Bailey, J. Michael, Michael P. Dunne, and Nicholas G. Martin. "Genetic and Environmental Influences on Sexual Orientation and Its Correlates in an Australian Twin Sample." *Journal of Personality and Social Psychology* 78, no. 3 (2000): 524–36.

Balsam, Kimberly F., Theodore P. Beauchaine, Esther D. Rothblum, and Sondra E. Solomon. "Three-Year Follow-up of Same-Sex Couples Who Had Civil Unions in Vermont, Same-Sex Couples Not in Civil Unions, and Heterosexual Married Couples." *Developmental Psychology* 44, no. 1 (2008): 102–16.

Barrs, Jerram. *Through His Eyes: God's Perspective on Women in the Bible*. Wheaton: Crossway Books, 2009.

Barth, Karl, *Church Dogmatics*. Edited by G. W. Bromiley and T. F. Torrance. Translated by G. W. Bromiley. 4 vols. 2nd ed. Edinburgh: T&T Clark, 1955–75.

Bartkowski, John P. *Remaking the Godly Marriage: Gender Negotiation in Evangelical Families*. New Brunswick, NJ: Rutgers University Press, 2001.

Works Cited

Bauckham, Richard. *Jesus and the Eyewitnesses: The Gospels as Eyewitness Testimony*. Grand Rapids: Eerdmans, 2006.

Bennett, William J. *The Index of Leading Cultural Indicators: Facts and Figures on the State of American Society*. New York: Simon & Schuster, 1994.

Block, Daniel Isaac. *Judges, Ruth*. New American Commentary. Nashville: Broadman & Holman, 1999.

Blow, Charles M. "Real Men and Pink Suits." *New York Times*, February 10, 2012. http://www.nytimes.com/2012/02/11/opinion/blow-real-men -and-pink-suits.html.

Bock, Darrell L. *Luke*. 2 vols. Baker Exegetical Commentary on the New Testament. Grand Rapids: Baker, 1994.

Bogaert, Anthony F. "Biological versus Nonbiological Older Brothers and Men's Sexual Orientation." *Proceedings of the National Academy of Sciences* 103, no. 28 (2006): 10771–74.

Booth, Alan, David R. Johnson, Ann Branaman, and Alan Sica. "Belief and Behavior: Does Religion Matter in Today's Marriage?" *Journal of Marriage and Family* 57, no. 3 (1995): 661–71.

Bowlby, John, and Institute of Psycho-Analysis (Great Britain). *Attachment and Loss*. 3 vols. International Psycho-Analytical Library 79, 95, 109. London: Hogarth P.; Institute of Psycho-Analysis, 1969–80.

Brody, Leslie. *Gender, Emotion, and the Family*. Cambridge: Harvard University Press, 1999.

Brody, Leslie R., and Judith A. Hall. "Gender and Emotion in Context," In *Handbook of Emotions*, edited by Michael Lewis, Jeannette M. Haviland-Jones, and Lisa Feldman Barrett, 395–408. 3rd ed. New York: Guilford Press, 2008.

Brooten, Bernadette J. *Women Leaders in the Ancient Synagogue*. Brown Judaic Studies 36. Chico, CA: Scholars Press, 1982.

Browning, Dominique. "Alone Again, Naturally." *New York Times*, January 5, 2012. http://www.nytimes.com/2012/01/08/fashion/why-men-cant -stand-to-be-alone-after-a-breakup-or-a-divorce.html.

Bruce, F. F. *The Acts of the Apostles: The Greek Text with Introduction and Commentary*. 3rd rev. and enl. ed. Grand Rapids: Eerdmans, 1990. First published 1951.

Brunner, Emil. *Dogmatics*. Translated by Olive Wyon. 3 vols. Philadelphia: Westminster, 1950–79.

Bumpass, Larry L., and James A. Sweet. *Cohabitation, Marriage and Union Stability: Preliminary Findings from NSFH2*. Madison: University of Wisconsin, Center for Demography and Ecology, 1995.

Buxton, Amity Pierce. "Writing Our Own Script: How Bisexual Men and Their Heterosexual Wives Maintain Their Marriages after Disclosure." *Journal of Bisexuality* 1, nos. 2–3 (2001): 155–89.

Call, Vaughn R. A., and Tim B. Heaton. "Religious Influence on Marital Stability." *Journal for the Scientific Study of Religion* 36, no. 3 (1997): 382–92.

Calvin, John. *Commentaries on the Four Last Books of Moses, Arranged in the Form of a Harmony.* Translated by Charles William Bingham. 45 vols. in 22 vols. Calvin's Commentaries. Grand Rapids: Baker, 1981. Reprint. Originally published 1563. Translation first printed 1852 for the Calvin Translation Society, Edinburgh, Scotland.

Caplan, Paula J., Mary Crawford, Janet Shibley Hyde, and John T. E. Richardson, eds. *Gender Differences in Human Cognition.* Counterpoints. New York: Oxford University Press, 1997.

Clement. *The Epistles of Clement* (Complete Text), edited by Allan Menzies. In vol. 9 of *The Ante-Nicene Fathers. Translations of the Writings of the Fathers Down to A.D. 325*, edited by Alexander Roberts, James Donaldson, and A. Cleveland Coxe. 10 vols. Buffalo: Christian Literature Publishing Company, 1885–96.

Clinebell, Howard J., Jr., and Charlotte H. Clinebell. *The Intimate Marriage.* New York: Harper & Row, 1970.

Cohen, Jacqueline N., E. Sandra Byers, and Lindsay P. Walsh. "Factors Influencing the Sexual Relationships of Lesbians and Gay Men." *International Journal of Sexual Health* 20, no. 3 (2008): 162–76.

Colgan, Philip. "Treatment of Identity and Intimacy Issues in Gay Males." *Journal of Homosexuality* 14, nos. 3/4 (1987): 101–23.

Collins, C. John. *Genesis 1–4: A Linguistic, Literary, and Theological Commentary.* Phillipsburg, NJ: P&R Publishing, 2006.

———. *Did Adam and Eve Really Exist? Who They Were and Why You Should Care.* Wheaton: Crossway, 2011.

Coontz, Stephanie. *Marriage, a History: From Obedience to Intimacy or How Love Conquered Marriage.* New York: Viking, 2005.

DeMaris, Alfred, and Monica A. Longmore. "Ideology, Power, and Equity: Testing Competing Explanations for the Perception of Fairness in Household Labor." *Social Forces* 74, no. 3 (1996): 1043–71.

Denton, Melinda Lundquist. "Gender and Marital Decision Making: Negotiating Religious Ideology and Practice." *Social Forces* 82, no. 3 (2004): 1151–80.

Derlega, Valerian J., and Alan L. Chaikin. *Sharing Intimacy: What We Reveal to Others and Why.* Englewood Cliffs, NJ: Prentice-Hall, 1975.

Diamant, Anita. *The Red Tent*. New York: A Wyatt Book for St. Martin's Press, 1997.

Dindia, Kathryn. "Men are From North Dakota, Women are From South Dakota." In *Sex Differences and Similarities in Communication*, edited by Kathryn Dindia and Daniel J. Canary, 3–18. 2nd ed. Lea's Communication Series. Mahwah, NJ: Lawrence Erlbaum Associates, 2006.

Dindia, Kathryn, and Daniel J. Canary. *Sex Differences and Similarities in Communication*. 2nd ed. Lea's Communication Series. Mahwah, NJ: Lawrence Erlbaum Associates, 2006.

Donges, Uta-Susan, Anette Kersting, and Thomas Suslow. "Women's Greater Ability to Perceive Happy Facial Emotion Automatically: Gender Differences in Affective Priming." *PLoS ONE* 7, no. 7 (2012): 1–5. doi: 10.1371/journal.pone.0041745.

Doriani, Daniel. "A History of the Interpretation of 1 Timothy 2." In *Women in the Church: A Fresh Analysis of 1 Timothy 2:9–15*, edited by Andreas J. Köstenberger, Thomas R. Schreiner, and H. Scott Baldwin, 213–67 (app. 1). Grand Rapids: Baker, 1995.

Dowd, Maureen. "We Offer More Than Ankles, Gentlemen." *New York Times*, January 12, 2013. http://www.nytimes.com/2013/01/13/opinion/sunday/dowd-we-offer-more-than-ankles-gentlemen.html.

Ellicott, Charles J. *The Pastoral Epistles of St. Paul*. Rev. 3rd ed. London: Longman, 1864.

Elliot, Elisabeth. *The Mark of a Man: Following Christ's Example of Masculinity*. New pbk. ed. Grand Rapids: Revell, 2006.

Fee, Gordon D. *The First Epistle to the Corinthians*. New International Commentary on the New Testament. Grand Rapids: Eerdmans, 1987.

Feldhahn, Shaunti Christine. *For Women Only: What You Need to Know About the Inner Lives of Men*. Sisters, OR: Multnomah, 2004.

Ferguson, Sinclair. "The Church and the Sacraments." Class lecture. *Reformed Theological Seminary*. Orlando, FL. January 1999.

Freedman, David Noel, ed.. *The Anchor Bible Dictionary*. 6 vols. New York: Doubleday, 1992.

Field, Frederick. *Notes on the Translation of the New Testament*. London: Cambridge University Press, 1899.

Gage, Warren Austin. *The Gospel of Genesis: Studies in Protology and Eschatology*. Winona Lake, IN: Carpenter Books, 1984.

Gallagher, Sally K. *Evangelical Identity and Gendered Family Life*. New Brunswick, NJ: Rutgers University Press, 2003.

Gallagher, Sally K., and Christian Smith. "Symbolic Traditionalism and Pragmatic Egalitarianism: Contemporary Evangelicals, Families, and Gender." *Gender and Society* 13, no. 2 (1999): 211–33.

Gooding, D. W. "The Composition of the Book of Judges." In *Eretz-Israel, Archeological Historical and Geographical Studies, Vol. 16: Harry M. Orlinsky Memorial Volume*, 70–79. Edited by B. A. Levine and A. Malamat. (Jerusalem: Israel Exploration Society, 1982).

Gottman, John Mordechai. *What Predicts Divorce? The Relationship between Marital Processes and Marital Outcomes*. Hillsdale, NJ: Lawrence Erlbaum Associates, 1994.

Gottman, John M., and Nan Silver. *The Seven Principles for Making Marriage Work*. New York: Crown Publishers, 1999.

Greeley, Andrew M. *Faithful Attraction: Discovering Intimacy, Love, and Fidelity in American Marriage*. New York: Tor, distributed by St. Martin's Press, 1991.

Grudem, Wayne, ed. *Biblical Foundations for Manhood and Womanhood*. Wheaton: Crossway Books, 2002.

Hall, Judith A., and Marianne Schmid Mast. "Are Women Always More Interpersonally Sensitive Than Men? Impact of Goals and Content Domain." *Personality and Social Psychology Bulletin* 34, no. 1 (2008): 144–55.

Hallett, Judith P. "Women's Lives in the Ancient Mediterranean." In *Women and Christian Origins*, edited by Ross Shepard Kraemer and Mary Rose D'Angelo, 13–34. New York: Oxford University Press, 1999.

Hart, Archibald D., and Sharon Hart Morris. *Safe Haven Marriage: Building a Relationship You Want to Come Home To*. Nashville: W Publishing Group, 2003.

Hazan, Cindy, and Phillip R. Shaver. "Romantic Love Conceptualized as an Attachment Process." *Journal of Personality and Social Psychology* 52, no. 3 (1987): 511–24.

———. "Attachment as an Organizational Framework for Research on Close Relationships." *Psychological Inquiry* 5, no. 1 (1994): 1–22.

———. "Deeper into Attachment Theory." *Psychological Inquiry* 5, no. 1 (1994): 68–79.

Herodotus. *The Landmark Herodotus: The Histories*. Edited by Robert B. Strassler. Translated by Andrea L. Purvis. New York: Pantheon Books, 2007.

Hershberger, Scott L. "A Twin Registry Study of Male and Female Sexual Orientation." *Journal of Sex Research* 34, no. 2 (1997): 212–22.

Hezser, Catherine, ed. *The Oxford Handbook of Jewish Daily Life in Roman Palestine*. New York: Oxford University Press, 2010.

Hibbard, Judith H., and Clyde R. Pope. "The Quality of Social Roles as Predictors of Morbidity and Mortality." *Social Science and Medicine* 36, no. 3 (1993): 217–25.

Hill, Wesley. *Washed and Waiting: Reflections on Christian Faithfulness and Homosexuality*. Grand Rapids: Zondervan, 2010.

Hurley, James B. *Man and Woman in Biblical Perspective*. Grand Rapids: Zondervan, 1981.

Hyde, Janet Shibley. "Epilogue." In *Sex Differences and Similarities in Communication*, edited by Kathryn Dindia and Daniel J. Canary, 393–97. 2nd ed. Lea's Communication Series. Mahwah, NJ: Lawrence Erlbaum Associates, 2006.

Hyde, Janet Shibley, and Nita M. McKinley. "Gender Differences in Cognition: Results from Meta-Analyses." In *Gender Differences in Human Cognition*, edited by Paula J. Caplan, Mary Crawford, Janet Shibley Hyde, and John T. E. Richardson, 30–51. Counterpoints. New York: Oxford University Press, 1997.

Ickes, William, and Marilyn Turner. "On the Social Advantages of Having an Older, Opposite-Sex Sibling: Birth Order Influences in Mixed-Sex Dyads." *Journal of Personality and Social Psychology* 45, no. 1 (1983): 210–22.

Ilan, Tal. "Gender Issues and Daily Life." In *The Oxford Handbook of Jewish Daily Life in Roman Palestine*, edited by Catherine Hezser, 48–68. New York: Oxford University Press, 2010.

Jewett, Paul King. *Man as Male and Female: A Study in Sexual Relationships from a Theological Point of View*. Grand Rapids: Eerdmans, 1975.

Johnson, Susan M. "The Contribution of Emotionally Focused Couples Therapy." *Journal of Contemporary Psychotherapy* 37, no. 1 (2007): 47–52.

Johnson, Susan M., and Leslie S. Greenberg. "Emotionally Focused Marital Therapy: An Overview." *Psychotherapy* 24, no. 3S (1987): 552–60.

Johnson, Susan M., and Paul S. Greenman. "The Path to a Secure Bond: Emotionally Focused Couple Therapy." *Journal of Clinical Psychology* 62, no. 5 (2006): 597–609.

Johnson, Susan M., and Andrea K. Wittenborn. "New Research Findings on Emotionally Focused Therapy: Introduction to Special Section." *Journal of Marital and Family Therapy* 38, no. supp. 1 (2012): 18–22.

Jones, Stanton L., and Mark A. Yarhouse. *Ex-Gays? A Longitudinal Study of Religiously Mediated Change in Sexual Orientation*. Downers Grove, IL: IVP Academic, 2007.

Josephus, Flavius. *The Life. Against Apion*. Translated by H. St. J. Thackeray. Vol. 1 (LCL 186) of *Josephus*. Translated by H. St. J. Thackeray et al. 10 vols. Loeb Classical Library. Cambridge: Harvard University Press, 1926–65.

Josephus, Flavius, *The Jewish War*. Rev. ed. Translated by G. A. Williamson. Revised by E. Mary Smallwood. Penguin Classics. New York: Penguin, 1981.

Kendler, Kenneth S., Laura M. Thornton, Stephen E. Gilman, and Ronald C. Kessler. "Sexual Orientation in a U.S. National Sample of Twin and Nontwin Sibling Pairs." *American Journal of Psychiatry* 157, no. 11 (2000): 1843–46.

Klinenberg, Eric. *Going Solo: The Extraordinary Rise and Surprising Appeal of Living Alone*. New York: Penguin Press, 2012.

———. "One's a Crowd." *New York Times*, February 4, 2012. http://www.nytimes.com/2012/02/05/opinion/sunday/living-alone-means-being-social.html.

The Koran. Translated by N. J. Dawood. 50th anniversary ed. Based on the 5th ed. with revisions and additional notes. Penguin Classics. London; New York: Penguin Books, 2006.

Kornrich, Sabino, Julie Brines, and Katrina Leupp. "Egalitarianism, Housework, and Sexual Frequency in Marriage." *American Sociological Review* 78, no. 1 (2013): 26–50.

Köstenberger, Andreas J., Thomas R. Schreiner, and H. Scott Baldwin., eds. *Women in the Church: A Fresh Analysis of 1 Timothy 2:9–15*. Grand Rapids: Baker, 1995.

Kraemer, Ross S. "Jewish Women and Christian Origins: Some Caveats." In *Women and Christian Origins*, edited by Ross Shepard Kraemer and Mary Rose D'Angelo, 35–49. New York: Oxford University Press, 1999.

———. "Jewish Women and Women's Judaism(s) at the Beginning of Christianity." In *Women and Christian Origins*, edited by Ross Shepard Kraemer and Mary Rose D'Angelo, 50–79. New York: Oxford University Press, 1999.

Kraemer, Ross Shepard, and Mary Rose D'Angelo, eds. *Women and Christian Origins*. New York: Oxford University Press, 1999.

Kurdek, Lawrence A. "Are Gay and Lesbian Cohabiting Couples Really Different from Heterosexual Married Couples?" *Journal of Marriage and Family* 66, no. 4 (2004): 880–900.

———. "Change in Relationship Quality for Partners from Lesbian, Gay Male, and Heterosexual Couples." *Journal of Family Psychology* 22, no. 5 (2008): 701–11.

Langberg, Diane. *On the Threshold of Hope: Opening the Door to Hope and Healing for Survivors of Sexual Abuse*. Wheaton: Tyndale House, 1999.

Långström, Niklas, Qazi Rahman, Eva Carlström, and Paul Lichtenstein. "Genetic and Environmental Effects on Same-sex Sexual Behavior:

A Population Study of Twins in Sweden." *Archives of Sexual Behavior* 39, no. 1 (2010): 75–80.

Laqueur, Thomas Walter. *Making Sex: Body and Gender from the Greeks to Freud*. Cambridge: Harvard University Press, 1990.

Lewis, C. S. *Perelandra: A Novel*. London: John Lane, 1943.

Lewis, Michael, Jeannette M. Haviland-Jones, and Lisa Feldman Barrett, eds. *Handbook of Emotions*. 3rd ed. New York: Guilford Press, 2008.

Lipman, Joanne. "The Mismeasure of Woman." *New York Times*, October 23, 2009, 1. http://www.nytimes.com/2009/10/24/opinion/24lipman.html.

Longman, Tremper, and Daniel G. Reid. *God Is a Warrior*. Studies in Old Testament Biblical Theology. Grand Rapids: Zondervan, 1995.

Lorber, Judith, and Susan A. Farrell, eds. "The Social Construction of Gender." Newbury Park, CA: Sage Publications, in cooperation with Sociologists for Women in Society, 1991.

Lucian of Samosata. *Lucian*. Translated by A. M. Harmon, K. Kilburn (vol. 6), and M. D. Macleod (vols. 7–8). 8 vols. Loeb Classical Library. New York: Macmillan; Cambridge: Harvard University Press, 1913–67.

MacMullen, R. "Women in Public in the Roman Empire." *Historia* 29, no. 2 (1980): 208–18.

Metzger, Bruce M., and United Bible Societies. *A Textual Commentary on the Greek New Testament; a Companion Volume to the United Bible Societies' Greek New Testament (2nd Ed.)*. London, New York: United Bible Societies, 1994.

Middleton, J. Richard. "The Liberating Image? Interpreting the Imago Dei in Context." *Christian Scholar's Review* 24, no. 1 (1994): 8–25.

———. *The Liberating Image: The Imago Dei in Genesis 1*. Grand Rapids: Brazos Press, 2005.

Miller, Henry. "The Universe of Death." In *The Cosmological Eye*, 107–34. Norfolk, CT: New Directions, 1939.

Mills, Michael. "How Can There Still Be a Sex Difference, Even When There Is No Sex Difference?" *PsychologyToday.com*, The How and Why of Sex Differences (January 26, 2011).

Milton, John. *Paradise Lost*. Edited by Merritt Y. Hughes. New York: Odyssey Press, 1935.

Morris, Leon. *The First Epistle of Paul to the Corinthians: An Introduction and Commentary*. The Tyndale New Testament Commentaries. Grand Rapids: Eerdmans, 1983.

Mounce, William D. *Pastoral Epistles*. Word Biblical Commentary 46. Nashville: Thomas Nelson, 2000.

Murphy-O'Connor, Jerome. *St. Paul's Corinth: Text and Archaeology*. 3rd rev. and expanded ed. Collegeville, MN: Liturgical Press, 2002. First published 1983.

O'Connell, Robert H. *The Rhetoric of the Book of Judges*, Supplements to Vetus Testamentum 63. Leiden: E. J. Brill, 1996.

Ovid. *The Love Books of Ovid Being the Amores, Ars Amatoria, Redmedia Amoris and Medicamina Faciei Femineae of Publius Ovidius Naso*. Translated by J. Lewis May. Whitefish, MT: Kessinger Publishing, 2005.

Pearcey, Nancy. *Total Truth: Liberating Christianity from Its Cultural Captivity*. Wheaton: Crossway Books, 2004.

Perry, Gregory R. "Phoebe, Paul and Other Διάκονοι [*Diakonoi*]: God's 'Go-Betweens' for a New Social Order." Unpublished article. Covenant Theological Seminary, Creve Coeur, MO, 2010.

Peterson, Jennifer L. "Gender Differences in Sexual Attitudes and Behaviors: A Review of Meta-Analytic Results and Large Datasets." *Journal of Sex Research* 48, nos. 2–3 (2011): 149 (17).

Peterson, Jennifer L., and Janet Shibley Hyde. "A Meta-Analytic Review of Research on Gender Differences in Sexuality, 1993–2007." *Psychological Bulletin* 136, no. 1 (2010): 21–38.

Philo. *The Works of Philo: Complete and Unabridged*. Translated by C. D. Yonge. New updated ed. Peabody, MA: Hendrickson, 1993.

Piper, John. "A Vision of Biblical Complementarity: Manhood and Womanhood Defined According to the Bible," 31–59. In John Piper and Wayne A. Grudem. *Recovering Biblical Manhood and Womanhood: A Response to Evangelical Feminism*. Wheaton: Crossway Books, 1991.

Piper, John, and Wayne A. Grudem. *Recovering Biblical Manhood and Womanhood: A Response to Evangelical Feminism*. Wheaton: Crossway Books, 1991.

Plato. *Complete Works*. Edited by John M. Cooper and D. S. Hutchinson. Indianapolis: Hackett Publishing, 1997.

Porter, Stanley E. "What Does It Mean to Be 'Saved by Childbirth'? (1 Timothy 2:15)." *Journal for the Study of the New Testament* 49 (1993): 87–102.

Pratt, Richard L. *Designed for Dignity: What God Has Made It Possible for You to Be*. Phillipsburg, NJ: P&R Publishing, 1993.

Rendsburg, Gary A. "Unlikely Heroes: Women as Israel." *Bible Review* 19, no. 1 (2003): 16–23, 52–53.

Rhoads, Steven E. *Taking Sex Differences Seriously*. San Francisco: Encounter Books, 2004.

Richardson, John T. E. "Conclusions from the Study of Gender Differences in Cognition." In *Gender Differences in Human Cognition*, edited by Paula J. Caplan, Mary Crawford, Janet Shibley Hyde, and John T. E. Richardson, 131–69. Counterpoints. New York: Oxford University Press, 1997.

Ridderbos, Herman N. *Paul: An Outline of His Theology*. Grand Rapids: Eerdmans, 1975.

Rinzler, Carol Ann. *Why Eve Doesn't Have an Adam's Apple: A Dictionary of Sex Differences*. New York: Facts on File, 1996.

Roberts, Christopher Chenault. *Creation and Covenant: The Significance of Sexual Difference in the Moral Theology of Marriage*. New York: T&T Clark International, 2007.

Ross, Hugh. *The Creator and the Cosmos: How the Greatest Scientific Discoveries of the Century Reveal God*. 3rd expanded ed. Colorado Springs: NavPress, 2001.

Satlow, Michael L. "Marriage and Divorce." In *The Oxford Handbook of Jewish Daily Life in Roman Palestine*, edited by Catherine Hezser, 344–61. New York: Oxford University Press, 2010.

Schaefer, Mark T., and David H. Olson. "Assessing Intimacy: The Pair Inventory." *Journal of Marital and Family Therapy* 7, no. 1 (1981): 47–60.

Schaps, David. "The Woman Least Mentioned: Etiquette and Women's Names." *Classical Quarterly* 27, no. 2 (1977): 323–30.

Schwartz, Pepper. *Love between Equals: How Peer Marriage Really Works*. New York: Free Press, 1995.

Sherman, Amy L. *Kingdom Calling: Vocational Stewardship for the Common Good*. Downers Grove, IL: InterVarsity Press, 2011.

Shriver, Maria. *A Woman's Nation Changes Everything: A Study by Maria Shriver and the Center for American Progress*. Edited by Heather Boushey and Ann O'Leary. Washington, DC: Center for American Progress, 2009.

Smith, Christian. *Christian America? What Evangelicals Really Want*. Berkeley: University of California Press, 2000.

Solomon, E. Sondra, Esther D. Rothblum, and Kimberly Balsam. "Money, Housework, Sex, and Conflict: Same-Sex Couples in Civil Unions, Those Not in Civil Unions, and Heterosexual Married Siblings." *Sex Roles* 52, no. 9/10 (2005): 561–75.

Spanier, Graham. "Measuring Dyadic Adjustment: New Scales for Assessing the Quality of Marriage and Similar Dyads." *Journal of Marriage and Family* 38, no. 1 (1976): 15–28.

Spanier, Graham B., and Linda Thompson. "A Confirmatory Analysis of the Dyadic Adjustment Scale." *Journal of Marriage and Family* 44, no. 3 (1982): 731–38.

Starks, Tyrel J., Brenda O. Gilbert, Ann R. Fischer, Rebecca Weston, and David L. DiLalla. "Gendered Sexuality: A New Model and Measure of Attraction and Intimacy." *Journal of Homosexuality* 56, no. 1 (2009): 14–30.

Stevenson, Betsey, and Justin Wolfers. "The Paradox of Declining Female Happiness." *National Bureau of Economic Research* Working Papers Series, no. #14969 (2009): 48.

———. "Marriage and Divorce: Changes and Their Driving Forces." *Journal of Economic Perspectives* 21, no. 2 (2007): 27–52.

Sumner, Sarah. *Men and Women in the Church: Building Consensus on Christian Leadership*. Downers Grove, IL: InterVarsity Press, 2003.

Tada, Ken. "Caregiving: A Cause for Christ." *Tabletalk*. October 1, 2011. http://www.ligonier.org/learn/articles/caregiving-a-cause-for-christ/.

Tavris, Carol. *The Mismeasure of Woman*. New York: Simon & Schuster, 1992.

Thomson, James G. S. S. "Sleep: An Aspect of Jewish Anthropology." *Vetus Testamentum* 5, no. 4 (1955): 421–33.

Van Leeuwen, Mary Stewart. *Gender and Grace: Love, Work and Parenting in a Changing World*. Downers Grove, IL: InterVarsity Press, 1990.

Wall, Robert W. "1 Timothy 2:9–15 Reconsidered (Again)." *Bulletin for Biblical Research* 14, no. 1 (2004): 81–103.

Waltke, Bruce K. *The Book of Proverbs*. 2 vols. New International Commentary on the Old Testament. Grand Rapids: Eerdmans, 2004.

———. *Genesis: A Commentary*. Grand Rapids: Zondervan, 2001.

Waltke, Bruce K., and Charles Yu. *An Old Testament Theology: An Exegetical, Canonical, and Thematic Approach*. Grand Rapids: Zondervan, 2007.

Ware, Bruce A. "Male and Female Complementarity and the Image of God." In *Biblical Foundations for Manhood and Womanhood*, edited by Wayne Grudem, 71–92. Wheaton: Crossway Books, 2002.

Webb, Barry G. *The Book of Judges: An Integrated Reading*. Journal for the Study of the Old Testament: Supplement Series 46. Sheffield: Sheffield Academic Press, 1987.

Wenham, Gordon J. *Numbers: An Introduction and Commentary*. Tyndale Old Testament Commentaries 4. Downers Grove, IL: InterVarsity Press, 2008.

West, Candace, and Don H. Zimmerman. "Doing Gender." In *The Social Construction of Gender*, edited by Judith Lorber and Susan A. Farrell, 13–37. Newbury Park, CA: Sage Publications, in cooperation with Sociologists for Women in Society, 1991.

The Westminster Confession of Faith and Catechisms: With Proof Texts. Lawrenceville, GA: The Orthodox Presbyterian Church, 2007.

Wilcox, W. Bradford. "The Evolution of Divorce." *National Affairs*, no. 1 (Fall 2009): 81–94.

Wilcox, W. Bradford, and Jeffrey Dew. "Is Love a Flimsy Foundation? Soulmate versus Institutional Models of Marriage." *Social Science Research* 39, no. 5 (2010): 687–99.

Wilcox, W. Bradford, and Steven L. Nock. "What's Love Got to Do with It? Equality, Equity, Commitment and Women's Marital Quality." *Social Forces* 84, no. 3 (2006): 1321–45.

Wilcox, W. Bradford. *Soft Patriarchs, New Men: How Christianity Shapes Fathers and Husbands.* Chicago: University of Chicago Press, 2004.

Wilson, Margaret R., and Erik E. Filsinger. "Religiosity and Marital Adjustment: Multidimensional Interrelationships." *Journal of Marriage and Family* 48, no. 1 (1986): 147–51.

Witherington, Ben. *The Acts of the Apostles: A Socio-Rhetorical Commentary.* Grand Rapids: Eerdmans, 1998.

Wolfinger, Nicholas H., and W. Bradford Wilcox. "Happily Ever After? Religion, Marital Status, Gender and Relationship Quality in Urban Families." *Social Forces* 86, no. 3 (2008): 1311–37.

Worthington, Everett L. *Hope-Focused Marriage Counseling: A Guide to Brief Therapy.* Expanded paperback ed. Downers Grove, IL: InterVarsity Press, 2005.

Yarhouse, Mark A., Christine H. Gow, and Edward B. Davis. "Intact Marriages in Which One Partner Experiences Same-Sex Attraction: A 5-Year Follow-Up Study." *Family Journal* 17, no. 4 (2009): 329–34.

Yarhouse, Mark A., Jill L. Kays, Heather Poma, Audrey N. Atkinson, and Jennifer S. Ripley. "Characteristics of Mixed Orientation Couples: An Empirical Study." *Edification: The Transdisciplinary Journal of Christian Psychology* 4, no. 2 (2011): 41–56.

Yarhouse, Mark A., Lisa M. Pawlowski, and Erica S. N. Tan. "Intact Marriages in Which One Partner Dis-Identifies with Experiences of Same-Sex Attraction." *American Journal of Family Therapy* 31, no. 5 (2003): 375–94.

Yarhouse, Mark A., and Robin L. Seymore. "Intact Marriages in Which One Partner Dis-Identifies with Experiences of Same-Sex Attraction: A Follow-Up Study." *American Journal of Family Therapy* 34, no. 2 (2006): 151–61.

Young, Iris Marion. *Intersecting Voices: Dilemmas of Gender, Political Philosophy, and Policy.* Princeton, NJ: Princeton University Press, 1997.

Younger, K. Lawson. *Judges and Ruth.* NIV Application Commentary. Grand Rapids: Zondervan, 2002.

Scripture Index

Sam A. Andreades is senior pastor of Faith Reformed Presbyterian Church in Quarryville, Pennsylvania. Previously, he was a pastor for ten and a half years in Greenwich Village, New York City, and is the founder of Higher Ground (originally called G.A.M.E.: Gender Affirming Ministry Endeavor), a New York City ministry of Christian discipleship serving those with unwanted same-sex attractions. He is a graduate of Yale University (B.S., geology and geophysics), Reformed Theological Seminary (M.Div., pastoral ministry), New York University (M.S., artificial intelligence), and Covenant Theological Seminary (D.Min., urban mission and ministry) where he wrote his dissertation on gender distinction in marriage. Sam is the husband of his wife of twenty-five years, Mary K., and the father of their four children, Thaddaeus, Jeremy, Veronica, and Enoch.